D1562748

DAFYDD

ap gwilym

the poems

Llawysgrif Hendregadredd, NLW MS. 668OB, fol. 120^r, showing (in faint scipt) the beginning of the poem to the Cross at Chester and the ascription to Dafydd ap Gwilym: *Eglynyon agant dauid llwyd uab gwilim gam yr groc ogaer* ("*Englynion* composed by Dafydd Llwyd ap Gwilym Gam to the Rood at Chester"). This manuscript is the subject of a forthcoming article in the National Library of Wales Journal (Summer 1981) by Daniel Huws, Keeper of Manuscrips at the National Library; Mr. Huws draws attention to the possibility that the poem (and therefore the signature) might be in the hand of the young Dafydd ap Gwilym. A facsimile of the conclusion of the poem is shown following the Introduction to the present volume. Reproduced by courtesy of the National Library of Wales.

gort dan gloew goleu gorelew babir me
uestir greludyt eulehyt gorth greith yn ll[..]
dum dir. gwyr a barchak lew a torchir
menenestir greluddy galchwed kyngreu[..]
yg kylchin y ndeui golehwy euuoir. pan
preibyd kaures taerwres trewy ddyr.
preit ostwg onilwg. a euuoir. menestir
nam ditaul ny m diuolir poed ym paradw[..]
ys ym kymwystir. gan teyruet ynn lwed
hir ys trewited. yny mae gyeled gwaraddred
gwir.

Ceslywon agant daud lloyd uab gwili gr ne .... gwir.

Ryf aherch yeo newdy nyt yn aet ureswyr eruys uguen ydos llyyth ddaer
hwyr maorgloe crocorym eurglaer eroe beus a hun o gaen gw[..]

lluryt erael maol can eys[.] mwen er......
deryt llinoll echwyell daen llodyp oer erlch........
llemy iony er ebuen goh ael eleunewyf..........
daugudeb uegreu llellenw bele oyes.......
anlaus y croerdaer llethyg san uaes......

lludde kylch haer er llacywlelo uys[.] lley lleslbyr...
daer lle 386 lyn crow[.] tya uet llrew lao lloud....
dyft dr erywydaer yn eurddelo loet yoy glau ra mordd[..]
lacyou uwre kyllaws yo oddeun diunu uay ryst oni a....
uyd coryf de tyyd didary erelueru kyslegoydaer herucoer....
tyll yo sow uewe gryydaydyr gwyrth ffruys ll ynglaer....
uoarhy lyef gwoch eis[.] or ygyot gynn lebuenn byryd....
sga euro oie orewhawl ddydyl ddau uelles............
lo eruvos uuenthe lo uyu aldoar............
daer dobedbes lenyey egryth gyee er due ll...........
wyn olyoue oredelis glae loll llwad llau yl befy...........
eu uuer er de wy dwrhawl ddael derdaer llot......
daer oyaur glou dwrn eryglaer donngeu....
Crosodnur oeduu adel y adwur ylbech deuyr soch....
eywer grewgrei aeuere enel eryos flleeu......
donn gwoter gwllelys[.] f wlbw yo euoe.........

medieval & renaissance texts & studies

VOLUME 9

DAFYDD

ap gwilym

the poems

TRANSLATION AND COMMENTARY
by Richard Morgan Loomis

Illustrations by Mary Guerriere Loomis

medieval & Renaissance texts & studies
Center for Medieval & Early Renaissance Studies
Binghamton, New York
1982

The St. David's Society of the State of New York
and the National Welsh-American Foundation
have generously provided grants to help defray
the costs of publication of this volume.

© Copyright 1982
With revisions

Center for Medieval & Early Renaissance Studies
State University of New York at Binghamton
Binghamton, New York

Library of Congress Cataloging in Publication Data

Dafydd ap Gwilym, 14th cent.
    Dafydd ap Gwilym.

    (Medieval & Renaissance texts & studies; 9)
    Includes bibliographical references and indexes.
    I. Loomis, Richard Morgan, 1926–   II. Title.
III. Series.
PB2273.D3A27   891.6'611   81–16968
ISBN 0–86698–015–6   AACR2

PB
2273
.D3
A27
1982

Printed in the United States of America

JESUIT - KRAUSS - McCORMICK - LIBRARY
1100 EAST 55th STREET
CHICAGO, ILLINOIS 60615

For Mary

Contents

Facsimiles: frontispiece and page 46
(National Library of Wales, MS 66808)

Maps: *The Wales of Dafydd ap Gwilym*
Streams and Other Natural Features   11
Lands and Districts   12
Residential and Religious Centers   13

Birds in the Poems   47
The birds shown on this page are the following,
clockwise from the top left corner, with the numbers
of some of the poems in which they are featured:
Thrush (28, 122, 123); Blackbird (63, 76);
Nightingale (25, 122); Seagull (118); Magpie (63);
Woodcock (61, 115); Owl (26); Skylark (63, 114).

Acknowledgements

My principal debt is to Sir Thomas Parry and the University of Wales Press for permission to base these translations on *Gwaith Dafydd ap Gwilym*. I am also grateful to Sir Thomas Parry and *Poetry Wales* for permission to quote a comment of his on Poem 139. In addition, Dr. Parry read and helpfully criticized fifty of the translations.

The commentaries of Rachel Bromwich have instructed and guided me in ways I often point to in my notes. I am grateful for her permission to quote the titles of some of the Welsh triads from her edition and translation of *Trioedd Ynys Prydein*.

R. Geraint Gruffydd has permitted me to include a translation of a revised text he has proposed for some lines in Poem 122. Professor Gruffydd, who is now Librarian of the National Library of Wales, has generously assisted me in obtaining publications I have needed. Professor Bedwyr Lewis Jones of the University College of North Wales has helpfully responded to my inquiries. The bibliographical note following my translations identifies other scholars whose works have been at my side as I have studied Dafydd. I thank them all.

My wife's pen and ink drawings of eight birds featured in the poems are based on figures in the following sources: for nightingale, skylark, and thrush, the article "Bird" in *The World Book Encyclopedia* (Chicago: World Book-Childcraft International, Inc., 1980); and for blackbird, gull, magpie, owl, and woodcock, S. Vere Benson, *The Observer's Book of Birds* (London: Frederick Warne, 1977). I am grateful to the publishers for permission to use these illustrations as models for the drawings.

It is not possible to name all the individuals who have aided me, but I must note my gratitude to the officers and staffs of the following institutions, for assistance of many kinds and access to library holdings:

First, my thanks to the faculty and administration of Nazareth College of Rochester, who have supported my work through a sabbatical leave and summer research grants. In Wales, I was made welcome at the National Library of Wales; the University College of Wales at Aberystwyth; and the offices of the University of Wales Press. The libraries of the following American universities have permitted me to use materials in their collections: Catholic University of America; Cornell University; Harvard University; and the University of Rochester. Professor Emerson Brown of Vanderbilt University read several of the translations at a critical stage in the preparation of the manuscript, and his encouragement was invaluable. Professor Mario A. Di Cesare and his staff at Medieval & Renaissance Texts & Studies have by their faith in the work and their many detailed suggestions helped to improve its substance and shape. But mine alone is the responsibility for inaccuracies and awkwardnesses that may remain. I hope that my translations will awaken the interest of readers in studying Dafydd ap Gwilym in the beauty of his Welsh language.

The St. David's Society of the State of New York and the National Welsh-American Foundation have contributed funds to help defray the cost of publishing these translations; I am most grateful for their support.

My family have been patient and helpful: with zest for cliff-climbing, stream-wading, cathedral-hunting, and embracing the Welsh, Mary explored Wales with me and later made — beautifully — the graphics for this book; Mario sang Welsh songs for us; Leonard read the manuscript.

The poet himself has grown to seem a friend. May his judgment of these efforts to sketch in English some of the golden lineaments of his Welsh verse be that of a friend — tolerant, amused, inattentive to lapses, *hael*.

Preface to the Second Printing

Some three dozen emendations are listed below, most of them based on suggestions generously offered by Dr. Parry. Dr. Bromwich's translations (no. 11 in my Bibliographical Note) are now in print, and I have found them most valuable. There are corrupt passages in the Welsh texts which my renderings may make too free of question.

Unless otherwise indicated, the numbers are of poem and line; the printed text is given first, the emended reading, second.

Emendations

Page 24, second line from bottom. *Delete* egn

2.3.   Christ of fair cross / Christ holy in His cross,

4.41.   Consider the wise / The wise man considers the

22.12.   brave / expensive

23.23.   spotless / perfect

23.43.   Mantled / Full of puddles

23.48.   Tears shall nourish it / It provokes tears

24.14.   lively head of a summer birch / head of a lively summer birch

26.26.   mousewoman / mouser

26.45.   wait for / suffer

33.21.   because of May's longing / rather than seek out May

34.15.   Fertile it's flying / Prolifically it's running to seed

34.23.   marvelous lady / wondrous number

39.27.   *Delete* what I did

42.4.   brow / crest

42.29.   Beautiful from the body of dawn / A beautiful body by day

45.7.   Despite this / From that time

52.51.   a good moon for long / long a gracious moon

66.   headnote. The mills, ducks, enclosures may be metaphors for parts of the clock.

67.12. over to the home / across the township
71.33. My counsel is constrained / I am perplexed
80.17. shall / does
89.24. dead / mortal
89.45. An agreement was made / You made an agreement
117.29. heather-husks / heap of husks
124.41. They fell from the table / The table fell
128.60. Make her one of an / Do that in any alehouse
148.19. He throws / He who throws
Page 280, line 5. as boars / bands
Page 290, line 3. above / below
Page 317, line 14. *For* 17 *read* 7
Page 332, line 19. *For* tomb *read* stone coffin
Page 334, line 12. Move the accent mark to above the letter *o*.

Introduction

Dafydd ap Gwilym is a poet of fourteenth-century Wales who has come to be recognized as one of the great lyric poets of medieval literature.

The modern critical edition of the work of Dafydd ap Gwilym (*Gwaith Dafydd ap Gwilym*) appeared in 1952, edited by Sir Thomas Parry; a second edition was issued in 1963, and a third, in 1979; all were published by the University of Wales Press. In the introduction to his first edition, Dr. Parry lists 267 manuscripts which he examined and collated over a period of more than two decades; in these manuscripts some 358 compositions are ascribed to Dafydd. The Parry edition presents a total of 150 poems as by Dafydd, together with twenty poems of doubtful authorship, eight poems by contemporaries of Dafydd (four are part of a debate with Dafydd, four are elegies), and two elegiac stanzas on Dafydd. The first printed edition of the collected poems of Dafydd ap Gwilym had appeared in London in 1789, edited by Owen Jones and William Owen, with the title *Barddoniaeth Dafydd ab Gwilym*; Welsh scholars refer to it as *BDG*. A second edition of *BDG* was issued in 1873, edited by the bard Cynddelw and published in Liverpool. One poem ascribed to Dafydd ("Y ferch o'r fynachlog faen," not included in *GDG* by Dr. Parry) had appeared in print in the sixteenth-century Welsh grammar by Gruffydd Robert — a learned Welsh priest in the service of Cardinal Borromeo — which was printed in Milan in the 1580's.

Sir Thomas Parry's critical edition builds on the work of Sir Ifor Williams, the pioneering Welsh scholar who, with Thomas Roberts, edited a selection of poems by Dafydd and his contemporaries under the title, *Cywyddau Dafydd ap Gwilym a'i Gyfoeswyr* (Bangor, 1914; second edition, 1935).

I have undertaken to translate all the poems in the Parry text. More than half of these poems have not before now been published in English translation. Indeed, many an American reader of this book — even if he is a teacher of British literature — may never have heard of Dafydd ap Gwilym.

He was a contemporary of Chaucer and Boccaccio, older than Chaucer, younger than Boccaccio; his estimated dates are 1320–80. He was a native of Ceredigion, the Welsh land known in modern centuries as the county of Cardigan. His birthplace was probably at Bro Gynin; his parish was Llanbadarn. His bardic master was his uncle, Llywelyn ap Gwilym, who was constable of Castellnewydd Emlyn and who had other courts in Dyfed (southwestern Wales). The patron to whom Dafydd addressed most of his poems of tribute was Ifor Hael, whose court was at Basaleg near Cardiff. Dafydd also wrote poems dealing with persons from the Welsh lands of Gwynedd (northwestern Wales) and Powys (eastern and northerly). He often mentions Anglesey (by its Welsh name, Môn) and seems to have had a predilection for the Anglesey town of Rhosyr (re-named Newborough by the English). A dominant tradition is that he is buried beneath a yew tree at Strata Florida, near the uplands where the Teifi has its source. Thus, while he has associations with Ceredigion from birth to death, he knew all the regions of Wales.

The accompanying maps of Wales (devoted principally to showing places mentioned by Dafydd) will bring the point home. I list first some of the Welsh place names that are known to English readers by different names or under a significantly different spelling. The maps show streams and other natural features; the political divisions of lands and districts; and residential and religious centers.

Welsh Place Names with Modern English Equivalents

Abermaw.	Barmouth
Aberteifi.	Cardigan (the town)
Bae Aberteifi.	Cardigan Bay
Brycheiniog.	Breconshire
Caer.	Chester
Caerdyf.	Cardiff
Caerfyrddin.	Carmarthen
Caer yn Arfon.	Caernarvon
Ceredigion.	Cardiganshire
Ceri.	Kerry
Dyfi.	Dovey
Dyfrdwy.	Dee
Gwy.	Wye
Hafren.	Severn
Is Aeron.	Lower Aeron (south of the river Aeron)

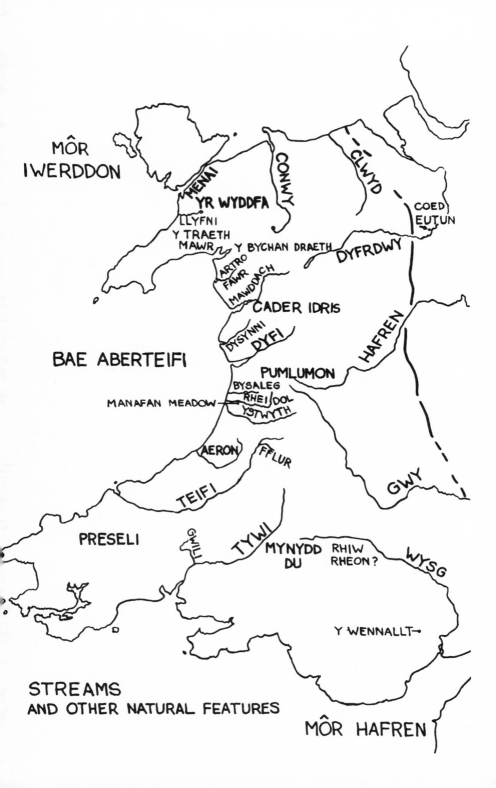

MÔR
IWERDDON

MENAI

CONWY

CLWYD

YR WYDDFA

COED
EUTUN

LLYFNI
Y TRAETH
MAWR

Y BYCHAN DRAETH

DYFRDWY

ARTRO
FAWR

MAWDDACH

CADER IDRIS

HAFREN

DYSYNNI   DYFI

BAE ABERTEIFI

PUMLUMON

BYSALEG

MANAFAN MEADOW

RHEIDOL

YSTWYTH

AERON

FFLUR

TEIFI

GWY

GWILI

PRESELI

TYWI

MYNYDD
DU

RHIW
RHEON?

WYSG

Y WENNALLT

STREAMS
AND OTHER NATURAL FEATURES

MÔR HAFREN

LANDS AND DISTRICTS

ST. CYBI'S ✠
LLANFAES
ABERFFRAW ○
RHOSYR
LLANDDWYN ✠
✠ BANGOR
CAER YN ARFON ○
ST. ASAPH'S ✠
CAER

MAESTRAN ○
▲ EITHINFYNYDD
ABERMAW ○ ▲ NANNAU

ST. CADFAN'S ✠
✠ LLANLLUGAN
TALYBONT
ELEIRCH ○
ABERYSTWYTH ✠ ▲ BRO GYNIN
LLANBADARN

✠ YSTRAD FFLUR

▲ TYWYN
LLANDUDOCH ○ ○ ABERTEIFI
▲ EMLYN ▲ Y DDÔL-GOCH
LLYSTYN ▲ CRYNGAE

✠ MYNYW—[ST. DAVID'S]
CAERFYRDDIN ○

CAERLLION ○
BASALEG ○
GWERNYCLEPA ▲
CAERDYF ○

○ CITY, TOWN, OR VILLAGE
✠ RELIGIOUS CENTER
▲ COURT, MANSION, HOME

Llandudoch.	St. Dogmael's
Meirionnydd.	Merioneth
Môr Hafren.	Bristol Channel
Môr Iwerddon.	Irish Sea
Mynyw.	St. David's
Rhosyr.	Newborough
Swydd Gaer.	Carmarthenshire?
Tywi.	Towy
Uwch Aeron.	Upper Aeron (north of the river Aeron)
Wysg.	Usk
Yr Wyddfa.	Snowdon; also known in Welsh as *Eryri*; though Dafydd names none of them, I note, in addition to Yr Wyddfa, these mountains and mountain-ranges: Cader Idris, Pumlumon (Plynlimon), Mynydd Du (Black Mountain), and the Preseli.
Ystrad Fflur.	Strata Florida

Y Wennallt is a wooded spot near Ifor Hael's court, mentioned in Poem 9; "Manafan meadow" is named in Poem 119. *Traeth* means "beach"; *coed* means "wood"; *rhiw* means "slope" or "hill." Because they are named by Dafydd, or in my notes, I also mark the location of churches dedicated to the Welsh saints Cybi, Asaph (the Welsh spelling is Asaff), and Cadfan.

Dafydd's family was a noble one that cooperated with the English authorities — the Conquest of Wales had been achieved under Edward I at the end of the thirteenth century — yet Dafydd evinces Welsh nationalism. He declares that his poems will honor a patron as far as Welsh is spoken and implies no doubt that that is a goodly distance. Not so much less, compared to the modern difference, than the domain of English, which in Dafydd's century was just reasserting itself as the principal language of government and letters in England, after three centuries of Norman-French domination. The world empire of the English language lay yet in the future.

We know Dafydd through his reputation, certain physical remains, and the poems. His reputation has been constant: he is a peerless poet. He is, more specifically, the greatest medieval Welsh poet, the greatest Welsh poet of love. His contemporaries acknowledged his supremacy, even while quarreling with him. Gruffudd Gryg, for example, criticizes some of the content of Dafydd's poetry but identifies him — with a casualness that indicates he is citing common opinion — as *y prydydd prif* (Poem 147, line 16), "the chief poet."

The number of manuscript copies of Dafydd's verse is a measure of his popularity. One of the earliest extant manuscripts, Peniarth 52A, may be in the hand of a fifteenth-century poet, Dafydd Nanmor, a tribute therefore by a later poet. In the eighteenth century, the brothers Lewis and William Morris of Môn would similarly honor Dafydd by making the transcriptions that were to become the primary source for *Barddoniaeth Dafydd ab Gwilym.*

One is helped in coming to know Dafydd by visiting places associated with the poet. Bro Gynin, the site of his probable birthplace, is marked today by a memorial plaque and stones from a residence later built on the spot. If no building stands that might have been his first home, the quiet valley itself retains its physical features: ridges running from the inland mountain mass of Pumlumon toward the sea, a clear stream (Afon Stewy, known to Dafydd as Masaleg or Bysaleg) passing the birthplace site, groves of trees such as the hazel and ash that are named in his poems, farm fields laid across the valley floor and up its slopes. It was and is a rural community, not wild but not populous. Here (or not far from here) Dafydd ap Gwilym formed his first attachments, may first have seen and heard some of the animals that figure in his poems, such as the skylark, owl, gull, crow, magpie, blackbird, thrush, woodcock, fox, hare, squirrel, roebuck, oxen, dogs, cats, chickens, geese. Here he could observe the skies of Wales, try his country's roads and some of its trackless ground.

The thirteenth-century church of Llanbadarn, four miles away, is the very church in which Dafydd gazed at the women of the parish.

A yew tree where Dafydd's body may lie grows at Strata Florida, about fifteen miles southeast of Aberystwyth, though the great Cistercian abbey, where Welsh loyalty was affirmed in the thirteenth century at an assembly of Welsh princes, is in ruins. The arch of the west door stands, but the rest of the abbey survives as a grassy, rubbled floor plan, with only some glowing fourteenth-century floor tiles (showing a griffin, a young nobleman hunting, geometric designs) to suggest the old splendor.

There is a description of Dafydd preserved in a note by David Johns, vicar of Llanfair Dyffryn Clwyd. The following is my translation of the note (the Welsh original is quoted in Dr. Parry's introduction, *GDG*[3], p. xxiii):

> I saw in 1572 an old woman who had seen another who had talked with Dafydd ap Gwilym. He was tall and slender with loose, curly yellow hair and that full of clasps and silver rings, she said.

The old woman must have been old indeed, to have talked with someone who had conversed with the poet two centuries before. But the description may derive from an authentic tradition.

From the poems, we may make such inferences as these about their author:

He is a nobleman, of recognized and reputable Welsh family. He has the prejudices of his class, race, and culture, using terms meaning "farm laborer" as epithets for the crude and the evil; admiring other noblemen who give gifts, not admiring merchants who are careful of their goods. Elements of wealth such as gold and jewelry, like all things white and bright, from gossamer to foaming water to snow and sun, supply him with metaphors for beauty. In social manner, style of dress, and speech, he assumes traditional standards, so that words meaning "suitable" and "appropriate" carry the senses of "good" and "beautiful." Those who are not only regular of body and manner but also delicate are irresistibly attractive. Delicacy, fineness, and gentleness are traits understood to result from breeding, so that describing a girl as of good lineage is short hand for the highest praise.

Dafydd wrote poetry for a lifetime, this being marked by references to his hair, now blond, now gray, now curly, now falling out (though the poems' references to being "old" may pertain more to decrepitude from his toils than from years; some scholars believe Dafydd's life was not a long one). He was not a warrior, though he carried a sword and was credited by others with a certain martial force of personality, at least in poetry and love. A fellow poet, Iolo Goch, called him "hawk of the girls of Deheubarth" (perhaps meaning by *hawk* "trained favorite" as well as "predator"). As a poet, he enjoyed patronage from noble benefactors and gave them thanks in formal poems of praise. What is striking in Dafydd's patronal tributes is their celebration of a way of life. Strength, valor, exuberance, playfulness, high fashion, taste, amiability, honor, service, fidelity, knowledge of the cultures of Wales, Christendom, and the great world: these qualities are praised in praising those who are credited with possessing them. And the feeling and courtesy of his style demonstrate that gratitude can be a moving art.

Some of Dafydd's poems resemble troubadour forms, such as the *pastorela* (pastourelle, Poem 41) and *alba* (dawn song, Poem 129). As in the troubadour tradition, there are in his poems lovers' conversations and quarrels, love-messages, salutes to spring (often bittersweet), memories of love-meetings, laments for separations, serenades outside the woman's house, outpourings of contempt for jealous husbands and slanderers, debates on the nature of love, greetings and asides to a sophisticated audience. Dafydd's poems also develop topics and modes of earlier Welsh poetry, as in the praise poem, the elegy, and the satire. The lover's boast of his conquests (as in Poem 98) has a Welsh antecedent in work of the twelfth century Hywel ab Owain Gwynedd, and the rejected lover's complaint appears in poems of Cynddelw Brydydd Mawr, also of the twelfth century. The poet Dafydd names most often (fourteen times in the poems in the Parry edition) is Ovid, who was also cited by Hywel ab Owain Gwynedd (and a host of other medieval love poets). Dafydd names Virgil (as a magician), Taliesin (four times), and Myrddin (or Merddin, a legendary Welsh warrior-poet, credited with prophetic powers, who is a source for the Merlin of the later romances). There are Biblical and Christian references (Adam and Eve, Noah, Christ, Mary and Joseph, Anna, the apostles; Dewi Sant — Saint David — and other Welsh saints). There are references, of largely military connotation, to Greece and Troy; Rome; France; the ancient northern English kingdom of Deira; Hercules, Hector; the swords of Charlemagne's knights. There are many references to Celtic and Arthurian heroes and heroines: Branwen, Deirdre, Eigr (Igraine), Enid, Esyllt (Isolt), Gwenhwyfar (Guinever), Luned (Lunette), among the women; and Arthur, Cai (Kay), Gwalchmai (Gawain), Tristan and Peredur (Percival) among the men. These allusions may remind us of the antiquity of Welsh literature (Taliesin belongs to the sixth century) and of its range: the sages, the religious themes, the heroic figures and legends, the patriotic tributes to Welsh lords, and the celebration of women and love that constitute the native literary tradition upon which Dafydd's work rests. The allusions to foreign literatures are indicative of his knowledge of continental culture and his freedom from a merely provincial taste.

The Wales of the poems of Dafydd ap Gwilym exhibits a wide range of crafts: clothmaking and brewing, woodcrafting, leather and metal working, building and painting, arts of ornamentation and feasting. But these crafts are not just indigenous; there is cultural commerce with other nations. Dafydd mentions the shop-goods and wines of France, the horses of Gascony, the woodwork, leather, and furs (and commercial travelers) of England. Mead flows plentifully, and there is good wine. Music and poetry are produced in delicate designs. Adornments of goldwork and jewelry are worn profusely, at church and fair, in hall and tavern. Ancient Welsh ways of rule, by law and the military arts, survive ambiguously in England's shadow, for the Welsh laws would not be suppressed until the reign of Henry VIII, and the last armed struggle for an independent Wales was to occur under Owain Glyndŵr (Owen Glendower) at the beginning of the fifteenth century. There are sports — falconry, hunting, archery, ball games, swimming — that are still known to us, as well as board games for which little more than the names survive today.

It is a culture close to two kinds of nature: domesticated nature and the wilderness. The first was the agricultural setting for daily living that even a nobleman-poet like Dafydd would have experienced: a place of grains, fruits, flax, wool; cultivated fields and tended livestock; animal shelters and farm workshops; cheesemaking and its gear; the farmyard with its noises and smells, its ordure and its vigorous animal life. In addition to this, there was near at hand the wild country. Dense groves fine for trysting, slopes conveniently out of the way, sea-strands free of people, beds of leaves and clover, the company of sun and breeze, of songbirds and deer. But wild nature could be malign as well, in its storms and frosts, its impassable streams, its bogs, its shrouding mists or its too bright moonlight, its grotesquerie of lurking, darting, shrieking, noisome creatures.

At the center of the world of Dafydd ap Gwilym is his Welsh language, not only because it was the medium through which he exercised his poetic craft, but also because, like any language, it provided the means by which his culture articulated its lore. Meanings, values, and associations embedded in words comprise, with sounds, the elements of language that poets turn to music.

The Welsh language (like its congeners, Breton and Cornish) developed from the language of the Celtic Britons who were colonized by Rome. It bears the imprint, therefore, of four centuries of early Roman influence, in addition to later infusions from medieval Latin and borrowings from English, Norse, and French. The name *Welsh* is of Germanic origin and was applied by the migrating Anglo-Saxon tribes to the Romanized Celts whose lands the Anglo-Saxons seized. By the Roman period, Celtic speech was represented by two main groups:

1. *Gallic* (in Gaul) and *Brythonic* (in Britain, including a variety in Pictland).
2. *Goidelic* in Ireland.

Later, Brythonic evolved into Welsh in North Britain and Wales, Cornish in the southwestern peninsula, Breton in Brittany (possibly superimposed on a remaining Gallic element); and Goidelic evolved into Irish, which was introduced into the Isle of Man (where later it became Manx) and into Scotland (where it became Scots Gaelic).

The Roman influence upon Welsh appears in a host of Latin loan words such as these:

Welsh	Latin	English
aur	aurum	gold
bas	bassus	shallow
braich	bracchium	arm
calan	calendae	first day of year or month
canol	canalis	middle
corff	corpus	body
dysgu	disco	to learn
eglwys	ecclesia	church
ffenestr	fenestra	window
gwag	vacuus	empty
Pasg	Pascha	Easter
pont	pons	bridge

Many such words derived from Latin are common to Welsh, Breton, and French, illustrating an affinity of Welsh to the Romance languages:

Welsh	Breton	French
aur	aour	or
braich	breh	bras
calan	kala	calendes
corff	korv	corps
eglwys	iliz	église
gwag	vag	vacant
Pasg	Pask	Pâques

The kinship of Welsh and Breton may be illustrated by the following Celtic terms in these two languages not derived from Latin (though some have Latin cognates):

Welsh	*Breton*	
aber	aber	mouth of a river, confluence
bara	bara	bread
blinder	blinder	weariness
bro	bro	region, country, neighborhood
buan	buan	swift
cad	kad	combat
cas	kas	hatred
coed	koad	forest, wood
cryf	kreñv	strong, brave
chwarae	c'hoari	play, game; to play
chwerthin	c'hoarzin	to laugh
dŵr	dour	water
du	du	black
eryr	erer	eagle
gaeaf	goañv	winter
genau	genou	mouth
gŵr	gour	man
hiraeth	hiraez	longing
iar	yar	chicken
llwyd	loued	gray
mawr	meur	great
nam	namm	defect
pump	pemp	five
tâl	tal	forehead
uchel	uhel	high

Welsh has only one phoneme not found in other languages: the un-voiced *L*, represented in modern Welsh orthography by the combina-tion *LL*. It is pronounced by sharply emitting air while touching the tip of the tongue to the palate just back of the upper teeth.

The following is the Welsh alphabet, with phonetic symbols, non-Welsh illustrations of the sounds, and Welsh examples. Note that the vowels have more than one value and that *I* and *W* may be consonan-tal. *R* is lightly trilled. *H* is normally aspirated strongly in Welsh. The diphthongs *AI, AE, AU, EU, EI* may be pronounced like English *eye* (though native speakers of Welsh pronounce them variously).

a	[ɑ]	father	da
	[a]	hat	mam

b	[b]	bet	beth
c	[k]	cat	ci
ch	[kh]	loch	chwarae
d	[d]	day	da
dd	[ð]	hither	Dafydd
e	[e]	état	de
	[ɛ]	get	pren
f	[v]	of	afon
ff	[f]	off	ffals
g	[g]	get	gorau
ng	[ŋ]	length	deng
h	[h]	hand	Hafren
i	[i]	lean	ci
	[ɪ]	pin	disgyn
	[j]	halleluia	iar
l	[l]	like	lol
ll	[λ]	— —	llam
m	[m]	mom	mam
n	[n]	nap	nant
o	[o]	tone	o
	[ɔ]	on	goddrych
p	[p]	peep	pi
ph	[f]	phone	ei phren
r	[r]	Roma	mirain
rh	[ρʻ]	Sir Hugh	rhag
s	[s]	say	sarn
	[ʃ]	shop	siop
t	[t]	top	tes
th	[θ]	thin	gwaith
u	[i]	lean	du
	[ɪ]	pin	cynnull
w	[u]	loot	gŵr
	[ʊ]	look	lwc
	[w]	won	gwen
y	[i]	lean	dyn
	[ɪ]	pin	llyn
	[ʌ]	sun	yn
	[ə]	father	yr

Among Welsh speakers, there are variations in pronunciation, particularly of the vowels and of the diphthongs formed from them. The above list indicates only the standard sounds of Welsh speech, but it should be helpful to the non-Welsh reader in pronouncing the Welsh names and terms that appear in this book. In scanning verse, these further principles should be borne in mind:

The accent in Welsh normally falls on the penult.

The unaccented vocalic *W* in words like *gwlad, marw,,* or *berw,* though lightly pronounced, does not count as a separate syllable. Similarly, the *Y* in *eiry* does not constitute a syllable. The same is true for the *L* and *R* in words like *dadl* or *mawr.*

The Verse Forms

Dafydd writes in these Welsh verse forms: *englyn, awdl, traethodl,* and *cywydd.*

The *englyn* is a short stanza. Two types of *englyn* appear in Dafydd's poems: *englyn proest* and *englyn unodl union. Englyn proest* is a stanza of four seven-syllable lines ending in the Welsh half-rhyme known as *proest* (the final consonants are the same, but the vowels — which must be of the same length — vary). The following example is from Poem 13, lines 49–52:

> Gwae fi weled, trwydded dr*w*g,
> Neuaddau milwr, tŵr t*e*g,
> Annawn oes, un yn ys*i*g,
> A'r llall, do gwall, yn dŷ gw*a*g.

These lines also exhibit *cynghanedd. Cynghanedd* is the repetition of sounds within a line of verse, following fixed patterns. The principal patterns, in highly simplified description, are:

CYNGHANEDD LUSG: the accented penultimate syllable rhymes with a word earlier in the line.

> O weilch dig*el* weh*élў*th

> Myn y Gŵr a f*edd* h*édd*ĩw

> Ac i'm t*ál* mae gof*ál*glw̃yf

CYNGHANEDD GYTSAIN: three kinds of consonantal correspondence, named *cynghanedd groes, draws,* and *groes o gyswllt.*

CYNGHANEDD GROES: the consonants before the caesura

alliterate, in the same sequence, with consonants after the caesura; accent determines three kinds.

> G1   A*m* aur o *ddýn* | *m*arw y*dd* wýf

> G2   *H*udó*l*iŏn | a'i *h*adéi*l*ẅs

(*Note:* A final consonant just before the caesura does not figure in the *cynghanedd* of G1 or G2; a consonant ending a line of verse never figures in *cynghanedd; n* may occur at the beginning of the first or second half of a line without affecting *cynghanedd.*)

> G3   Y *b*u'*r* *b*ái, | w*b* o'*r* *b*ýwẏd

> G3   *Ll*awn o *h*úd, | *ll*un e*h*édfäen

(*Note:* In G3, a consonant after the accented vowel just before the caesura — if such a consonant occurs — must be repeated after the penultimate accented vowel of the line (as is *d* in the example just above.))

CYNGHANEDD DRAWS: only the beginning and end of the line alliterate; in the middle are non-alliterating consonants; the distinctions as to accent are similar to those for *cynghanedd groes.*

> D1   *N*a *b*ai *d*ég f 'wyne*b* a *d*á

> D2   Yn *d*ý*ll*äu terydr *d*éi*l*liŏn

> D3   *P*ún*t* er dyfod o'*r* *p*éintiẅr

CYNGHANEDD GROES O GYSWLLT: repetition of consonants begins before the caesura; since this pattern rarely occurs in Dafydd's verse, I do not offer illustrations.

CYNGHANEDD SAIN: two words within the line rhyme; the second of these rhyming words is linked by alliteration (roughly on the principles of *cynghanedd groes* or *draws*) with the word constituting the end-rhyme of the line; there are four kinds, distinguished by accent.

> S1   Mae gwayw i'm p*en* am w*én* *w*íw

> S2   Pan dd*êl*, ós*gêl* i és*gÿ*rn

S3   Drwy na thorro, *tró tr*éiglfrẙs

S4   Ang*au* a'i *chw*arél*ău chw*ẏrn

Englyn unodl union is a stanza of four lines, of different length. The first line has ten syllables, the second line, six, and the last two lines, seven each. The last syllable or syllables of the first line are separated from the rest of that line and constitute what is called the *cyrch*. The main rhyme of the stanza occurs just before the *cyrch* and is repeated at the end of each of the other three lines. The *cyrch* is linked by rudimentary *cynghanedd* to the second line. *Cynghanedd* also appears in the first line (up to the *cyrch*) and in the third and fourth lines. The first two lines are called the *paladr* ("shaft") and the last two lines are called the *esgyll* ("wings").

Poem 6 is a sequence of *englynion*; the following stanza of *englyn unodl union* is the fourth stanza of that poem:

S1   O ufudd-dawd, ffawd a ff*ẏdd* — a *chi*ried,
      A *cha*ru ei brýd*ẏdd*,

S4   Ofer bedwar, rwyddbar r*ẏdd*,

G2   Wrth Ifor, araith Óf*ẏdd*.

The *awdl* is a long poem in a variety of meters, usually devoted to a serious subject, as in the poems of praise and the elegies. In the *awdl*, Dafydd uses, in addition to *englyn* stanzas (Poems 2, 6, and 13 consist entirely of *englynion*), the following meters:

Cyhydedd Naw Ban: rhyming couplets of nine-syllable lines.

      Nid un gwin naddfin â mynyddfaidd,
      Nid un y paun gnu o blu â blaidd

Toddaid: couplets interlocked by rhyme; the first line has ten syllables, the second, nine; the main rhyme occurs before the end of the first line and is repeated at the end of the second line; the words following the main rhyme in the first line are the *cyrch*; the *cyrch* rhymes with a word at the middle of the second line.

      Gwyndir cryf lle tyf tafarnwri*aeth* — h*oed*,

      A gwedr egn egin c*oed*, gwiw dirieg*aeth*.

A four-line stanza formed of *cyhydedd naw ban* and a *toddaid* couplet is called *gwawdodyn*. Poem 14 consists of 12 *gwawdodyn* stanzas; Poem 15 consists of 3 *englynion* followed by 8 *gwawdodyn* stanzas. *Toddaid* couplets also occur in the following poems:

Poem 1:   1 *englyn* followed by
          19 *toddaid* couplets

Poem 11: 4 *englynion*
          15 *toddaid* couplets

Poem 12: 3 *englynion*
          20 *toddaid* couplets (the second line of the
          eighth *toddaid* couplet is missing)

Poem 5:   4 *englynion*
          8 stanzas consisting of 2 *toddaid* couplets
          each

Poem 16: 9 *englynion*
          11 stanzas of 2 *toddaid* couplets each

Poem 21: 16 *englynion*
          12 *toddaid* couplets

Traethodl, a form from which the *cywydd* may have developed, has rhyming couplets of seven-syllable lines; the rhyming final syllables may be accented or not; *cynghanedd* is not required. The only instance of *traethodl* in *GDG* is Poem 137. The following are lines 43–50 from that poem:

Merch sydd decaf blodeu*yn*
Yn y nef ond Duw ei h*un*.
O wraig y ganed pob d*yn*
O'r holl bobloedd ond trid*yn*.
Ac am hynny nid rhyf*edd*
Caru merched a gwrag*edd*.
O'r nef y cad digrif*wch*
Ac o uffern bob trist*wch*.

The remainder of the canonical poems by Dafydd in *GDG* — 138 poems — are all *cywyddau*. The full name of Dafydd's *cywydd* form is *cywydd deuair hirion*. This form has rhyming couplets of seven-syllable lines; the rhymes are on alternating accented and unaccented final syllables (as in the English, d*en*, hidd*en*); the sequence of the accented and unaccented final syllables may vary from couplet to couplet; each line is to have *cynghanedd*, although fourteenth century poets occasionally omitted *cynghanedd* in lines of the *cywydd*.

The following lines illustrating the *cywydd* are from Poem 49 (lines 25–38). I have marked the key accents, italicized the sounds that figure in *cynghanedd*, and identified the type of *cynghanedd* by abbreviations at the left of each line. The caesura is marked only in lines of *cynghanedd groes*. *G* at the end of a word followed by *G* at the beginning of the next word makes one sound that may alliterate with hard *C*. The sound represented by *NG* is joined to a preceding vowel sound (as in gu*ng* ho).

Poem 49: lines 25–38

D1	*M*air! ai *g*wáeth bod y *m*ur *g*wýn
G3	*D*an y *c*álch, | *d*oniog *g*ýlch*y̆*n,
S4	No phe rhodd*id*, *g*éubr*ĭd g*w̄ŕ
D3	*P*únt er dyfod o'r *p*éin*t*iw̄r
G1	I *b*eintio'n *h*árdd, | *b*wyn*t*iau'*n h*óyw,
G2	*Ll*e árlo*ĕ*s | a *ll*iw eúr*l*oy̆w,
L	A lliwiau gl*án* ychw*á*n*ĕ*g
S4	A llun*iau t*ari*á*n*ău t*ég?
D2	*D*íl*y̆*s, fy nghorff, lle *d*él*w*y̆f,
G1	*D*eu*l*iw'r s*ê*ŕ, | *d*o*l*ur*us* wýf.
S4	Dith*au*, d*if*ród*iău* dy *f*ráwd,
S2	Dyn*yn* dan*h*éd*d*w*y̆*n *h*áed*d*w*ă*wd,
S4	Gwell *w*yd mewn pais *w*énll*wy̆*d *w*íw
D2	No*g* iá*rll*ĕs mewn gwis*g* éur*ll*ĭw.

To achieve the intricate harmonies of Welsh verse is clearly a test of craftsmanship, but Welsh poets enjoy a license that expedites *cynghanedd* even as it complicates understanding their poems. It is the license to interrupt sentences, phrases, and even compound words or names. There are two kinds, *sangiad* and *trychiad*.

Sangiad is a poetic license permitting parenthetical interruptions in a sentence, the parenthesis consisting not only of words or phrases in apposition to elements of the principal sentence, but also the disjointed development of a counter sentence. *Trychiad* is the separation of words that normally are a close unit; a common *trychiad* is dividing a name into genealogical fragments: first name in the first line, father's name with patronymic (*mab,* son; *merch,* daughter; mutated by principles of Welsh phonology to *fab* and *ferch*) in the second line, the names being separated by other words in the sentence. While *sangiad* and *trychiad* are devices that expedite *cynghanedd,* they seem also to have been used as a poetic ornament in their own right, a word-mix riddlingly different from straightforward prose. Dafydd ap Gwilym skillfully employs these interruptions for the enrichment or complication of meaning and the expression of vehement emotion.

Dafydd's vocabulary is extensive and varied, mixing the archaic and the colloquial, plain words and figurative compounds. He uses English words, including several like *mwnai* ("money") and *mwtlai* ("motley") which are not now current in Welsh, suggesting commerce with English-speaking communities consistent with the openness to foreign cultures that he shows elsewhere in his poetry. He draws on French words as well as English, though Middle English might have been the medium for his learning many of them. If he never visited France, he could still have heard French in places of Norman settlement in Wales or the Marcher lordships along the English border. My guess, from his references to Gascony and Paris (he never names London) as well as his references to the hazards of sea-crossing, is that he did visit France. But Wales itself, with its southern and northern lowland roads and its peninsulas out to sea traffic, was sufficiently cosmopolitan to have been Dafydd's lifelong home and still have made a European of him. He refers often to the international medieval church, to its liturgy, papacy, friars, nuns. He uses technical language, especially in extended conceits: terms from law (as in Poem 82, "Begging for His Life" and Poem 123, "The Cock-thrush II"), agriculture (as in Poem 87, "Love's Husbandry"), warfare (as in Poem 140, "A Fortress Against Envy"), political administration (as in Poem 117, "The Wind"). Musical terms abound (the exact meaning of some being lost to history). But he is a master also of homely, vivid description, particularly of the natural world.

The variety of his diction, like the parenthetical weavings of his verse, reflects his complexity. I hope I have done justice to his puzzles, while expressing his meanings. After experimenting with various forms and strategies, I have settled on translating the poems in prose, line by line so far as sentence-sense would allow. The translated poems appear (and are numbered) in the same order in which they stand in Sir Thomas Parry's edition; the lines also follow the numbering of the Welsh text. This should make it convenient for readers to use my translations in conjunction with *Gwaith Dafydd ap Gwilym.* But I have rearranged words and phrases wherever adherence to the Welsh word order would have been meaningless or too unnatural in English. Welsh syntax permits things that English does not. For example, in Welsh, the beginnings of words may be changed to indicate function or relationship within a sentence. To cite only a few of the many mutations in Welsh, there is such a mutation of certain modifiers; of objects of certain prepositions and verb forms; of compounded words. Like inflected endings (and Welsh has some of those), the mutations convey information that in English may be indicated only by position. On the other hand, the genitive in Welsh may be indicated by position alone: *allor serch* means "altar of love." Consequently, a translation must depart from word-for-word rendering of the Welsh by moving words to the positions required by English syntax or adding the function words required in English.

I have tried to match the economy of Dafydd's Welsh, but that is sometimes impossible. For example, Dafydd frequently refers to a beautiful woman by an elliptical phrase such as *unne geirw*. The words mean "same-color" and "foam." In context, the sense of the phrase would be "one of the same color as foam." It is a tribute, a variation on the theme of the woman's light complexion and radiant beauty. Such an expression may be deftly introduced into a Welsh line, but needs more words in English. Poem 67 begins with the line, *Digio 'dd wyf am liw ewyn,* which I translate, "I'm vexed because of a girl bright as foam." The Welsh expresses "a girl white as foam" with just the words, *liw ewyn,* "color of foam." The word-by-word equivalent of the line in English would be something like "I'm vexed because of the color of foam," but that is not what the Welsh means. The Welsh reader understands "color of foam" as shorthand for "one of the color of foam," and that must be made clear in English. My specifying "bright" is not literal (nor is my specifying "girl") but that is the sense of the comparison, a sense that can be muted in an English translation long on abstractions and function words.

The *cywydd* line has only seven syllables; one of the lines in my translation of Poem 67 has sixteen syllables. In addition to having to open up a Welsh shorthand-phrase, I had to struggle in this case with some packed Welsh monosyllables. There are many words of one syllable in Welsh that translate into polysyllabic English. *Teg,* for example, which means "beautiful, fair, fine." *Fair* works well as a translation of *teg*. Though it has an archaic flavor, it carries the same meanings of "beautiful" and "admirable" as the Welsh word; and *fair* also expresses the lightness of color that is so often noted as a quality of beauty in medieval love poetry. But one cannot be using *fair* all the time. In addition to *teg* (and polysyllables like *prydferth, golygus, lluniaidd,* and *gweddaidd*), Welsh has several other monosyllables that mean "beautiful" (such as *hardd, glân, glwys, tlws, syw, cain*.) Each of these has distinctive connotations that must be respected in translation. To avoid overuse of "fair" and to find terms of the right connotation, one must turn to polysyllables in English: beautiful, lovely, handsome, good-looking, comely, attractive, radiant, elegant. The same is true for *fine*. Besides *teg*, these Welsh monosyllables mean "fine": *cain, syw, coeth, gwych, gwiw, pur, glân, braf*. The English monosyllables that might translate these words are few: brave (in its archaic sense of "excellent"), right, fit, pure, choice. Again, one must often search among English polysyllables for an appropriate translation: excellent, refined, elegant, cultured, splendid, brilliant, fitting, proper, worthy.

Bright, like *fair* and *fine*, is a word that occurs often in my translations. Together with *shining*, it is a frequent translation for several terms used in Dafydd's poems to express radiance. So often does Dafydd mention brightness, with so many bright images and lively words, that his poetry sparkles and flashes. I have sometimes felt that I had only a couple of light bulbs to switch on in contrast to all his jewels of words: *gloyw, claer, golau, disglair, llachar, llewyrchus*. To this list must be added the words for "white," which often mean "bright" or "luminous": *gwyn, can, cannaid*. The feminine of the adjective *gwyn*, *gwen*, may also be used in Welsh to mean "fair maiden," "pretty girl," "pale beauty." It is another instance of the enviable resources of many a short word used by Dafydd ap Gwilym.

And *gwen* is but one of several words (many of them monosyllables) that Dafydd uses for "woman" or "girl":

bun:	woman, maiden, sweetheart
dyn:	woman, maiden
dynyn, dynan:	little woman
gwawr:	lady
gwraig:	woman, wife
merch:	girl, daughter
morwyn:	girl, maid, virgin
rhiain:	maiden

To this list should be added such terms as the following, by which he may refer to one who is loved:

annwyl:	dear
anwylyd:	beloved
byd:	treasure, darling
cariad:	lover, love
crair:	relic, holy thing, treasure

enaid:	soul
gem:	gem
glain:	jewel, bead
lleuad, lloer:	moon
trysor:	treasure

Modern translators tend to use *girl* to translate the terms for "woman"; it is the plain, affectionate, uncomplicated modern choice. But the Welsh terms Dafydd uses carry varying connotations that deserve some recognition: distinctions of age, rank, intimacy, elegance, innocence, experience. Even the figurative expressions pose problems: *relic* can sound like anything but a complimentary way of saluting a woman! Expressions like "my dear" or "my darling" may seem stilted or ironic in modern English. The problem is complicated by the fact that Dafydd does have complex tones and ironies in his verse. At any rate, I have used *girl* most of the time for Dafydd's women; but I have also used *woman* and the alternative expressions wherever it seemed natural and right to do so: a *maiden* here, a *sweetheart* there, occasionally a *lady*. I keep the figurative terms as metaphorically intact as possible (moon, soul, gem, jewel); *crair* I usually translate as *treasure*.

The following are some more Welsh monosyllables that I have wished I could use in my translations, without having to hunt for English words of the same force and meaning:

aur: gold; money; treasure, beloved; fine, splendid. Dafydd often uses *aur* in its figurative senses, but I have kept it "gold" or "golden" whenever I could. The alternative would have been another drain on *fine*. Thanks in part to Housman and Shakespeare, "golden girl" has about the same meaning for us as it had for Dafydd — a trace archaic, but still suggesting (without footnotes) a glow of solid worth.

berw: boiling, seething; tumult, turbulence. A favorite image of Dafydd's is to speak of the composition or recital of poetry as *berw*, a boiling. Energy, excitement; life, air, light; bursting, rapid, overflowing movement. Poetry.

glas: blue, sky-blue, sea-green; grass-green, blue-green; pale blue, gray-blue, pallid, pale; silver; iron-gray; gray, holy; cool, faint, scornful; raw, fresh; bright. All that and more. The Celts use color-terms not for one fixed hue but to name a range of colors that wash into various shades and qualities.

gwas: lad, youth, man-servant. Dafydd often applies the term to himself. *Lad* says it, but with tones from Housman or Shakespeare that may make the term less ordinary, less plain and modest than it is. Like *boy* in the United States, the word can be used condescendingly. In such cases, I usually translate it as *fellow,* sometimes as *boy.*

hoyw: one of Dafydd's favorites. It means: lively, active, sprightly, nimble, brisk, cheerful, vivacious. A wonderful word in every way, the more wonderful for being short and simple.

hud: magic, enchantment, charm. The English equivalents have associations with show-business, adornment, or sweetness that are not irrelevant but which divert us from the Welsh word's core meaning of a powerful, otherworldly spell.

mad: good, fitting, lucky. The word suggests Aristotle's notion of the happy man. I often translate *mad* as *fine*, but feel the need of a footnote explaining "*fine* in the sense of *good, fitting, lucky.*"

trais: violence, rape, oppression. Dafydd often uses the term in contexts not involving literal violence. "Forcible coercion" appears to be the underlying sense. The word is a whiplash that cracks in many a line of Dafydd's. Is it a reminder of the element of force in medieval Welsh political strife (as in the murder of Dafydd's bardic uncle)?

In his use of detail for descriptions and comparisons, it is characteristic of Dafydd ap Gwilym to attend closely to the object his senses apprehend. I have tried to express these perceptions justly, to reproduce his images as exactly as I could. Here, as much as in translating words, phrases, and sentences, translators differ. The picture or detail that one sees, another will omit or fit into a different configuration or simply understand differently. An illustration of my handling of Dafydd's imagery is the opening section of Poem 63 (a poem devoted principally to a quarrel between the poet and a magpie), where there occur these five lines on the skylark, in my translation:

> And the skylark, a calm voice,
> Dear, gray-cowled bird of wise speech
> Going in utter weariness
> With a *cywydd* to the sky's height
> (From the bare field, gentle prince,
> Backwards to his chamber he climbs).

This translation is fairly literal. But what does it mean to say that the skylark climbs backwards to the sky's height? Kenneth Jackson, in *A Celtic Miscellany* (Penguin Books, 1979, p. 317), notes that the skylark does drift backwards in its fluttering flight. There may also be this figurative logic, that the skylark flies from the field to the sky as one entitled to soar, as a "gentle prince," as one flying back to his high place. Why, then, does he go "in utter weariness?" Jackson translates *lludded* (fatigue, weariness, exhaustion) as "ecstasy." I keep the literal sense because it conveys the strenuous character of the small bird's flight. The difficulty of his flight makes more admirable the fact that the bird sings as it hovers in the sky. And what he sings deserves note: a *cywydd*. The skylark is a poet like Dafydd (in Poem 114, line 44, Dafydd hails the skylark as "my privileged brother"). The bird has brown, striated plumage with a small crest; Dafydd calls him gray-cowled. His word for "gray" is *llwyd* (the same word the magpie will later apply reproachfully to Dafydd himself); it means not only "gray" but also "pale," "brown," and "holy." Thus, it suits the phrase "gray-cowled" that links the bird to a cowled monk (like the Cistercians, whose cowls were of this color). The skylark is unlike the jabbering, earthbound magpie who chides the poet; the skylark has a "calm voice" and "wise speech." He is a prince of the sky.

Indeed, in Poem 114, Dafydd calls the skylark *modd awdur serch* (line 23), which I translate, "image of the author of love," that is, like God. There are abundant references to God in the poetry of Dafydd ap Gwilym (listed in my Glossary). From so bold a love poet, one does not expect ordinary pieties. But Dafydd is not unbelieving. The persons that medieval religion made spiritually present to man-kind — the Persons of the Trinity, the saints — are present in Dafydd's poetry with a realness that is heightened by his forthrightness. He quarrels with God, enlists the help of heaven in earthy pursuits, consigns those who oppose him to the devil. This is not nice, hardly proper, though amusing. Some readers are content to read such poems as boisterous fun needing no justification. Yet there is a shadow of pathos to his merriment. And also, despite the honest sadness, a recurring note of equally honest and profound exultation. God is involved in it all. He made Paradise, He renews nature, He offers His life for love, He is the source of beauty and joy — and He forbids any love that obstructs the soul's union with Him. In this universe of love, love contends with love. The power of Dafydd's poetry lies in his depiction of that cosmic contention of loves. The struggle has turns and counterturns, but among those contending, God is active as a skylark.

Although I have not attempted a verse translation, I have tried to retain something of the woven quality of Dafydd's poems. Dafydd often speaks of poetry as a debate and as a weaving. Within the fabric of sounds in his *cywyddau*, with their rhyming couplets and their intricate patterns of *cynghanedd*, there lies another fabric of woven meanings. A first strand is the poem's central line of thought or action, often begun abruptly, developed with description, concluded neatly and pungently. A second strand consists of parenthetical compliments and complaints, scattered through the poems like irrepressible sighs and groans. A third strand consists of parallel or contrasting topics that are developed against the main thread of the poem.

At times, these weavings resemble stream of consciousness fiction. At times, they suggest the patter of a comedian. In fact, they are the tapestries of a medieval Welshman exploiting the liberties of parenthesis allowed him by his poetic tradition. What paradoxes, what conflicts, what ambiguities he can represent through his self-interrupting style, I shall discuss later in this introduction. At this point I would only draw attention to the necessity of attending to these strands in Dafydd's verse. To assist the reader, I have added some reinforcement to the punctuation in Sir Thomas Parry's edition. In particular, I add parentheses and a few slashes and dashes. It is not possible to mark all of Dafydd's parenthetical utterances thus. Sometimes the phrases are too closely knit to be separated. But when a sentence is broken by a tribute or reproach, by a counter sentence, by a fragment of reminiscence or a hint of something about to be discussed, and when the broken sentence is hard to follow because of this break, I mark off the interruption. I hope thereby to help a reader not lose a main sentence while adverting to a secondary element.

Though I have supplied these signposts and have simplified the structure of other passages, yet I have tried to keep the original fabric where I could. For the interruptions are not so much interruptions as they are separate motifs or voices. The poems offer us a many-layered music that we hear — once we have learned how to listen to it — not as disjointed fragments but as polyphony.

As we would expect from one sensitive to voice, Dafydd ap Gwilym is a master dramatist. He did not write for a theatre, since none existed adequate to his talents. But he composed dramas, in which he plays a central role.

Five poems begin with the phrase, "Fal yr oeddwn," meaning, "as I was"; some forty more have in their opening lines a verb or phrase containing or implying "I am," "I was," or "I did"; some twenty-five have in their opening lines such time-words as *yesterday, today, last night, day* (or *night*) *before yesterday, the other night, at dawn*; more than sixty of the poems present an incident as their subject, their setting, or a key part of their development.

A characteristic method of his is to mingle times he has experienced or is experiencing or may experience. The opening of Poem 131, "Yesterday," exhibits a typical development: the poet compares a happy yesterday of love with an unfulfilled day before yesterday, asks whether God will give him in the future another yesterday, and in the present moment of the poem affirms his stubborn commitment to love.

More than forty poems are addresses, explicitly directed to persons, places, or things: to Christ (1, 2), to Ifor Hael (5, 6, 7, 10), to the Dean of Bangor Cathedral (15), to Rhys Meigen (21), to the father of the noble girl Dyddgu (45), to Dwynwen, patroness of lovers (94), to the town of Newborough (134), to the poet Gruffudd Gryg (148, 150, 152, 154). Thirteen are addressed to various women (recurring names being those of Morfudd and Dyddgu). Several are addressed to messengers, including some of Dafydd's most imaginative compositions, the poems commissioning a love-messenger (*llatai*) to take his appeal to a woman he loves; among the messengers are a lark (114), a woodcock (115), a stag (116), a storm-wind (117), and a seagull (118). Other addresses are to summer (27); a birch hat he's received as a love-token (59); a haystack where he hides (62); a wave at the estuary of the Dyfi (71); his own wayward heart (108).

Many of Dafydd's poems contain dialogue. Where it has seemed helpful, I have identified the various speakers, in italic letters at the left margin. These identifications are my addition and do not appear in the Welsh text.

There are passages of dialogue in some twenty-six poems. Most of the talking (besides Dafydd's) is done by his women. They often tease him, but do not always deny him. The women who speak in the following poems are affectionate or at least encouraging:

> Poem 32: A Garland of Peacock Feathers
> Poem 77: Doubting Wrongly (Morfudd denies that she
>   is not true to him)
> Poem 126: The Goose Shed
> Poem 129: The Dawn

In these last two, the girl hurries Dafydd on his way, but promises a tryst with him later.

In the following poems, the woman expresses a challenge of anxiety or criticism, but does not altogether reject the poet; the poet responds, usually at length, with self-defense:

> Poem 33: The Plain-dealing Poet
> Poem 58: The Girl Mocks His Cowardice
> Poem 91: The Frost

In Poem 41, "A Stubborn Girl," the girl teases him with ambiguous promises that she does not keep.

In Poem 48, "The Girls of Llanbadarn," and Poem 142, "The Song," the girls ridicule him.

The proud woman in Poem 128, "Insulting His Servant," is outspokenly contemptuous of Dafydd's overtures.

Other speakers in the poems are the poet Madog Benfras (25), an old woman who favorably interprets a dream of the poet's (39), a fellow poet who joins him in a game of prognostication by nuts (50), certain persons who report that the girl he loves is getting married (86), an English huckster worried about his pack in the tavern where Dafydd attempts a tryst (124), friars who condemn illicit love (136, 137, 138, 139).

Finally, there are the fantasy poems in which Dafydd represents these non-human creatures or personifications as speaking to him:

> Poem 27: Summer
> Poem 36: A Cock-thrush
> Poem 63: A Magpie
> Poem 92: Longing
> Poem 115: A Woodcock
> Poem 141: His Shadow
> Poem 144: A Ruined House

Conversations in the poems of Dafydd ap Gwilym do more than invest his scenes with life. They provide an articulation of contrary attitudes and convictions, a genuine dialectic. Dafydd uses the Welsh words for debate (*dadl, ymryson*) with relish. He likes to debate, with girls, fellow poets, his critics, animals, cosmic powers. It is natural for a reader to assume that the speaker of the poems, the *persona* Dafydd, is expressing the poet's mind; but it is, I think, a misreading to dismiss all those other voices as not also part of the poet's mind. At any rate, what the poet often gives us are debates, and we should read carefully both his arguments as a character in the poems and the arguments of his adversaries. Fourteenth-century poets, like those famous contemporaries of Dafydd's, Chaucer and Boccaccio, were not incapable of ironic self-portraits.

That Dafydd's debates reflect inner contests, were debates that held his own mind in tension, is suggested by the fact that this poet who argues so impudently with friars (136, 137, 138, 139) also wrote devotional poems (1, 2, 3, 4). Readers may choose to regard the devotional poems as merely conventional and to judge the posture against friars as embodying Dafydd's "serious" convictions. But I am persuaded—by the poems—that his position was indeed ambivalent.

The devotional poems, to begin with, are intelligent and impassioned. Themselves well-crafted works of art, they contain indications of their author's appreciation of craft, as in the fourth poem, a meditation on a contemporary painting of Christ and the apostles. Here we find Dafydd's love of color and of life-likeness, together with a capacity to match the painting with apt brief sketches of the figures there represented. The *Anima Christi* stanzas, appropriate to a sequence of the mass, are sacramental yet personal, orthodox yet original, an elaboration, prompted by individual feeling, of a central theme of medieval belief. Like the solemn praise poems that follow in Dr. Parry's edition, these religious poems fix an orientation of standards and commitments reflected variously in the more innovative love poems.

As for the friar poems, we note that in none of them does Dafydd assail the friars on grounds like those in, say, Chaucer's satirical portraits. Dafydd's friars are not outrageously irregular. Indeed, their offense lies chiefly in their austere advice to Dafydd to repent, in that wisdom of renunciation which accompanies the love poetry of the later Middle Ages and the Renaissance like Hamlet's faithful friend who was not passion's slave.

Though Dafydd rejects this wisdom while debating the friars, he announces a death-fearing repentance in Poem 106. And even as he flings abuse at the friars for their busy, authoritarian, world-roaming preaching, the language he gives them is dignified. The friar of Poem 136 graciously compliments Dafydd on his gifts and urges him to dedicate them to praising God. The friar in Poem 137 is grave but not so deferential; he denounces all secular love poetry as an inducement to sin. This criticism provokes Dafydd's longest apology. His defense seems sane and untroubled enough and easily persuades modern readers; but we should remember its ironic setting: the confessional.

In Poem 138, Dafydd accuses the friar of contaminating the world with his nonsense. What nonsense? The friar is quoted as saying two things, that flesh rots in the grave and that lust is punished in hell. The first is a fact undoubted in all ages (save when a miracle intervenes); the second was (at least as regards unrepentant lust) a certainty of medieval theology. Dafydd's defiance of this "nonsense" makes high and mournful comedy, but he does not exactly confute the friar's warnings.

The last of the friar poems, Poem 139, is closer to tragedy. Here we have what may be Dafydd's last poem on Morfudd; it is, at any rate, the one that represents her at the latest stage of her career: Morfudd grown old. It is one of Dafydd's bitterest poems. Not only the friar who urges Morfudd to cover her body but God Himself comes in for denunciation, for laying waste to Morfudd's beauty. And Morfudd too must bear the poet's lash, for so enchanting him that even when her beauty is gone, he cannot rest easily without her.

The introduction to the 1789 *Barddoniaeth Dafydd ab Gwilym* offers a narrative-frame for the Morfudd poems; Dr. Parry scrupulously avoids anything more than setting forth some of the evidence for recognizing Morfudd as an historical figure and not merely one of the poet's fictions. Eurys Rowlands, a leading modern commentator on Dafydd ap Gwilym, has written of Dafydd (in his review of *GDG*[2] in *Llên Cymru* 8: 1–2, p. 111; my translation): "It is extremely likely that one of the facts in his life that most influenced his poetry was his relationship with Morfudd."

There are 36 poems in which Morfudd's name appears: Poems 34, 35, 38, 42, 43, 50, 52, 53, 57, 59, 67, 69, 71, 72, 73, 76, 77, 79, 83, 85, 87, 89, 93, 94, 96, 98, 102, 103, 106, 108, 109, 113, 117, 122, 131, 139; Gruffudd Gryg also mentions Morfudd in his first *cywydd* in his debate with Dafydd (Poem 147). These Morfudd poems engage us, even more than do the friar poems, in debates on love. While we may refrain from attempting to fix a narrative sequence for the poems, we do find, upon comparing and relating them, some help in understanding their debates. And as we read them together, we perceive elements of a situation and of a changing relationship that yield, if not a story, at least *dramatis personae* and myriad compelling scenes.

Morfudd was not the only woman for whom Dafydd professes love. In Poem 98, "Choosing One of Four," Morfudd is the first to be noted as loved by the poet; followed by Helen (wife of a burgess); Dyddgu; and an un-named woman of rank. The woman of rank might have been Angharad, wife of Ieuan Llwyd of Glyn Aeron, who was a patroness of the poet's for whom he had such an attachment as to provoke gossip (see Poem 140 and the elegy on Angharad, Poem 16). Nest, wife of Ifor Hael of Basaleg, is praised with feeling in poem 11, but presumably not amorous feeling, given Dafydd's friendship for Ifor.

One poem each is allotted to women, perhaps only imaginary types, named Efa (Poem 97, "Being Forgetful"), Deifr (Poem 66, "The Clock"), and Luned (Poem 133, "A Kiss"). Such traditional names as these might also be pseudonyms for women whose identity Dafydd chooses to keep secret.

Of the many love poems that do not name the woman who is their subject, some agree, some do not agree with consistent features of the Morfudd poems.

Remembering Dr. Parry's caution — as in his note on Poem 57 — that some of the Morfudd poems may not be by Dafydd, we can assemble from the Morfudd poems this conjectural portrait of her: She was blonde and, before she aged, beautiful (*passim*), tall (96), well-born (102), possibly born in Eithinfynydd (57) in Merionethshire, her father's name being Madog Lawgam (93). Dafydd's courtship of her was public (108), and he celebrated her in poems that became famous throughout Gwynedd (34). A religious girl, she had scruples about returning his love (57), but at last pledged her love to him (43). This pledge may have been part of a ritual marriage, though not a marriage sanctioned and witnessed by the church. In any event, a canonical marriage with another man was arranged for Morfudd by her family, leading Dafydd (in a poem, 86, that does not name Morfudd but fits the circumstances of his love for her) to declare that he would have no other wife. Morfudd's husband, named Cynfrig Cynin (73), bore the nickname "Bwa Bach" (131), meaning "Little Bow," that is, "Little Hunchback." His home in Uwch Aeron (117) was in Dafydd's own home country (the parish of Llanbadarn in north Ceredigion). Morfudd bore Bwa Bach children, but did not cease to love Dafydd (79). Dafydd's love for her lasted, as I have noted above, until she grew old (139). After her marriage, he sought (and sometimes won) secret trysts with her, in the woods (successfully in 53) or by night at her home (unsuccessfully in 89). But her husband's jealousy was savage enough that Dafydd was virtually exiled from his native territory in Uwch Aeron (117), his covert incursions involving a risk to his life. Of this risk he speaks in commissioning animals to bear his love messages; their fleet natures should enable them to evade the jealous husband's attacks (as in 117). It is, doubtless, of this dangerous little man that Dafydd speaks in 75, a poem wishing death on Eiddig ("the jealous one"). Eiddig's very breath, Dafydd charges in 81, has spoiled the face of the wife whom we may take to be the same Morfudd whose loss of beauty from age is mourned in 139.

In one Morfudd poem (122), the poet observes that Morfudd has sent a thrush to greet him from *Swydd Gaer*, perhaps meaning Carmarthenshire. Dr. Parry (*GDG*[3], p. xxvii) sees no reason why Morfudd might not have resided at some time in Carmarthenshire, but he believes that it is not of Morfudd that the poet speaks in poems referring to women from the following places: Dyfed (84), Is Aeron (88), and Maelor (44).

Three Morfudd poems (34, 57, 98) link her in some way with Gwynedd. If Morfudd is also the woman referred to in poems 86, 114, and 137, these further Gwynedd ties would apply to her: her family are "hawks of Gwynedd" (86); she is the "moon of Gwynedd" (114); the poet who praises her sees himself as entertaining an audience of "girls of Gwynedd" (137). Perhaps she is the girl from Gwynedd who has spoiled Dafydd's face (105). All these Gwynedd references could be accounted for as having to do with her place of birth, if we accept the testimony of Poem 57 that Morfudd is from Eithinfynydd (and if we locate Eithinfynydd in Merionethshire — see *GDG*[3], p. 490). Other poems having to do with a girl from Gwynedd imply that the girl lives now in Gwynedd: Poem 51, which deals with a first meeting; Poem 128, a tavern encounter. Dr. Parry doubts that Morfudd is the girl at Bangor Cathedral (Poem 111) whose love-spear wounds Dafydd, to the satisfaction of husbands in Môn. There are these further instances of poems concerning an unnamed Gwynedd woman: the girl in Môn referred to in Poem 8; the object of Dafydd's going to Gwynedd in Poem 10; the married woman from Môn who, after first granting him her love, has so far rejected him that Dafydd charges her with wanting him hanged (82); the girl called a nun (it could be the devout Morfudd herself) whom Dafydd imagines as making a pilgrimage to St. David's in reparation for having "slain" the poet (99). Morfudd is associated with nuns in Poem 113, namely the nuns of the Cistercian convent of Llanllugan in Powys, who are called her "sisters in baptism" (which may mean simply that they are all Christians; or, as Dr. Bromwich urges, that Morfudd is as inaccessible to Dafydd as the nuns).

Certain of Dafydd's poems to unnamed girls suggest mere promiscuity, without the sustained relationship of the Morfudd poems: for example, Poem 47, "Bargaining," and these tavern poems: 124, "Trouble in a Tavern"; 132, "Carousing"; 135, "Stealing a Girl."

Whatever complications the poet may stumble over in pursuing these other women, all are relatively simple affairs compared to Dafydd's relationship with Morfudd. Consider Poem 79, in which Dafydd compares the brunette Dyddgu and the blonde Morfudd. They differ in more than hair color. Dyddgu is the ideal love, beautiful and gracious. Morfudd is not ideal. She loves "those who rebuke her," being married to a fiercely jealous man who does not know how to love. Therefore, the poet concludes that he'll choose Dyddgu (if he can win her). A neat conclusion; but in the other eight poems that name Dyddgu (Poems 37, 45, 92, 95, 98, 116, 119, 142) there is no mention of successful love. Dyddgu remains beautiful and gracious — and not to be won by Dafydd. Morfudd is the girl he won and lost and won again and lost again; the girl he admires not casually nor from a distance but intimately; and she is the girl he chides, criticizes, condemns, with an acerbity he never uses toward the remote Dyddgu. For Morfudd knows how to give him her love and how to withhold it; she can betray her husband by trysting with Dafydd, yet she remains respectably married; she prays to Mary — and not only permits the poet's advances but enchants him herself, with a magic she never loses, even in age.

In Poem 54, several details fit the Morfudd relationship, though she is not named. The poem is Dafydd's assertion of his claims over those of a rival. He who has mocked a jealous husband must now feel the sting of jealousy himself. Dafydd reminds the woman that his rival has not travailed or travelled as Dafydd has, has not wept such floods, has not sung a hundredth part of the canon of poems Dafydd has composed to her. This last detail fits Morfudd alone: only to her did he sing such numbers of famous tributes. Morfudd, then, has entertained a rival, at least according to report; and this cruel fact must account for her present coldness toward Dafydd: not piety, not marital fidelity, not fear of an angry spouse or an enraged family, but love for another lover!

No wonder Dafydd feels (as he twice declares) a spear-pang in his head for Morfudd.

For he loves her and does not love her. In one of the Morfudd Llwyd poems, Poem 76, "Against Trusting in the World," Dafydd identifies Morfudd's love as one of the fickle goods of this unstable world. He has lavished his own goods on the pursuit of her, only to lose her to Eiddig. Better to be a blackbird singing blithely in nature's good custody! And singing, at least, the poet will continue to be, recovering thereby (since he is well patronized throughout Wales) the wealth he's lost. Yet he cannot refrain from closing with the cry that he was tricked out of his light, his "candle," the Morfudd Llwyd who had sworn to love him always.

Love is no unmixed delight for Dafydd. In Poem 30, he likens love to a fowler snaring him; in Poem 104, to a costly and ungrateful foster son. Poem 108, "The Heart," begins with what seems to be praise of love: "Hail, short, round, little heart. . . ." But the loving heart is then crudely indicted as a source of troubles prompting Dafydd to ruinous extravagance. Still, in Poem 90, "A Lover's Affliction," after cataloguing his ruins (accomplished no doubt by time as well as love's betrayal), he concludes that no love is left in him — "unless a girl asks."

In his elegy on Dafydd ap Gwilym, Gruffudd Gryg, a younger contemporary, says of him: *Gwawr serch ar y gwir y sydd.* This I translate as: "Lord of love, he is for the truth." The judgment may reflect an admiration that Gruffudd Gryg attained as he himself grew more accomplished as a poet.

Gruffudd had battled with Dafydd on the subject of love poetry. As I have noted earlier, Dafydd employs themes, situations, and forms of continental courtly love literature, especially the troubadour conventions. These would have reached him probably through French poetry (such as the *Roman de la Rose*), or through popular minstrelsy (including English as well as Welsh lyrics). His bardic uncle's courts were no doubt polyglot literary centers where he could have learned more than Welsh poetic lore. As Rachel Bromwich has demonstrated, the debate between Dafydd and Gruffudd Gryg may be read as a protest by the conservative, northern Gruffudd Gryg against these foreign fashions. For the continental Ovidian modes stress the helpless misery of the poet-lover, which is what Gruffudd ridicules in Dafydd.

Several of Dafydd's poems, on the other hand, incorporate native customs relating to love. Among them are Poem 31, "Madog's Birch Wreath"; Poem 32, "A Garland of Peacock Feathers"; Poem 38, "The Lady Goldsmith"; Poem 50, "A Game of *Cnau i'm Llaw*"; Poem 59, "The Birch Hat"; Poem 85, "Disappointment." Each of these tells of objects taken from nature (birch stems, peacock feathers, hazel nuts, sticks of hazel and willow) which are conferred as gifts that carry a love meaning. The birch hat of Poem 59, for example, has been made and given to Dafydd by Morfudd Llwyd. If it really means that she loves him, the sign will spell sorrow for her jealous husband. Jealous husbands do not love; they possess their wives coldly. Their season is winter, not summer. The poet in his grove boldly affirms a claim to Morfudd that supplants the husband's.

Yet Dafydd honors the married love of his patron and friend, Ifor Hael, and Ifor's wife, Nest, and appears himself to have wanted to marry Morfudd, even to have been pledged to her in a ritual resembling marriage. Poem 43 tells of an exchange of love-oaths between him and Morfudd, concluding thus:

> In cold water was ordained
> The oath that Morfudd Llwyd gave.

The holiness of water is an element of folk belief attested to by the holy wells still frequented in Celtic lands. Was it by dipping her hand in the water of such a well that Morfudd swore to love Dafydd? In any event, this reference to an oath by word, hand, and water is a dramatic instance of Dafydd's use of a folklore that links human love to the larger order of nature.

One of the conventions of medieval literature that appears often in Dafydd's poetry is the representation of birds as speaking a love like that of poets: they debate on love, compose verses, woo with song, complain in song, can serve as love-messengers, as well as preach and read the gospel with distinction.

It has long been recognized that Dafydd's use of nature is remarkable, so much so that some critics have urged that he be denominated primarily a nature poet. For one thing, there is the abundance of detail in passages of description in poems with a woodland setting or featuring an animal or a natural phenomenon. In medieval Welsh poetry, such passages usually entail an accumulation of comparisons, called *dyfalu*. These comparisons may be riddling. In Dafydd's poems, the comparisons often prove to be both surprising and exact, the riddle puzzling us and then, as we attend to it, yielding a keener impression or insight. The comparisons are frequently to things that are a part of Dafydd's human world, so that *dyfalu* descriptive of nature may simultaneously show us a good deal of the gear, the trappings, the folk of fourteenth century Wales: a fox is likened to a fire-dish (lamp) set at a shuttered window; mist, to a slovenly blanket; a haycock, to a burgess; a star, to a mass-wafer and a feast-dish and a pearl and a gold coin and a perfectly white loaf; the wind is a cloud-notary, a sportive boy on the seashore, a fluent author, a privileged laugher on the hill.

Poem 46, "Love Compared to a Hare," begins with 42 lines that describe the hare with lively precision. Rachel Bromwich notes that Dafydd's fox (Poem 22) is no Reynard, no humanized beast, but simply and extraordinarily a real fox. Dafydd manages to draw us into his act of perception: he sees the fox "sitting like a tame animal | On his haunches near his den." To suggest the fox's speed (when preying on farm animals), Dafydd gives this blurred impression of the fox as being in two places at once: "At both ends of a field there turns up | A dog-shape looking for a goose."

In several poems, Dafydd explores similitudes between elements of nature and his own experiences in love. Poem 42 likens the beautiful but changeable and hard-to-hold Morfudd to the sun, by aspects clearly distinguished and logically developed. In Poem 87, he likens the collapse of a courtship to the loss of a crop in a violent summer storm. Poem 30 asserts that Dafydd has been snared as birds are caught in birdlime—and that God has set the trap of love that holds him.

In Poem 83, "A Journey for Love," the poet tells of a walk he made over his native hills in quest of a meeting with Morfudd. He has previously made successful walks of this sort and notes one spot of moorland where he says leaves still retain the contour of his and his love's bodies. But the journey of this poem is without fulfillment. As he walks along, his mood is happy with remembrance and hope, yet grows increasingly disconsolate as he encounters no one. He hears himself calling for the girl, he waits for her as reverently as a monk in choir. He knows all the land by heart, its very names are dear to him, and he recites them for us joyfully. But his quest has failed. The poem's melancholy and transport are precisely located, attached to fitting sites, as Dafydd crosses a brook of hoarse voice, slips through reeds where a goosechick might shelter, runs along slopes like an exhausted hound, gazes proudly from a high pass, grimly endures bad weather, recalls in solitude a better time.

Poem 91, "The Frost," is about the poet's visit to a girl in a winter storm. Two afflictions have transfigured him: on his way, he fell through ice into water; and at her house, icicles hanging from the eaves threaten his "thin flesh." From inside, she asks him if he's comfortable; he answers that he doesn't know what he is. He's like some legendary survivor of a sojourn in a mountain of ice. If he's not to get relief within her house, he asks that the sun shine on him and melt away the leavings of this icy prelude to his call on her. The frost, vividly described, is nature's equivalent to the girl's indifference, as Dafydd's longing for a melting sun expresses more than merely a desire to get his chilled body dry and warm again.

Nowhere does Dafydd show so well his skill in wearing nature as the dress of his inner life as in the love-messenger poems commissioning an animal or force of nature to bear his love-message. On the one hand, he paints so accurate and sensuous a picture that we see and believe in these creatures of nature, as we see and believe in his fox or his hare. On the other hand, in their role as messengers, they take us beyond literal description.

Poem 115, "The Woodcock," is a dialogue. Dafydd tries to persuade a woodcock not to make its intended flight for shelter from winter snow, but to go to where his girl lives, there to spy on her. He assures the bird that its rapid flight and busy beak can out-trick the fowler who might try to shoot or snare him. The bird answers abruptly that Dafydd is too late, for the girl has already taken another lover.

The poem externalizes an inner debate, an anxious questioning as to the girl's fidelity. The bird seeking shelter counters the poet's scheme for an inquisition by giving him wintry truth. The woodcock was not, evidently, a favorite bird of Dafydd's, for all the courtesy he shows the bird in the dialogue of this poem. In an earlier woodcock poem, Poem 61, Dafydd tells of how a woodcock in winter startled him and his girl; they mistake the bird for *Eiddig* ("the Jealous One" — the husband) come in pursuit of the girl. This bird, concludes Dafydd in the earlier poem, is no singer of love songs; he knows only how to probe dung with his dark spear of a beak. Indeed, a fitting voice for the doubts expressed in Poem 115.

In Poem 116, "The Stag," Dafydd identifies with the creature he commissions, finding in the flight of the stag an image for the freedom and strength he would exercise in the pursuit of love. He has an affinity for the stag; he understands its anxieties while recognizing its noble endowments of muscle and antler. For the stag, too, must suffer hounding. Escape your pursuers, Dafydd tells him, go to my beloved and fetch me a kiss. He wishes for the stag an unobstructed life clear of human exploitation, as he wishes a wild liberty for himself.

In Poem 117, "The Wind," the poet asks a mighty storm-wind to convey a message of love. There is logic to it: Morfudd is inaccessible to Dafydd, so that he needs a powerful (and elusive) messenger to get to her. But the poem develops the paradoxical fantasy of a frustration that would speak through an uncontrollable freedom. Alone and constrained, the poet conceives of the wind as a glorious alter-ego. The wind moves swiftly, without limbs, without support; roars through trees, yet cannot be caught; can neither be deceived nor seen, though full of sound and rain; writes in clouds, bounds over wastelands. This prodigious being is "God's blessing" — breaking the tops of oaks! Where are you going, Dafydd asks, you who confound the sea and play on the shore? Go, man, where I cannot go.

And return: you are the sky's good, the sky's benefit, the power of the heavens that the poet would have obedient to a lover's will: serve me! It is as bold as any prayer, as desperate as any cry cast on the wind.

Though, on balance, Dafydd seems to suffer more than he is comforted, though complaint is more often his theme than triumph, though he did lose Morfudd and never got near Dyddgu and succeeded with girls who evidently meant far less to him and was rebuffed by others of possibly meagre credentials to be a poet's love, though he never presided over a family and court like those of Ifor Hael, though health and wealth too may have missed him in his later years when he could imagine a magpie calling him "gray, abject, half-mad old man," yet his poems offer evidence to confirm Gruffudd Gryg's judgment of Dafydd: "Lord of love, he is for the truth."

   The poems of Dafydd ap Gwilym affirm loves of remarkable range
and intensity, they have vision and insight, they strike an authentic
note. And his voice has proved singularly durable:

> Yesterday old Dafydd (the pain of hidden love)
> Was avenged with new love.
> After my wound (I am blind),
> I'm tough like a withe from an apple tree
> That bends easily (affliction's touch)
> And will not break after a strong blow.
> There is in me (faint memory of a smile)
> The soul of a shivery old cat;
> Let the wood-gray body be wounded, beaten,
> Whatever be at it, it will live.
>
> (Poem 131, lines 13–22)

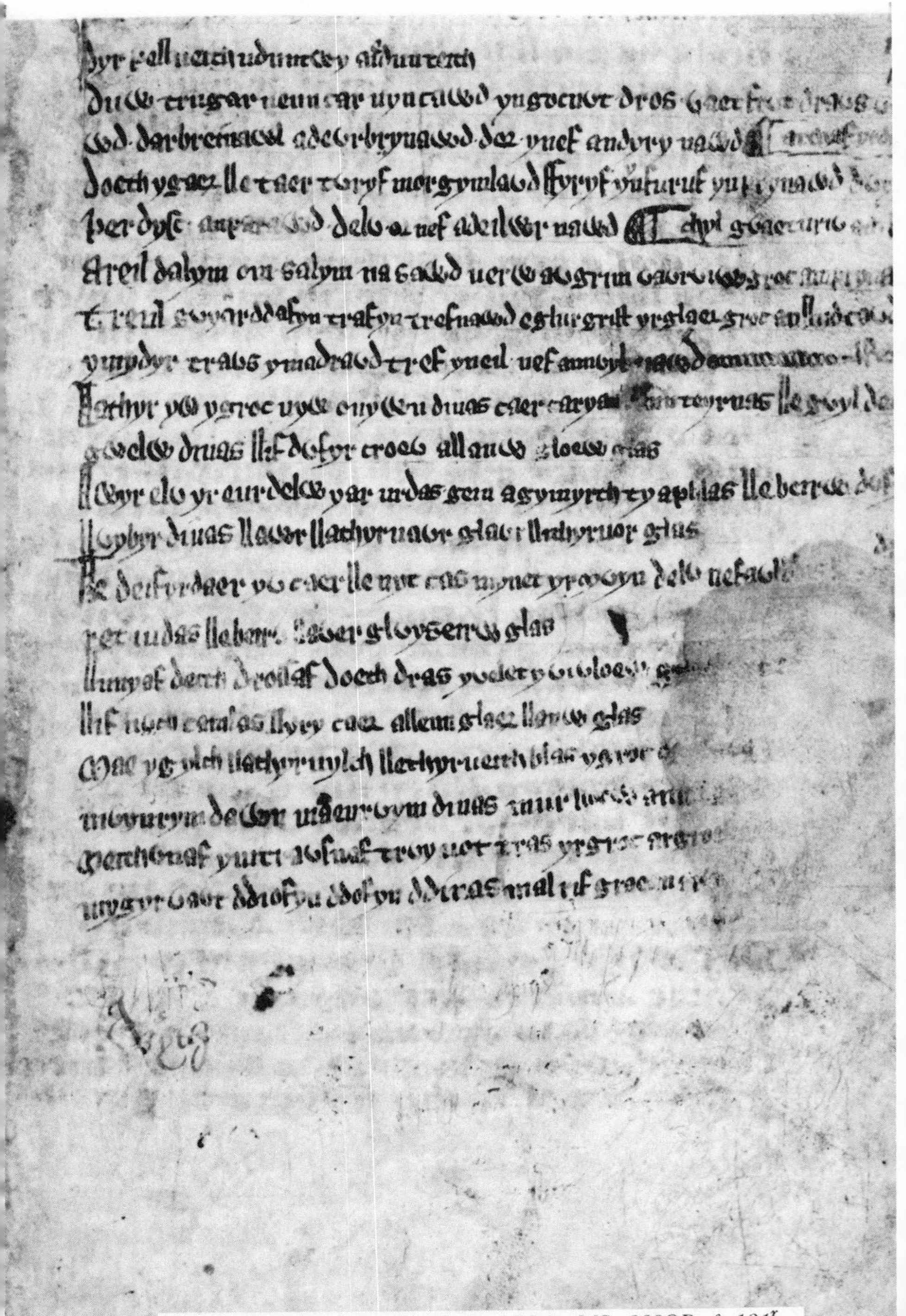

Courtesy of the National Library of Wales MS. 6680B, f. 121r

THE

POEMS

I. *To Jesus Christ*

Of great age are you, Jesus, Spirit of the good God,
    You suffered great penance,
  A weapon's wound, grim stretching
  On the wood of the Cross, for the world's five ages.

The world heard of your being wisely begotten
  Of a maiden, slim-browed and virginal.
After your birth, O God, early
  They call you from there, *Domine, Dominus.*
Three comforting kings, honorable and well-bred,
  Came to the land, as mindful men;   10
They brought three gifts, bright giving,
  Because of the might of Mary and Thee: gold, myrrh, and
                    frankincense.
The true Father, the Son of fair grace, and the Spirit,
  The true prince of salvation and a shining lord,
Ah, God of Three, is it not arrogant for anyone
  To betray your honor, kind miracle?
Folly of Judas, inept indeed,
  To give you to strangers, hard punishment.
An excess was it, gratuitous work and pointless obstruction,
  The twisting of your limbs, rightful lord.   20
To sit to judge you, the beggar-judge
  Of a flour-beggar's son was Pilate.
There came round you naked, with flattering speech,
  Jews, thieves too deceiving.
Nine went to bind you, in your strong sanctity,
  To purchase penance on wood of pine.
And with your cruel binding oppressively fixed,
  A great cry did tearful Mary make.
Even so, despite the Cross, gracious was the end,
  Your escape from the grave, says Matthew.   30
When we see for us your blessed Passion,

Why do we not think of the pitiful agony?
Your feet full of blood, remembrance of you is not evil,
    Your hands, O God, aching for me;
Marks of death on your beautiful forehead,
    A pang from the spear and paling of the lip.
And after that for your sad, aching wound
    A hundred ought to call you *Holy.*
From your affliction, harsh state, were we not blest
    In your coming to us, suffering God?   40
Afterwards your death is not evil for any;
    Good for Joseph was your life, Jesus!

2. Anima Christi

These *englynion* comprise a meditation on lines from the Latin eucharistic sequence, *Anima Christi.* The Latin means: Soul of Christ, sanctify me; Body of Christ,
save me; Blood of Christ, intoxicate me; water of Christ's side, wash me; Passion of
Christ, strengthen me; O good Jesus, hear me and do not permit me to be separated
from Thee, so that with Thy angels I may praise Thee. Amen.

Anima Christi, sanctifica me.
Renowned, merciful heart of Three and One,
        Glory of the prophets,
    Fair soul of Christ of fair cross,
    Like a jewel within, cleanse me.

Corpus Christi, salve me.
Body of Christ that is quite stricken from wrongful
                            hardihood,
        Flesh of Communion when it is sought,
    Cause of salvation of a pure spirit,
    Because you live, keep me alive.

Sanguis Christi, inebria me.
Blood of Christ, lest sadly, for what I do,   10
        I be exiled and lost,
    Rise, light of God's praise,
    Keep me from the sin of drunkenness.

Aqua lateris Christi, lava me.
Water of Christ's heroic, sorely wounded side,
     Happy to bear the cross,
   Divine breast, without abandoning,
   Faithful circle of life, wash me.

Passio Christi, comforta me.
Passion of heaven's Christ, lord of the world's prophets,
     Severe were your five wounds,
   Strong is the just, worthy power of prayer,
   Strengthen me, great nobleman.   20

O bone Iesu, exaudi me.
Gentle, kind Jesus, turn yourself toward me,
     Answer to the light,
   Lord of all altars of great praise,
   Listen without blaming me.

Et ne permittas me separari a te.
And, O my being, place me, a good increase,
     Near you, weal of the world;
   Like a bush, fit strength to serve,
   Praise without end, I'll praise you.

Ut cum angelis tuis laudem te.
With your host of angels, strong, true lord,   30
     In light that will not be lost,
   In heaven is it proclaimed,
   How near is salvation, so be it.

Amen.
May it be true that we are led to heaven's fair kingdom,
     In obedient homage,
   Land of the feast of high grace, lasting grace,
   Banquet of substantial form.

3. *The Good Works of God*

Good was the Trinity without stinting
Who made heaven and earth for us.
Good was the Father more than any
To give Anna of chaste countenance.
Good was Anna of righteous increase
To bear Mary, most immaculate maid.
Good was Mary of pure prayer
To bear God to mar the devil.
Good was the Lord God, sure joy,
By his cross to bear the Five Ages from their pain.   10
Well may Mary's Son do, confessed truth,
To bear us all each one to heaven!

4. *A Painting of Christ and His Apostles*

This is a meditation on a painting of Dafydd's time. The representation was
evidently iconographic, not scenic: Peter is on the Lord's right side; Paul —
who had no association with the Apostles until after Christ's death — is on His
left. Judas Iscariot (as well as his successor, Matthias) is not mentioned. A
twofold mission of the Apostles is indicated: the first naming of the original
twelve, and their dispatch to the ends of the world after the Resurrection. The
Christ figure in the painting may have combined signs of the Passion and the
Resurrection.

Well was it painted, right style,
The breast of God's Son above Who rules us.
Bravely was there set in a new picture
An image of the Lord on bright pieces of wood
For showing to His gold enclosure
All the Twelve and the Passion,
Gracious is it, on the cross which is where
God the Almighty suffered,
The Trinity, dear wisdom,
And Its grace one with Jesus.   10

Jesus the holy God was pictured well,
With able learning, and His disciples,

Mighty increase, growth above reproach,
Thirteen, is not the picture beautiful?
The holy Lord God is in the center,
Gentle image, well does He merit praise.
And the Twelve, a group cheerful and fair,
Were joined together around Jesus.
A share of six on each side,
They all came round the Lord God.   20

    On the right side, gentle Lord,
Of Him, noble God,
Is Peter, well does he know how to gaze,
And John of worthy, excellent inspiration;
Philip of best impulse of grace,
Blest are his feet; and good Andrew;
James generous, good and dear, renowned,
And Saint Simon, of flowing gifts.
Golden, on the other side
Of the learned and wise Lord   30
Is Paul, decent, good, wise,
And Thomas, amiable, refined;
Bartho- (he did not deny)
Lomew, of bright, seemly praise;
In delicate color, holy Matthew,
And James, these are without reproach;
Saint Jude in incense lively and fair—
There they are, a beautiful line.
Full of grace are they, of far-reaching wisdom,
Where they are set in undeceiving color.   40

    Consider the wise fine story
Of the time when the Twelve were allowed
To walk the world with Him,
Noble habitation, before the Passion.
After the pain on the Rood-Cross
That Christ bore, and His retching,
And His death too, it was not in vain,
And from the world to the grave,
When the God Jesus rose up
Our true friend from the black earth,   50
He brought into His party, no need for fear,
The honorable Twelve.

5. Awdl *to Ifor Hael*

This is the first of seven poems of Dafydd's celebrating his patron, Ifor ap
Llywelyn of Gwernyclepa near Basaleg (northeast of Cardiff); the epithet *hael*
means "generous."

A wheel runs well downhill (rough country)
    Or a gull on an estuary;
  Twice as well runs (a lord's good gain,
  Busy am I) your praise, Ifor.

Good, the sea's lucky plaiting that long wets it
    To a pirate ship of rope anchor;
  Better do I weave, bravest lord,
  The tongue's praise for you, Ifor.

Good fortune come to you from me, honored lord,
    And a friendly welcome;   10
  You're as good as an army, steel-weaponed lord,
  Strong men's fear, strong Ifor!

Swells not a sea-tide's stone-veil cover in a torrent,
    Lord like Arthur or Hector,
  Bright fulfiller, proverbial defender,
  As praise swells to you, Ifor.

Beautiful Lord of the folk of the four corners of the
    world's length
And the Lord of the bright choir of heaven's court,
May He be a strengthener on the sea and the earth's
    surface,
  Lord of the firmament, to stout Ifor.   20

A merchant, a mender of treasure and praise,
  The dismay of Norman wealth, praise's rudiment,
The hewing of a battle-host's weapon upon a steward's
    court, English-vexing,
  Mary's patronage be on Ifor, he has plied seas.

Of the stout nature of a Hercules, with brilliant,
                     purple gown bright-clothed,
  And a Nudd of open-handed prowess.
He's a lovely and strong ship at anchor,
  Not shallows has noble Ifor attained.

There's no place that might long dispense with him;
  May I not be without him, ready-handed lord.   30
No gift-giver is better, none higher,
  No one has ever equalled Ifor.

Handsome heir, he gives an unfailing gift of mead-drink,
  Brilliant kinsman of white-helmeted Llywelyn.
Today no guileless, clear-browed lord equals
  (Diligent claim) the celebrated Ifor.

Easy day for me when he gives fluent, clear counsel,
  Easy the night of the lively lord's dear peace.
Easy table converse, daily welcome,
  Easy the life of the mind of Ifor's obedient sworn-brother. 40

Easy praise like unrestrained Hector's in tumult,
  Easily with thick breastplate he scatters the skilled
                     men of Deira.
I asked and got with eager abundance
  A full feast from generous Ifor.

A great lord to handsome, blameless bards, with a
                     shield of sieve-device,
  Spirited plowman of Severn border fight.
Long-lived was Noah, excellent shield-lord,
  Longer, eloquent sojourn, be the life of Ifor!

6. Englynion *to Ifor Hael*

Ifor surpasses all; it is even a sorrow, a slave's provocation, to presume to liken any
other to him.

  For generosity, my Nudd and my gold fort,
    And my gold stag generous in giving,

It's a sorrow, slavekind's provocation,
Vain is one compared to Lord Ifor.

For a quick sword's courage, bold-bright assertion,
    And skill to throw back an army,
For unimpeded, great attack, my gold fort,
Vain two compared to fervent Ifor.

For wisdom, no Norman is nearer him
    Than from France to the Isle of Man;   10
To dispose of weighty argument,
Vain three compared to Ifor there.

For obedience, fortune, faith, and gift,
    And loving his poet,
Vain four, fluent and liberal lord,
Compared to Ifor, speech of Ovid.

For nobility, lineage, straight is his sword,
    And frequent, unfailing success,
For hawks of famed pedigree,
Vain five compared to Ifor ever.   20

For strength, my strong man of thick wrists, gold-fair,
    Bearing gold-topped irons,
An Ovid of battle who will dare champions,
Vain six compared to swift Ifor.

For beauty, most generous, honored, stout lord,
    Prince of the pride of lineage,
I'm his bard, for deep cunning,
Vain seven compared to fine Ifor.

For humility in office, bard's disposer,
    Soul of poets and their haven,   30
Battle-grief to strike a traitor,
Vain eight compared to Ifor the warrior.

For the champion feats I love in a man,
    I judge him eagle-like,

For frequent and most abundant gifts,
Vain nine compared to Lord Ifor.

For excellence, my chief of Fulke's vigor,
    Morgannwg's wall-support,
    For casting down a man, wild aim,
    Vain ten compared to tall Ifor.   40

7. Cywydd *to Ifor Hael*

Ifor, the best of fine stewardship
Is mine, pleasant tending;
I am, generous, spirited leader,
The steward of your wealth, great is your gift.

    It's brave and considerate you are,
My store, you're a good man.
I paid you lively tongue's praise,
You paid me black-bright bragget.
You gave me treasure, a sign of love,
I give you Rhydderch's epithet.   10
Well-armed with a weapon, weapons shall not hinder you,
Friend and bondsman of the poets.
Mighty lord of the stock of mighty men,
Minstrels' slave, rich leader.

    You are the bravest and strongest man
To·follow, not a weakling.
Your ancestry was good and proud.
By the God who rules, doubly more obedient
Are you to your bard (of blameless, discreet prudence,
Leader of a host) than one hand to the other.   20

    I go from my land, lord's shoot,
And come, Ifor, with your praise.
From my language is fashioned,
Not a crude term, the truth about you.
From my own mouth, assemblies' chief lord,

Eight times twenty hosts praise you.
As far as the farthest man travels,
As far as the bold course of summer's sun turns,
As far as the wheat is planted,
And as far as the lively, bright dew moistens,   30
As far as unobstructed sight sees
(It's strong) and as far as ear hears,
As far as there's Welsh language,
And as far as beautiful seeds grow,
Handsome Ifor of lively custom,
Long is your sword, your praise shall be sown.

8. *Ifor's Court at Basaleg*

In this poem, the poet explains to a girl in Môn, through a bird-messenger,
why he has been staying in Glamorgan.

Go, servant (he loves choice green,
A fine, elegant world), above green birch.
From Morgannwg, bring good day
To Gwynedd, a mead-feast path,
Where I'm beloved (the world's bright joy)
And greet the country of Môn.

Say (I've not been allowed to go from my land,
God knows, you are not guilty)
That I have been for some time, Song of Songs,
Loving a person above Cardiff.   10
Not crude or wrong is my state,
Not love for a smooth-lipped, slender girl.
Great love of Ifor held me,
It's greater than love for a concubine.
Love of Ifor have I praised,
Not like the love of a foolish-natured Englishman.
And say that I'll not go, most perfect lord,
If he asks, from love for Ifor,
Either one day to wicked towns,
Or one night from Morgannwg.   20

He's of the lineage of a best-bred lord,
With fine retainers, gold helm, liberal, great.
A wealthy, venerable hawk,
His body very firm on a stallion.
Swift, tenacious, expert overthrower in fight,
An accomplished, wise hawk of comprehensive discourse.
Deathless stag, he brooks not the men of Deira,
Very faithful would vassals find him.
Humble and good in his speech;
Vain is any but handsome Ifor.   30

Great honor came to me:
I shall have, if I live,
Hunting with hounds (no more bountiful lord)
And drinking with Ifor,
And shooting straight-running, great stags,
And casting hawks to sky and wind,
And beautiful verses,
And solace in Basaleg.
Is it not fun in a crowd
(Minstrels' target, shooting at a clear mark)   40
To play *ffristiol* and *tolbwrdd*
On the same level as the powerful man?
If anyone (courteous agreement)
Were to get the better of the other, most refined,
Freely with song I grace him,
I shall get the best of Ifor.

None is generous, as we seek for his equal,
None brave; is he not a monarch?
I shall not go from his court, proud lord,
None's obedient but Ifor.   50

9. *Giving Thanks for Gloves*

Ifor was gold-prodigal:
No finger went from his court without gold.
Yesterday I was at dinner
In his court getting wine from his hand.
I swear with my tongue,
Weaver of song, wherever day turns,
O best wife as far as Ceri,
Your man is the best husband!
While happily laboring,
Among praises he labored.   10

    The day I came from his house
With his gloves and double-money,
The loan of his gloves to a poet-
Receiver did Ifor give:
White gloves thick and beautiful,
And in each glove some money.
Gold in the one, the two grasp,
It's a sign, for the right hand,
And silver, the praise of thousands,
In the other, my winning was it.   20

    Every girl asks
Me for a loan of my gloves.
No girl might have, despite begging them,
More than a man, my gloves.
I'll not give, I'll bear neatly,
The gift of Ifor of fluent speech.
I won't wear wether-skin wrinkled
Gloves to wither my finger;
I'll wear, I don't want his wrath,
The hospitable man's stag-skin.   30
Holiday gloves on my hands,
Rain will not often wet them.

    I'll give to him, I know his gift,
Active in patronage, hall of Rheged,

Wine-endowed Taliesin's blessing,
Which, without a word of boasting, lasts always.
At table's head to take a meal,
There may he go in the home
Where I dispense some part of my praise,
Where the son is brave, the daughter chaste,   40
Where aristocracy dwells,
In feasts, luxuries, nourishment,
With handsome women, with offspring,
With hawks, with greyhounds, with wine,
With beautiful, gracious scarlet,
With wrought gold, with lovely words.
There is no tree in the Wennallt
Whose head and hair are not green,
With its branches woven closely,
With its gown and its tunic one hedge.   50
Is it not sweet for a chief bard
To see a bright, handsome assembling?
Lordship was (a comely dukedom)
Established at Basaleg.

    Gloves from his dwelling I got,
Not like an Englishman's English gloves;
Gloves that were a lord's sincere New Year's gift,
Pleasing wealth are Ifor's gloves.
Gloves of Dafydd's liege-lord,
Ifor Hael, who greater gives them?   60
My winnowed blessing
Shall come to the court of Ifor Hael.

10. *Parting from Ifor*

With obedient lovers' speech,
Ifor, handsome, royal lord,
Going as I might desire
(It's very hard) to Gwynedd am I.
Not going (of famed double-gift)
Is he who may come again.

Two months on the banks of Dyfi
I could not be without you.
The full, round heart, lord,
Rises not (farewell, Ifor!)
Nor the land-honored eye of wet cheek,
Nor hand nor thumb, where you're not.
Not great is my strength here,
It was neither wise nor of good understanding
For anyone who loved the nine
Drinks of wine to leave you.

You're my lord and the mightiest man,
Farewell, noble, bright tower!
An easy course, Rhydderch's equal,
Is before you, a knowing sense of love;
During war's wrath, some full caring,
And during peace, Ifor of bright gift.
Long you're loved more than any,
Great, fair lord of sea and land.

Lord of a birch-wood, the shrines of a harmony
Of heaven and this world, praise-pillar,
I would have what gift I might desire
(I'm rich and famous)
Of beautiful words, of silver,
Of fine gold, as a hundred know,
Of clothing, no finding fault,
Of splendid weapons of French mode,
Devoted expense, of mead and wine,
Of jewels, a second Taliesin.

Strong deeds, king of Christendom,
You, Ifor, father of drink,
Fame of taverns, magistrate of spirited custom,
Honor of generosity, gave them!

11. *Elegy for Ifor and Nest*

In medieval Wales, elegies were sometimes written while their subjects were
still alive, as a form of eulogy; Dr. Parry (*GDG*³, p. xl) holds that to be the
case with this poem for Ifor Hael and his wife Nest; the fourth stanza has a
reference to the poet's harp-playing, the traditonal accompaniment for Welsh
verse. The Welsh text of this poem begins and ends with the word *henaint*,
meaning "old age," the first a reference to the poet's old age (which will be sadder now), the second a reference to Ifor's old age (committed now to heaven's
sleep). Rachel Bromwich takes such clues as these as evidence that Dafydd
and Ifor were contemporaries, and she reads the poem as a literal elegy,
noting the tradition that the cause of the simultaneous deaths of Ifor and Nest
was the plague, perhaps the midcentury Black Death (*DG*, pp. 34, 35).

Clumsy old age and longing and pain
    And penance like an arrow's point:
  Ifor dead, no excellence,
  Nest is dead, Wales is the worse.

Worse is it because of a foster father; there's a door
                between me and him,
    Confined at chancel's end;
  Dead is Nest (my harp-string's a sea),
  Heaven's maiden; dead is righteous Ifor.

Best was Ifor with his straight body (our lord,
    Putting the men of Deira on a bier)   10
  Of those who have been, dear one of the ancestral line,
  Those who are and those who will be forever.

Never will I go from my nest with the passion of a minstrel
    Who has walked around the world;
  My two arms shall not play a while,
  I shall not gain, I shall not have ease.

Ease provokes rage of heart
    And longing in this breast, and old age.
From weeping of rain, prodigy of a silver bath,
  For Nest and Ifor, brooks are swelling.   20

Generous God, an event causes me, a seer, heavy sickness,
  Nest the treasure cannot be seen, perverse utterance.
A war-leader's grip is it or the anguish of pain
  (Fine hue of summer brilliance, veil of a flood)
To see the generosity in giving of the saints' own love
  And the wise beloved whom they sustained.
Pale, fine Nest, wine-wise, white-toothed, and Ifor,
  With more than predilection they gifted me!
With bright wine from a glass they pampered me at a feast,
  And with mead from a drinking-horn they indulged me
                                                more.   30
They gave me both red gold and rich stones each hour,
  And with great hawks they endowed me.
Long gifts for the two: reluctantly they would go, secretly
  Together, to shelter in their hiding places.
And the same are they who did not delay my gain,
  And the same revelation of gain shall they be.
A fortress-destroying leader in battle, they would not act
                                                weakly,
  Would venture nine thousand in a tournament.
Welcome they led at fair Basaleg court,
  Lord of its gold pavement, a place of great drunkenness,   40
Where there's conversation, a flood from wine vessels,
  A bright cup-bearer and slenderness of brow.
Broken-bladed, scattering the English in the right good
                                   style of bathèd Llŷr,
  And a many-privileged battle-bruised lion.
Widely-loved defense of the rich kindred-host in the region:
  May the lord of sleep steer heaven to old age!

12. Awdl *to Llywelyn Ap Gwilym*

Llywelyn ap Gwilym, an uncle of Dafydd's who instructed Dafydd in poetry,
was constable of Castellnewydd Emlyn. D. J. Bowen (*LlC* 8:1–2, 7) suggests
that this poem of celebration may have been occasioned by Llywelyn's ap-
pointment as constable.

Dyfed's custom is to summon wine-houses

To Llywelyn's district;
A glade, let all men's greeting go
(Place of a warm court for a throng) to Emlyn.

A lake for Emlyn park, a canal to Teifi,
    And taverns everywhere;
Let him prevent disgrace, let him slay his foe,
Where the hammer-blow might be, a path of honor.

Path of honor of a great spear striking an eminence, clear
    Provocation of England and Scotland;   10
    Wherever he comes, the whole world draws
    (Generous hand) to Llywelyn's fame.

Llywelyn wills me energy and strength,
    Happy son of Gwilym, high, mighty lord.
An unconstrained place, vexation ceased to vex me,
    He exercised lordship, nourished me.
He labored, he adorned (in order to feed the good)
    A court on the bards' hill, a place of handsome men is it.
A place where it's customary to get shelter and lively clothes,
    An open house of constant welcome,   20
A place where wine is familiar and the serving of drinking
                        horns,
    An active place, taverns' way, where Teifi churns.
Sweet, sparkling place of wonderful feature,
    Where the world's guests play without ceasing.
A long place busy filling the drinking-horn,
    Where there's sharp, right wine for getting drunk.
Where by Thy might, resplendent God, I return

                *   *   *   *

A place where there's wine of France; furnished with a bench
                        veiled in silk brocade,
    A place with rooms full of a tide of gold vessels.   30
A leisurely court that a host of carpenters made stately;
    A fort painted with fresh lime; lamps burning.
Most bountiful, faultless goodness of courtesy,
    The ordering of the generous, fertile country, praise-laden,

Well-traveled land of Gwri Golden Hair's love,
   Llywelyn the strong shall go over it.
Ruler, reeves' chieftain as far as Elfed,
   He is Dyfed's leader, taming many.
Tribe's defense, his lineage penetrates as far as Gwili;
   Meek, judicious, like Pryderi.   40
With smooth hand gilding guests; spears are his knitting
                     needles,
Having the anger of Pyll with a weapon in three fragments,
   Rhodri's stroke.
Fine spear like Beli's spear in a battle,
   Of a nature fully like quick, strong Llŷr, a lion of valor.
Cheerful, endearing man who rouses us, causing a prosperous
                     custom,
   He gave us good cheer for our lifetime.
Llywelyn ardent to break a spear,
   The bravery of men and their goodness.
Llywelyn ardent to break an army in battle,
   Of a good hand (with red gold) that knows giving.   50
Advance, don't diminish, One and Three, henceforth,
   Let favor to him thrive, God keep him!

13. *Elegy for Llywelyn Ap Gwilym*

This elegy was provoked by the death — evidently a political murder — of the
uncle who was Dafydd's bardic master (see Poem 12). Dr. Parry dates
Llywelyn's death as between 1346 and 1349, the murder probably having
been instigated by Llywelyn's successor in office, Richard de la Bere (*GDG* [3],
p. xv). Repetitions of words and initial consonants link the stanzas; note, for
example, that the poem begins and ends with the word, *Dyfed*. The lines of
asterisks indicate what Dr. Parry judges, from breaks in the linking of stanzas, to be missing stanzas. The poem, a tour de force of technical design, is
yet — especially when read in conjunction with the preceding joyous tribute to
Llywelyn alive — genuinely moving. Llywelyn had courts at Llystyn, Y Ddôl-
goch, and Cryngae, in addition to the administrative center at Newcastle
Emlyn; Emlyn and the first two courts are named in this poem.

Dyfed's hope has been made void, her boast broken,
   Because of the eagle of the Land of Enchantment;

Yesterday, a good time, speaking,
He was gifted, and today, mute.

Before this, Llywelyn, wealth of the land,
    You closed no house against me;
  Mighty lord of song were you:
  Open to me, silent man!

Handsome-featured, wise father of the chief of lands, great
                     author
    Of prophetic word, proud, straight, brave,   10
  You of prime, good praise, try to speak,
  Poet, linguist, don't be mute!

Lifeless my fine leader, Deira's scourge, why
    (A flood of tears in earnest)
  Did you leave me, my support,
  My gold-giving friend, my mute stag?

Prince, lord of the land of enchantment, deep below,
    Perfectly you taught me;
  You knew every mastery;
  I have felt pain since you fell silent.   20

My tears are deep, not quiet is my cry
    For my strong, brave leader;
  Not painless, that you don't answer me;
  Not easy to speak with one who's mute.

Lord of true heaven and earth, an exile's cry is this:
    It was harsh that you did not hear it;
  Alas, God of all wealth,
  Wretched is my condition because of a mute man.

Woe is me (praise's boon for one like Clud ceased not for him)
    That he's not able to speak;   30
  I know a deal of care from sadness,
  A cry of great words for a mute man.

Alas, Lord Christ, hard was my pride,

(Was I not punished too much?)
Fine were we all before the loss,
That the jewel of Christendom's virtues has fallen!

Alas, Lord Christ, a pierced heart is mine,
    I'm sad for a hard loss:
He of splendid weapons holding the land around,
That the lord of all virtues has fallen!   40

Alas, my Lord, placing in your design, God!
    The taking of the music-loving, strong hawk,
No feast-day gift, grief's fluent,
That there's no freedom to fix blame for a kinsman's sake.

Alas, taking (like rushes, the illusion of a privileged
                society)
    The peoples' government,
The throng's profit, death of hosts;
Cheerful, he was men's joy.

Alas, that I have seen, bad welcome,
A soldier's halls, fair tower,   50
Life's misfortune, one damaged,
And the other, roof gaping, an empty house.

Alas for the nephew who grows cold, who suffers seeing
    (Depth of memory wakes me)
The motley court disintegrating above,
And Llystyn an empty house.

A court of wine and steed, just revenue,
    Woe for the loss of him who had made it!
Court of a golden lord, the gain of many,
The lord of benefit if he were alive, everybody's court
                was it.   60

A small, fleeting gain, to be bravely rash;
    And the whole world is formed like a wheel;
A proud lion of abundant courtesy,
The pillar of praise was slain with a blue weapon.

Lion-like knight, Llywelyn, if you have been killed
    In your fair court in Emlyn,
  There's less learning of book and harp,
  Say many downcast men after you.

Running tears are mine of a sweet kind; alas, that it was
               possible
    With mercenary knife,   70
  Many a bitter cry in public,
  Bright wrists, to kill a handsome sovereign!

I give a cry because of Llywelyn's taking, wise man;
    His land gives a cry;
  A free cry I give the next day,
  A cry daily; his day has come.

Woe, woe, Dôl-goch, to hold a reverential feast,
    Because of your loving master;
  Woe upon sad double-woe,
  Woe, what but woe? Who weeps not?   80

I wept where I saw my lord's bedchamber,
    Was this not a great wound?
  Say a word, I'm your kinsman;
  Good, wise man, open your house!

A man, no lad, slain from the pain of a steel wound,
    And terrible was the hard loss;
  He of manly claim in a shattered helmet,
  A sad word for the best of all.

Sad retinues of a lord of taverns, wound of tongue-work,
    Worse now is it to take thought;   90
  A strong buckle, empty is the breast,
  After a lord of praise, men are weaklings.

Blind will be, as after sin, from taking out the eye,
    The world that was in England or Wales;
  Bring to your feast (you will not refuse me,
  Men's security) the good nobleman, O high God!

This is a proverb, it will be verified in the region:
    Whoever kills shall be killed.
  The point of this may be guessed,
  Endless woe, and God, let it be true!   100

He who fashions a grave, woe and want for the South,
    He will be dealt swift vengeance;
  He who does evil by an unwise stroke
  By hand, let him await another.

  Not carefree (firm, strong of brow)
  The enemy who may do grief:
  He who may kill a man with bright steel
  To end a life, will be killed.

                    *   *   *   *

Forlorn theme of a sad blow for a golden lad is this,
    To make known a great murder,   110
  The proper claiming of full dignity;
  He hears horns (the lament for a lord) since he's been slain.

Righteousness he was, the reconciliation of noble peoples,
    The wisdom of poetry,
  The keystring of fidelity,
  Praise-column, no one was of the same courtesy.

Well-bred heir, of noble fleur-de-lis lineage,
    Deliverance of a Paris bell-house;
  A brave Welshman has left us;
  One is taken, Wales is less.   120

If my uncle's dead, it's a great wonder
    (Arabian gold of great Wales)
  That I did not go, nephew who cares for him,
  That I do not go mad, God my Lord!

                    *   *   *   *

  Disfigured and hurt for a generous lord:

Wine-cellared, table-heaping, poet-maintaining,
Of the champion instinct of a gift-giving environment,
O that the world's combined triumphs have forever fallen!

*   *   *   *

Both base and brilliant who may love justice,
    Let him go tonight to Llandudoch;   130
Wisdom has gone there,
Devout treasure under sand-gravel.

The lively feast-provisioning flower has died,
    Of two bright cheeks;
Wholly, wine-enslaved purpose,
Has iron taken the memory and judgment of the world.

*   *   *   *

A warrior was Llywelyn (a sober, true song,
    Before placing the earth around him);
A master of warfare without hiding himself,
He was lord of great Dyfed.   140

14. Awdl *to Ieuan Llwyd of Genau'r Glyn*

Ieuan Llwyd, another of Dafydd's patrons, lived at Morfa Bychan and later at
Genau'r Glyn (both in Ceredigion).

It's May, flawless are the bird-bards on the beach,
    There's underbrush in the woods, stuff for weaving,
Shrill and persistent is strict musicianship from a bird;
    I paid it honor; heartache is mine.

Since I may not get (bright joy's food)
    New presents in Môn and nourishment,
There's need for banquets, the world's generous service;
    There's no beloved, there's sorrow of breast.

There are benches, tables, poets' booty,
There's a fair family of welcome,   10
Love's service — it was not for me, holy God!
The great desire is worse than for a girl's greeting.

Neither do I see Ieuan of perfect breeding
Nor does he, lord of the race, see me;
I shall go to him, dearest communion;
I am not bold without him, fearless support.

Wild am I, while I may see the plenty of youth;
The service of wine has turned to poison within me;
Afterwards, a legacy of fear,
From open weeping, the craft of song turns hard
                                against me.   20

A strong enclosure is where he is, I shall declare it,
The sport of government, true love-craft,
A strong, fair land where longed-for tavernship flourishes,
With glassy forest shoots; a choice region.

I see supreme his supremacy,
A hawk of Llawdden's line, of the hawks for hunting;
He's a saviour of bards, a liquor that fosters,
A singing lord who loved the cry of the minstrelsy.

I shall be an idle lad in my state as a guest;
The golden chief's a reliable host;   30
I'll be the same captive of a fine feast
In spring, winter, autumn, and hospitable summer.

The author keeps well, fair custody,
Wishes me well, by custom he caused me to be without fear;
Steel-latticed is the battle-door on the land by the crumbling
                                shore of the sea,
A fearless door of supremacy, he has homage of Deira.

Perfect is the intercession of one with a chieftain's energy,
All say that he provides food perfectly;
Welcome, clothing, protection he maintains,.
Huail's customs, an abundant feast.   40

Of keen, courageous aristocracy,
Unfailing, no other man is an equal in valor;
Unflawed, splendid door, of brave purpose, proud and swift,
A perfect gold lord of profound nobility.

Good weapon-threat of men, warfare's Llŷr,
He reassured me, good shepherding;
A doublet to me, powerful binding,
A double coat of mail, fortunate honor, is my foster father.

15. Awdl *to Hywel Ap Goronwy, Dean of Bangor*

Dafydd praises Dean Hywel of the Cathedral Church at Bangor both as a
poet and as a generous, civilized lord. He is likened to holy men of learning:
the apostles, Simon and Jude; St. Giles, the monk and abbot for whom
St.-Gilles in southern France is named; Welsh saints, including heroes of
Welsh monasticism: St. David ("Dewi"), St. Cybi, St. Eilian, St. Mordëyrn.
Gwinau Dau Freuddwyd was the great-grandfather of St. Llywelyn of Y
Trallwng (Welshpool) in Powys; Bran was a legendary king of Britain. For
another reference to the Bangor organ, see Poem 149.

Lord of canonical office like Mordëyrn
        And Dewi in the Land of Enchantment,
    Cybi of heavenly wealth,
    Companions of Simon, Jude.

Of the same manner as St. Jude, he was bordered by the family
        Of Gwinau Dau Freuddwyd,
    A Saint Giles, incense of a hearth,
    Saint Elien's psalm, a holy man of letters.

Holy ruler, a prophet of Bran's line, a rare man's
        In Bangor, with a fur gown,   10
    Of a foam-white house with a lovely organ,
    Choir's harp-string, without faltering does he play it.

My tongue sings wheaten praise:
One does not find a bent ruler beside a straight one;

Not hidden from lively, friendly Hywel
Is the path of clear, easy poetic gift.

Peaceful, often-visited helper that I got,
A Welsh gift, he won't allow violence to me;
   Nine would not petition him, wise one, and would not dare
               to there
If he made a trial of anger, the prelate-lord.   20

In Gwynedd he gets bold, lively mead;
A noble lord, he loves, he who interprets
   The full, manly praise that reaches (in the Môn
Of the bards) my bardic Dean.

Not shallow is the genial, dignified man,
He's a poet of strong word with a well-formed hand;
   This is no cracked, senile judgment in the mind;
No world is there without the man of Gwynedd of poet-like
               feature.

There lives not under the stars a lord like my
               bright-lineaged, brave leader,
Grace of a virile life: 30
   A sprightly, proud, bold hawk of live eyes that abides
               in fields
Is not the same as a wren chick.

The clear speech of a wandering minstrel is not the same
As the way of a swift warrior, in love;
   Not the same standing for a young boy as for elders;
Mown wheat is not the same as scorched barley.

Not the same is a carved cup's wine and mountain whey;
The peacock's feather-fleece is not like a wolf 's;
   Not like Bleddyn (a man not endowed with craft)
Does a skilled lad sing a Cynddelw-like outpouring.   40

Wholly dismayed, no generous Welshman knows
How to give like Rhydderch to suppliants,
   Except Hywel of learned rule,
Solemn and discreet, lord of Môn, a shining, lordly Dean.

16. *Elegy for Angharad*

Angharad was the wife of Ieuan Llwyd of Glyn Aeron; this mid-Ceredigion family was noted for its patronage of poetry. The Angharad mentioned in Poem 140 may be the same woman.

There runs a long and constant tear from my eye
        From how sad it is for me to remember
The placing of spirited, generous Angharad
Under earth (her eyebrows were black).

It is sad that the lady of ripe wine is not alive;
        It is the ruin of inspired poets.
Warrant and true foundation of the praise of riches,
Frequent were feasts from her lively hand.

Serving wine was she, say a host, a luminary, an elegant
                Indeg,
        Before the day of decay.   10
Except for God's heaven, home of a life of peace,
Life is a bewitchment for many.

Many a breast in Pennardd is disfigured for her,
        A second Esyllt, fine, comely, beautiful;
Many a comrade to the sad poet
(Complete grief) does not play, does not laugh.

Laughs not the faithful poet fulfilled and fortunate
                (a grim lament),
        For Angharad has gone;
It does not leave my breast, it is a betrayal to me,
Like a foaming flood, it is a bitter cry.   20

Very sad, unhid bereavement, was the obligation
        (Tan of cheek with proud, blackberry eye,
Maidenly woman, she shared wealth)
To bind oak between us and her two cheeks.

A slender, pale-cheeked lad, I'm sick for a beauty,
        A golden candle in fine dress,

That there came (deep tear-gain)
Her end, bountiful, chaste woman.

Most giving, most amusing, best woman in a fort
  Was well-shaped Angharad,   30
  Of lively hue, good learning, there was not one,
  Sky-sun, not one her equal.

Who's like my golden lady of so short a life-day?
  Frequent, profuse tear wearies me;
  Lapse of a fostering circle, sad, short-lived prudence,
  Radiant niece of the sun, what breast does not break?

Anxious heart-swoon, a seizure that afflicts me,
  Has overtaken me from her departure.
Bright woman with ancestors of long, noble seed,
  She checked frivolous words, modest of bearing. 40

Praise's gold-lord, upon You, Lord God,
  Is my rebuke because of Angharad,
Since You chose (she was ever wise) to take her
  Very suddenly sadly into earth's gross trap.

As perfectly as You gave an excellent endowment
  Of righteously gained gifts to the one in gold-worked
      fine cloth,
You consummated (a course too severe) her life-day;
  Her kinsmen know, and God the Father.

Kinswoman of hawks war-proud, gold-fine, and diligent,
  Great grand-daughter to Cynfrig, pillar of the family's
      eminence.   50
Of choice Eigr's hue and beauty, like Uthr's beloved,
  Terrible, at one swoop, was our despoiling.

Excellent, slim, black-browed woman, it's sad she's not alive,
  Woe for the kin of a lady like Eigr from the wine-graced
      fort.
Hue of the breast of a quick wave's flight on a white beach,
  Her foster brothers know grief's song.

Strength of the honor of a gold-giving lord,
   Womanly beauty, the moon of women.
Bearing a fine spear, a champion's mate in the encampment
   Of Ieuan of fire-edged spear, of battle-feat.   60

The lord with blood-filled spear (the land's bond and its grip)
   Gets praise, liberal, devout lord, rich sustainer.
He resists enemies, a camp-defender comrade,
   Strong spear, a wine-loving oak tree, lord of lovely song.

Strongly did grief wound me (longing is it called)
   For one of the fresh look of a long lily snowy as the moon,
The gentle bee knew her grace,
   Gossamer of Ceredigion, rough her removal.

After lament for life-bereavement, I'm a singer
                heart-shattered,
   For one of the look of grass dressed with a snow-trail,
                fortunate Buellt's lady.   70
Perfect, pale maiden, bounteous hostess at a feast,
   Wine-board and riches, the support of happy poets.

The pang of remembering her, a thrust through me, lays siege
                to me,
   Gem of a bright brooch, woe for my eye!
Bitter hurt, a tear-shower dampens the face,
   My cheek livid and lined; elegy of a great infirmity.

Bitterness for me is the plaint for her; there was not had for
                my side
   (Bulwark of an honest court) a scarlet gown.
Bad work for the sight is long weeping in captivity;
   Worse (confined heartache) is remembrance of Angharad.   80

17. *Elegy for Rhydderch*
(For Llywelyn Fychan of Glyn Aeron)

Rachel Bromwich (*DG*, p. 23) identifies this Rhydderch as the son of the
Angharad of Poem 16; the famous manuscript, "The White Book of Rhydderch," possibly a product of the scriptorium at Strata Florida Abbey, is
associated with his name.

Yesterday I heard (I sought a hiding-place)
Three cries on a high slope.
I did not think (I know a hundred cries)
A man could ever give such a cry.
There has been in my country (liberal giver)
Neither a flood of lament nor the shout of a master
of hounds
Nor a slim horn above a brushwood slope
Nor a bell greater than the cry that was given.

What tumult is this, anxious cry?
Obvious ache, who gave the cry?   10
Llywelyn (from the house of love)
Gave it for Rhydderch,
Fychan beside his handsome court,
Faith-brother of haste-hushed Rhydderch.
Amlyn's cry from his sad home
(A nurse of sorrow) for Emig;
Cry of a man that keenly loved
His beloved, it was from great grief;
And the third cry (bell of the Glyn)
That Llywelyn gave matches theirs.   20

When Rhydderch's mouth was closed (seven-
fold love was buried,
A wine-giver),
There died (I know I too shall be disarmed)
Blessed Deheubarth's head indeed.
Done, the great custom of mead,
Done, the interring of bravery.

The white swan in captivity,
Lying in a stone grave is he.
A grief to nature, the grave's no longer
(Straight, brave, proud one) than seven feet.   30

        A strange sermon was it to lay
Under this black turf
Knowledges, senses of love,
Expert Rhydderch's range of gift;
And his prudent, perfect worth,
And his white, strong body; pleasant, wise;
And his virtues, a recital of grace's talents;
And his bright learning and his enlightenment;
And his grace, friendly linguist;
And his praise — alas, that his day has come!   40

        Cold trouble sadly to inter,
A merciful knight he was.
Through the simple mode of love,
God give mercy to Rhydderch!

18. *Elegy for Gruffudd Ab Adda*

Poems 18, 19, 20, and 21 are about poets contemporary with Dafydd, the first three tributes, the fourth a lampoon. The three tributes have the form of elegies. Dr. Parry doubts that Gruffudd ab Adda died by having his head split as geese were killed; hence, though some readers have found this poem convincing, others take it as a mock-elegy.

A great distinction by a whitewashed wall
Where there may be orchard trees (a proud host)
Is that there should be below the apple trees
A nightingale calling night and day;
A long-singing bird of pure, bright cry,
With a hollow nest, like a chick from heaven:
Cry of golden praise on a graceful bench,
Fine timepiece on a fair, green branch.
Should there come afterward (keen to fashion praise)

A wild archer, a sharp leaper,   10
From the grim effort of betrayal toward destruction,
With a birch bolt of four barbs,
Though the orchard were full (a gift of joy)
Of sweet fruit, the trees' graceful load,
Metrical song will be (with mighty longing)
Without the forest-blossoms' bright jewel.

Powys — a land liberal, lovely, fruitful,
Generosity's sweet drinking-horns of bright taverns —
Was a pleasant orchard
Before a wise lad was slain by a blue sword.   20
Now it is, alas for widowhood,
Hawks' land, without a nightingale of song.
The overthrow of bards (*awdl* without respect)
Is this (hateful foes).
If there's great grief these three months,
Alas, there has not been a grief that wasn't less,
Because of the blow (a cry of great distress)
Of a weapon's edge where loving was not.

Gruffudd (bird of sweet music)
Fab Adda, most blameless man,   30
Everyone not base called him
"Prince of the Fair Crest of May,"
And an organ of most pleasant resonance,
And an amorous gold nightingale,
A bee of ready, true praise,
The wise springtime of Gwenwynwyn-land.

It was depraved for his kinsman to strike him,
Bold from anger, with steel in his hand.
A weapon gave (essence of terror)
My brother a deep sword-stroke,   40
Through the fine hair of a hawk of proud lineage;
Ah me, how good its edge's edge!
The three edges of the sword (is it not pitiful?)
Through the blond hair of a brave, decent man.
A stroke of the same cut as a saw,
Ugly cut through a charming skull,

I rage, same cut as a goose's,
Two pieces, was it not crude?

Cheeks colored like a blond angel,
Tower of gold, the man has died.   50

19. *Elegy for Madog Benfras*

Poems 25 and 31 are evidently about the same man as the subject of this
elegy. Madog probably survived Dafydd; see his elegy on Dafydd among the
Supplemental Poems below.

An enchanted, broken sieve,
That's the sort of world it is, its whole length.
The lord cheerful tonight
Whose life may be pleasant
(A terrible dream, quick and harsh)
Tomorrow turns dead.

Why does the swift muse pain me,
Radiant inscribing, a great, bright path?
For Madog (a twin of bard-speech)
Benfras, no servant of praise was better.   10
He was a brave and bold — there will not be for
                              a long time —
Victor of meter — a man like Madog
For mastering many meters,
For good verse (he was a portent),
For utterly intense song, for learning,
For generous wit and friendliness,
For love more than anyone,
For a wise name, for wisdom.

Harsh for a year my shout,
For the taking of Madog, he was my grace.   20
Terrible is the pang for men's teacher,
He does not cast away a disciple of the bards.
Far-clear sovereign of judgment,

Peacock of good debate, was he not without guile?
Battle auger, tender heart,
The carpenter's plane of sense and sound.
Couples of Merddin's poetry,
Couple of a shelter, eyes of wine,
And a choice bell of May-month,
And the trumpet of verse and its horn,   30
And the choir of affection and love,
And song's copper lustre and strife's debate,
A bright organ, jewel of the best,
The chieftain of poets' poetry.

  The downcast poets are without a happy land,
Without a *cywydd* will the world be.
Seldom did he not deserve wrought gold;
May's small leaves will be neglected.
Without song will be the small, bright,
       beautiful nightingale;
Increase of plague, abject tears.   40
Without respect will be the birch that he
      does not salute.
Good was he; ash trees are forlorn.

  Ready couple, the muse's chapel;
Compared to him, everyone's a copper; a fair
      girl's empty-handed.
Churlish would it be (he visited lands),
As long as there is a world, that he lives not.
Alas, throng of bards (decent his bard-speech),
He's been left with God.

20. *Elegy for Gruffudd Gryg*

Gruffudd Gryg's verse debate with Dafydd appears at the end of this collection of Dafydd's poems (Poems 147–154); Gruffudd's elegies on Dafydd are among the Supplemental Poems. D. J. Bowen argues (*LlC*, 8:1–2,9–12) that the *ymryson* (verse debate) with Gruffudd Gryg occurred early in Dafydd's career and that this fictitious elegy on Gruffudd is a later work, reflecting

Dafydd's mature esteem for a Gruffudd Gryg who had himself come to master the "Ovid-art" of writing love poetry.

Bitter was the taking, a very seizure,
Of a jewel from our midst, a Taliesin of praise.
I mourned (not gentle is the seizure),
Heavy and sad (as happens to the dead).
Praise was diminished, no need to deny,
The world over, the crudest seizure was it.
Across my cheek, slow flood,
Tears course for an agreeable man.

Wise Gruffudd Gryg was he, of eloquent praise-speech,
By the Cross.   10
There is grief for the sake of his *englynion*,
The carpenter's square of praise, nightingale of the men
                            of Môn.
Fashioner of every right understanding,
And lawbook of correct language,
Alphabet of the good wise ones,
And song's fountain and refined head,
And its tuning-horn, unreproached, good,
And its pitch-string. Alas, noblemen!

Who sings by his lovely book,
Bard of water-bright Goleuddydd?   20
Ready from his head is inspired song,
The primate and dignity of song.
No mention to be had of a word of love,
None sings, with a sigh, a song
Since he went (constant sorrow)
Under a grave to fall silent, a mute.
No moaning bard laughs, for grief,
There will be no entertainment in the world.
Not living is a fair bird who used to sing,
Not proud is the blackbird-cock of May.   30
No increase in love's urging,
There sings neither nightingale nor cuckoo;
Nor will there be a thrush of twice-doubled language
After Gruffudd Gryg;

Neither *cywydd* of dales nor of leaves,
Nor poems. Farewell, green leaves!

A sad tale for a sorrowful girl
Is it to bestow in the full-marbled choir of Llanfaes
Surely as much (a gem that belongs to us)
Of song as all that has been bestowed.   40
Love's rudiment has been bestowed
In a chest at the edge of the choir.
Of a treasury of songs (great payment)
No chestful has ever been found so good.
Chest and oak (terrible chest-load)
Hide the hawk of fine, proud verse.
For a song of golden songcraft,
Since yesterday we are all finally constricted.
Fashioner of exact accomplishment of gentle song,
Behold, a chest full of song!   50
Alas, great Christ, God's generous treasure,
That there's no one who might open the chest!

Should a fine, brilliant girl love
To hear sweet praise with harp-chord,
I judge verse-craft to be widowed
And now praise is enfeebled.
Beautiful poetry went
As if in pawn, *englyn*-sequences are sad.
The best verse after Gruffudd
Will be worse and worse without Ovid's art.   60

Bird of sweet paradise-cry,
He was a bird from the land of heaven.
From heaven he came, fine warbler,
To compose praise to the woods' face;
Inspired poet of a wine-bred muse,
To heaven, he was worthy, he went.

21. *A Satire on Rhys Meigen*

Tradition has it that Rhys Meigen, the man ridiculed in this poem, died after hearing Dafydd recite it. The story was that Dafydd's attack was provoked by a scurrilous *englyn* that Rhys Meigen sang to Dafydd in the course of a Christmas dinner given by Dafydd's uncle, Llywelyn ap Gwilym. From the manuscript (Peniarth 49) assembled by the Renaissance humanist Dr. John Davies, Dr. Parry quotes in his introduction (*GDG* ³, p. xl) the offending *englyn* ascribed to Rhys Meigen. The following is a translation of it: "Dafydd, false, sluggish, blasted dog, you're the son of all fathers: I pierced your mother, evil seduction, above her arse, alas, in her hole."

A pretty mad bungler of broad offense is there,
    Not of Gwalchmai's office;
    Dogs from every region would bark at him;
    He'd get neither respect nor favor.

Hard-headed Rhys Meigen would foster indignation
    (Dark, hollow boy) where he'd come;
    Gangling fellow, a dog that would stray,
    Trifle of song of the whey-drink of May.

The false, beastly beggar, he'd boast with his tongue
    From Teifi to Menai;   10
    Slow-witted dwarf, no one would trust him,
    Short-limbed, without grandmother, without nephew.

Love, flushing red, where he used to put pressure,
    Confession's nature, he wouldn't get it;
    A song of wormwood he'd let loose,
    Jaw of a sick ape; I won't do what he'd do.

The stiff, parched mouth — he didn't excel in words —
    Of a flatterer spoke them;
    Plain buffoonery he used to noise,
    The dirty smock of a persistent, household flour-poet.   20

Crafty churl of sod, though he'd try to meet
    With the swift, he couldn't do it,

Often racing, halfpenny-saddle,
He sums up every such fault.

Sickest, lewdest love-messenger to sick women,
      Using puny weapons;
   The hateful corn-thief is a shitty dog,
   Leg of a cliff-gull, ebb's travelling-woman.

Clumsy ragamuffin, from his trousers, a hundred thongs
                  of coracle-skin,
      Old, despised leatherpiece;   30
   He couldn't manage meter's law;
   He wouldn't go to combat or tough battle.

Hackney of a poor, stinking sort of song, drummer-boy
      Of the muck of stretched-lip scum,
   He'd turn over a hundred thousand beetles,
   False, surly lad, between each one.

Brawling verse of a poor-mouthed, garrulous,
                  ass-shaking dog,
      Long-wandering, belly-shaking, slow ebb;
   Lattice-boat of a skinny flour-thief,
   Bark boat that stands without a surplice.   40

Lad odious, dirty-legged, clumsy, trouser-puffing, bent,
                  and feeble,
      Blest is whoever would hang him;
   Dish-spending pressure-work of a soup-beggar's belly,
   Nape of a tough tomcat busily prying.

Quarrelsome, quick-lipped, shriveled stammerer at beer,
      A noisy pig when he vomited;
   Flawed failure of the odd pomp of a meat-beggar's cockles,
   Wild bolts that blemish the harsh hue of the ebb-turn.

A bandit that is a sharp-edged, intractable guest,
      And he cast a dirty hand;   50
   The devil's shears, alas where he came,
   Cowardly cup-bearer of clay minstrel-water.

Truly a body like a beggar's, not brave Cai Hir,
    Reluctantly would he stand in battle;
  A tallow-cake of draff would he suck;
  Empty, gray-brown, hollow skin.

A liquor of lees would suit the worm,
    Timid lamb weak for battle,
  Big-bellied bravery of a beggar;
  Coarse plumage, an ape was not less.   60

He sang to everyone a work of abuse,
    Without knowing what it might be;
  The harp-string of a mouse of the privies,
  The worst place (filthiest calf) would be where he was.

Rhys Meigen, a halter under strong timber
  Will be your finish, O lord of wrists;
Frustrated and angry, your teeth thresh,
  Wonder of a lard-feast, tough-looking, infested sole.
Loose lip familiar with stinking mouth-loads,
  Cocky on boar-meat, not on mead-horns.   70
You'd gulp suet and the marrow of the big bones of the gut,
  Gaping at flesh before drink, by Cyndeyrn!
A marvel is the whelp of a hundred fetters with the
                meat-spit head,
  Red-assed minstrels' bell, glands of white suet.
A coward as a soldier, he's a wonder in battle,
  A fiery statue's nod, not a Dinbyrn.
Guilty, louse-heavy, the look of a fox of a worn-out tribe,
  Unworthy face without profit, a chop of the kettles,
Ungentle, loose breeches, undignified, constipated,
  Skin and bones of a very withered shadow.   80
Your eye's roving is a pryer without a lantern,
  Rhys meanly stained with meat-gulps, a swaddled tomcat.
Sound of a gaping, constipated gut sucking dregs of the
              hollowest sour apples,
  Belly of road-dirt, not regal.
Since you don't know (angry thruster with sticky, shit-lump
             pants)
  Awdl or *englyn*, leather-fisted thief,

Run, mad, spouting, sour, immeasurably wild boy,
Run! It's proper for you to drink tavern dregs.

22. *The Fox*

Yesterday was I, sure of purpose,
Under the trees (alas that the girl doesn't see it)
Standing under Ovid's stems
And waiting for a pretty girl beneath the trees;
She made me weep on her way.
I saw when I looked there
(An ape's shape where I did not love)
A red fox (he doesn't love our hounds' place)
Sitting like a tame animal,
On his haunches near his den.   10

    I drew between my hands
A bow of yew there, it was brave,
About, like an armed man,
On the brow of the hill, a stirring of high spirits,
Weapon for coursing along a district,
To hit him with a long, stout bolt.
I drew for a try a shaft
Clear past the jaw.
My grief, my bow went
In three pieces, luckless disaster.   20

    I got mad (I did not dread him,
Unhappy bear) at the fox.
He's a lad who'd love a hen,
A silly bird, and bird flesh;
He doesn't follow the cry of horns,
Rough his voice and his carol.
Ruddy is he in front of a talus slope,
Like an ape among green trees.
At both ends of a field there turns up
A dog-shape looking for a goose.   30
Crows' beacon near the brink of a hill,

Acre-strider, color of an ember,
Likeness of a lure for crows and magpies at a fair,
Portent looking like a dragon.
Lord of excitement, chewer of a fat hen,
Of acclaimed fleece, glowing flesh.
An awl of hollowed-out fine earth,
Fire-dish at the edge of a shuttered window.
Copper bow of light feet,
Tongs like a beak of blood.   40

   Not easy for me to follow him,
And his dwelling toward Annwn.
Red roamer, he was found to be too fierce,
He'd run ahead of a course of hounds.
Sharp his rushing, gorse-strider,
Leopard with a dart in his rump.

23. *The Month of May*

God knew that it suited well,
The start of the gentle growth of May.
Unfailing green stems would sprout
On the first day of the kind, lovely month of May.
Unwithered tips of the wood detained me,
Yesterday the great God gave May.
Bards' jewel that would not cheat me,
A good life for me was the coming of May.

   Fine, handsome lad who'd give me gifts,
A great, generous, sure-handed fellow is May.   10
He sent me valid money,
The fair, green slices of the sweet hazel of May.
Treetop florins that would not vex me,
Fleurs-de-lis riches of the month of May.
Uncut, he'd keep me from betrayal
Under wings of leaves of the mantles of May.
I'm filled with anger that it would not stay
(What is there for me?) always May.

I'd tame a girl who greeted me,
A well-born, gentle girl under a choir of May.   20
Handsome poets' foster father, who ordained me,
Gentle lovers, is May.

Godson of the spotless God,
Bright blue-green, great is the dignity of May.
From heaven did he who purified me come
To the world; my life is May.

Green is the slope, happy the love-messenger,
Long is the day in the greenwood of May.
Light green (he would not hide)
Are the slopes and the crests of the small trees of May.   30
The night is short, no journey a burden,
Handsome are the hawks and blackbirds of May.
Glad is the nightingale where it tarried;
Talkative are the small birds of May.
He taught me active vigor;
No great glory is there but May!

A green-winged peacock of a townhouse,
Which one of the thousand? Supreme is May.
Who could construct it from leaves
In a month's time except May?   40
He nourished a blue-green wall,
The radiant, small, fresh hazel slices of May.
Mantled (it's best that he failed)
Is winter; gentlest is May.

Spring ceased, it would concern me no more;
Refined gold is the fine, golden wealth of May;
The bright beginning of summer would trample it;
Tears shall nourish it; pleasant is May.
The green-barked hazel's leaves would clothe me;
A good life for me is the coming of May.   50
God wise and strong has resolved,
And Mary, to maintain May.

24. *Summer*

Alas for us, Adam's weak descendants,
A tide of grace, how short is summer!
By God, true that it's most wicked,
Because of its end, the coming of summer —
And a gentle sky quite clear,
And a cheerful sun and its color in summer,
And the air relaxed and mild,
And the world pleasant in summer.

A very good crop, perfect flesh,
Comes from the old earth in summer.   10
For growing (loveliest greening)
Leaves on trees was summer given.
I laugh to see how goodlooking
Is the hair on the lively head of a summer birch.
A paradise, I sing to it,
Who doesn't laugh when summer's fine?
With great perseverance I praise,
Sweet style, oh what a gift is summer!

A girl pale as foam I love
Under the twigs, and her rashness is summer.   20
If I ask, the amorous cuckoo
Sings at the start of the sun of summer;
Refined gray bird, a beautiful
Vesper bell at midsummer, I grant.
Eloquent is the voice of a very pretty nightingale,
Well-groomed and bold under a summer house.
The thrushcock (I steal away from strife)
Has bright baby talk of summer.
Ovid's man (handsomest long day)
Roams through summer, reckless in speech.   30
Eiddig, Adam's bastard son,
Doesn't care whether summer comes.
Winter was given for those his age,
And lovers' share is summer.

For me, under birches, in the houses of a grove,
I desire only summer's mantles.
Wearing a fair web around me,
A sturdy cloak of summer's beautiful hair,
I shall unweave ivy leaves.
There won't be a cold on summer's long day.   40
If I greet a gentle girl,
Glad to court her at the height of summer.

Poetry does not prosper (saddest sign)
When summer is denied the lively poet.
The wind won't leave, I put on clothes,
Trees in their prime — ah, for summer yesterday!
There's longing (I won't apologize)
In my heart for summer's fine weather.
If snow and ice come, in autumn, then winter,
To drive away summer,   50
Woe is me, Christ, I ask,
Since they drive so abruptly, "Where's summer?"

25. *The Nightingale*

Dafydd: "Madog fab Gruffudd, heir of the woods,
You command gold praise, shining meter-instrument,
The increase of Mordaf and Rhydderch,
The carpenter's plane and wisdom of love,
You were more faithful than anyone,
The key-string of fidelity.
You came to Dafydd
Fab Gwilym with strong, free song.
Is our friendship all remembered
And my plaint at the little birch grove?   10
I'm suspecting that it's stripped,
Without fighting, without killing, without burning,
By Eiddig (a curse on him!)
With his mattock (alas for his greed!) and his shovel."

Madog: "No need for you to be dejected

For any tree or birch in the world,
While God lets the holly be;
Man shall not burn it and shall not strip it,
And in spite of what stormy weather may come,
It will not be bare nor bent nor withered.   20

"You'd have complained altogether, no doubt,
Had there happened to you (a world of great fear)
What happened to me, my sharp anger,
Of more fearful point is my grief.
There was no comfort for me
Nor consolation, sad lust,
Nor song on a white, seemly birch,
Except for a bright, fair, gray nightingale.
Take note of her if you see
A bold weaver of meter in the strong fort.   30
Loving, she sings under the leaves
A fine psalm beneath a covering of twigs.
Exiled woman, gentle of prayer,
Good flute in a wilderness grove.
The sanctus bell of lovers,
Clear, sweet, and lovely is her tone.
Eloquent will her noble song be
At the tip of the green stem.
Love's dawn-woman, comely girl,
A dark glance above thorn-tables.   40
Cuhelyn's sister, bright little girl,
A whistle six times faster
(Mistress of the organs of Maestran)
Than a hundred, from the treble string she sings.

"She did not leave a love-messenger in Gwynedd
When she went, worse and worse is the condition,
The little gray-tailed thief,
It contained none better.
May there be set on the top of the pillory
(Amen forever, if I have my way)   50
As many a one
As accused her in Coed Eutun!
In the region where she stays while she chooses,
There she shall remain for Christmas.

Where she is there shall be most love,
Good gittern, God keep her!"

26. *The Owl*

It's a pity that the lovely owl,
Cold and poor, gives no lull.
She won't let me sing my pater,
She's not quiet while there are specimens of stars.
I do not get (alas for the prohibition!)
To sleep nor to compose slumber.
House of a hunchback, of the bats,
Her back against drizzle and snow.
Nightly (small charm for me)
At my ears (memory's pennies)   10
When I shut (obvious pain)
My eyes (honor's chieftains),
These wake me, I did not sleep:
The song of the owl and her voice,
And her frequent shout and her loud laughter,
And her false harmony from her mouth.

    From then, as I live,
Till dawn, unhappy energy,
She's singing, unhappy cry,
"Hoo-thee-hoo," lively yearning.   20
Great strength, by St. Anne's Grandson,
She incites the dogs of night.
She's a whore, unfit double-shout,
Thick-headed, unfriendly shout;
Broad of brow, belly of rowan berries,
An old, wide-eyed mouse-woman;
Busy, profitless, drab,
Dry her voice, her color tin.
Loud her chatter in a fair wood,
Alas for the song, roebuck of a chain of trees,   30
And her look, the face of a tame girl,
And her form, the ghostwoman of birds.

Every dirty, exiled bird
Beats her; is it not a wonder she lives?

    She's more sharp-tongued in a wooded slope
At night than the nightingale of the hillside;
By day she does not draw (keen devotion)
Her head from a thick, hollow tree.
She'd wail with a sharp tongue, I know her face;
A bird to Gwyn ap Nudd is she.   40
Talkative owl who sings to the thieves;
Mishap to her tongue and her tune!

    In order to scare the owl
From me (I have a song),
I shall set, while I wait for frost,
Fire to every ivied tree.

27. *In Praise of Summer*

You, summer, father of daring,
Father of thick-set brushwood,
Handsome forester, thick slope's master,
Everybody's tower are you, every hillside's thatcher.
You are the cauldron (bravery's speech,
Perfect lord) of the world's rebirth.
You are, provoker of speech,
Each vigorous plant's nursery,
And the salve of growth, contention of doubled growth,
And the ointment of trees' encounter.   10

    By the God Who is loved,
Well does your hand know how to branch green trees.
Fond nature of the four parts of the world,
Awesome is it that from your grace also there grow
Birds and the beautiful earth's crop,
And swarms flying,
Moorland hay of glassy-topped meadows,
Swarms of wild bees, and strong droves.

Prophet of the highways, you are foster father
Of the heap of earth-load, the green garden-load.   20
Sprouter are you to my fine shelter,
Sprouter of a leaf-web's fair leafing.
And evil is it always
How near is August, night or day,
And knowing from the long failing,
Golden heap, that you would go away.

Tell me, summer, this is wrong,
I am able to ask you,
What place or what country,
What land do you go to, by wise Peter?   30

"Silence, praise-poet, your strict verse,
Silence, strong wizard of masterful boast.
It's my destiny, a mighty feat,
I am a prince," sunshine sang,
"To come for three months, to grow
The substances of a host of crops;
And when roof and leaves cease
To grow, and branches to weave,
To avoid winter's wind
To Annwn from the world I go."   40

Blessings of the world's poets
And their hundred greetings go with you.
Farewell, king of fair weather;
Farewell, our master and our lord;
Farewell, young cuckoos,
Farewell, weather of the slopes in June,
Farewell, high sun,
And the thick cloud, a white-bellied ball.
Monarch of an army, surely you will not be
So high, lord of sky-snowdrift above,   50
Until there come (unconcealed, lovely garden)
Summer once more and his beautiful slope.

28. *The Cock-thrush (I)*

The cock-thrush of loving sound,
Of pure-spoken, bright tone,
With beautiful, bright language, whose voice yesterday
(Lucky, joyous talent) I heard under birch —
What sort of thing could be a sweeter
Composition than his little whistling?

    Three lessons of matins he reads,
Feathers are his chasuble among us.
Far is heard above lands
His cry from the grove and his bright shout.   10
Hill prophet, great author of longing,
Chief bard of the bright passion of the glen.
Beside a brook, he sings every perfect cry
Out of his loving joy —
All love songs of fine meter,
Every organ tune, every poem,
Every gentle melody for a girl,
A contention for the best love.
Preacher and learned reader,
Sweet and nimble, pure his muse.   20
Poet of a faultless song of Ovid,
Sweet primate of the great dignity of May.

    He knows from his birch love-retreat
(Author of wood-birds' music,
Happy echo from a fair glade)
The rhymes and measures of love.
Consoling bird who sings on hazel
In a lovely wood, with the wings of an angel,
It would be unlikely for skilled birds
Of paradise who love him,   30
From right recall through passion,
To speak the poetry he sang.

29. *The Holly Grove*

Holly grove of a rightly loaded armful,
Sunny-faced fort with coral fruit,
Graceful choir that man does not uproot,
Yard with a snug roof, a house for two,
Tower for a girl to take care of me;
With points, with leaf-spurs.

I'm a man roaming past a hillside
Under woods, gentle, fine-haired trees;
Grace attends, a very pretty building,
I roamed the woods, of dales and leaves.   10
Who in winter found
The month of May wearing green livery?
It's worth remembering: today I found
A holly grove at the point of the hill.
There was the same love-seat, the same hosts,
The same livery as in May for me!
Branching woods where an organ was to be had;
Mighty mansion upon a fair, green pillar.
Song's pantry above a snow-hollow of discontent;
A bower; God's hand painted it.   20

Twice as well did the noble God make
A fine thing as generous Robert.
Hywel Fychan of generous life,
Of solemn praise-speech, he knows how to choose form,
Made a tribute, not churlish,
To a wood's angel in a fine bed.
Handsome branches near roadsides,
A stout, short-haired lad with a green tabard.
A chamber for birds of the land of paradise,
Round heap of comely green leaves.   30
Not like an old hut gluttonous of rain,
Two nights in this will be snug.
Holly leaves scarcely wither,
Having tips the same as steel.
No goat from here to Severn,

Nor an old buck, chews a mouthful of this.
Iron muzzle, when it's a long night,
With frost in each glen and moor,
The fair tree does not lose its tithe,
Despite a cold, bare spring-wind's cry;   40
A true camlet of green leaves,
Intertwined near the crest of the slope.

30. *The Fowler*

The fowler in winter places birdlime on twigs around springs, to catch
alighting birds. Dafydd has been snared in the trap of his beloved's face, God
being the fowler of that capture.

The fowler in eastern frost
Or snowdrift, fine snow shower,
Puts in the path, delicate, surely,
At hill-breast, a fine, glad winter moon,
Coltsfoot honeydew,
If he has with him
Sticky twigs (which freely ensnare them) that shelter
The shining banks of pure springs.
When a bird comes (pain's condition)
To Môn nearby above the shore,   10
He'll recognize (a very free turn)
The tenderness of waterland there.
If he stirs (he will descend),
His feathers fold in the water-lime,
Until there comes (a mind of war-wrath)
The hand of the plotter who successfully hunted him.

    Just so (father of divinity,
Good that he strikes me) did God with my love.
Like snow of the hill, beautiful color,
A sweetheart's face; I know who.   20
Deep fountains of blue tear
Are the glowing eyes of Eigr,
Lovely berries, they merit praise,

Goldsmithwork of Mary's Son above.
A hundred woes are mine (why do they afflict me?) —
Brooches of God, that they are not closed!
Love and bright liveliness adhered
(The bond of lime) between us as a wound.
The foolish mind (terrible grip)
Will not go from the courtly brow   30
(Radiant berries of a head of playful wit,
The intoxication of cheating eyes)
More than a bird (she's noble)
From the soft lime (greatly praised is her color).

Long loving, spoiler of a face,
Secret mind, far is your blow.
Her black and slender eyebrows
Are the lime-twigs, lasting capture.
More marked on a girl is a brow of blackbird plumage
Than a builder's tape on a white fort.   40
Likeness of a lordly cloud on a girl's brow,
Wearied intelligence
Was fettered, memory was chained,
A fetter of grace, it was nailed in me!

31. *Madog's Birch Wreath*

The Madog of this poem is probably Madog Benfras of Maelor (see Poems 19
and 25); he is contrasted with another poet, Iorwerth ab y Cyriog of Môn,
who is charged with asking silver or gold for his poems, while Madog and the
speaker of this poem are content with love as payment. The poem is consistent with Poems 19 and 25 in its depiction of a bardic friendship with Madog.
Conferring woven birch is a sign of love in Dafydd's poems: another wreath in
Poem 32 (the girl substitutes a garland of peacock feathers); a belt in Pem 38;
a hat in Poem 59.

A girl sent home
To Madog, love's chieftain,
A furnishing of love,
A roof of green leaves, he is well worthy of it.
Madog gives thanks to God
For getting the wreath from his generous sister.

Often he wears the forest fringe,
It is on his head daily.
A crown of the same form, skilled work,
Is my own, not of long gold.   10
The birch cluster was like a fetter,
And the girl gave it with pleasure.
Branch tips, a weary man loves them,
Braided from the midst of birds.
A thumb made it, birch of the glade,
A bud and stimulant of love.

Iorwerth prefers payment for
His verse rather than a gift from the woods.
A treasurer of poetry for silver
And refined gold, as a hundred know.   20
Some finger garment, there was given him
A beautiful circle that won't rust his hand.
Little need the man had
To bind a rhymer's whole finger.
A slender girl made a torque,
Generous is she, gave him her gold.

Two feet (a worthy young man, long-daring)
Of healthy land (good is the language)
From the same spot (a web of the pain of love)
Madog the poet allows   30
For Iorwerth (verse-lord of wise song)
And for everyone for loving girls.
If Madog of meter-wise cry wants
A prize for his tongue's praise,
He'd be liberal, and asks of her
Neither jewels nor gold, but her.
And Mab y Cyriog in Môn
Charges them for a correct *cywydd*.
A great difference (sweetheart's musician)
Is there between wealth and love.   40
A crown of twigs, though it does not pay
With goods his debt to him,
Distinguished star of birches,
A great portion, it pays it to me.

The kiss of a bountiful girl,
God knows it's good to get one;
There'd be won for pledging it
Neither mead nor wine, a lip nourishes it.
An old huckstress would be no more likely
To buy it than a rush.   50
The same sort of gift is this,
Made from the green birch of a handsome lad.
He desires gold from a lord,
An excellent lad loves fresh birch.

Concerning joy, not of the same mind
Are my brothers, the handsome courtly poets.
The merchant of song and its praise
Is Iorwerth who sells his verse.
And Madog, well-born stag,
Most sportive man of Ovid's tear,   60
Of one song with a young nightingale in a field,
He's my kinsman, loves.

32. *A Garland of Peacock Feathers*

In the morning, it was a dawn to desire,
There was for me an encounter with a girl,
One mind in love, right passion,
In the brow of a wood, weaving verse.
I asked my girl, of my age,
To braid a branch from the wood's midst,
As handsome horns, lively crown,
A garland for me, bright green:
Let it be a circle of love, if it be faultless.
And she answered her poet: 10

"Sincere your voice, a ready cry,
Why didn't you know, pain to say,
That it would be shame, not fun,
To strip birch in remote places.
There aren't on birch, it knows none,

Leaves that might be fit to take.
I will not weave branches;
It's not right to take leaves from the grove."

She gave me (it will be long-lived)
The gift I'll keep a long time —   20
A garland as good as a gold veil,
Of peacockwear to press the head.
Prime chaplet, bright, bold linen,
Handsome blooms of good, sprightly feathers.
Lovely weave of shining twigs,
Butterflies, jewels of leaves.
Royal work, a trim feat was it,
Heaps, and whorls of three colors.
Lamps of gadflies, men's eyes once,
Images of moons are they.   30
Good to get, surely no loss,
Mirrors from Virgil's fairs.
A lasting grace, I know, a pretty girl gave it,
A garland for her merry poet.
An affectionate, bright deed was its folding,
And its plaiting from wings and feathers.
A girl's love-gift to her kind bard,
God endowed this, fair array,
With all craft and good work of fine gold,
All hues as on a gold pavilion.   40

33. *The Plain-Dealing Poet*

I walked faster (long distress)
Than lightning for eighteen miles.
The front of my foot (my grief 's energy)
Last night (I'm rushing)
Did not touch (my end is sad)
The ground (youthful sign).
I'm of the same mind in the fair country
As fearsome Tristan in song.
A frail twig does not break, lively trick,

Under my foot, bold, mad man.   10
I did not turn, reckless rule,
My face back for anyone.
I went faster than wild wind
To the court of a girl like Esyllt.
I gave, and I did not name her,
Desire's gift, advice to her:

Dafydd: "Don't be debased, girl in sendal,
In your mind, color of untrodden snow,
After, gentle maiden,
Long keeping a virgin's privilege.   20
Don't desire, because of May's longing,
A clown, badly would he live with you.
Well-born, stately maiden,
Love him who loves you, elegant, shrewd girl."

She: "It's worse," says my fosterer,
"For me now because of my riches;
I've seen, Fab Gwilym, much of
Getting a man who'd deceive me."

Dafydd: "A lover is no deceiver,
He does not dwell in flattery or change.   30
I wouldn't want, could I manage,
To deceive you, black are your eyebrows.
I would not, handsome man from a bright house,
Entice you out of your house.
No man alive shall deceive you, a lord's kind
                            of protection,
Wherever I am, vain accusation.
Celebrated is your face,
My treasure, no one shall deceive you."

34. *Paying a Debt*

Morfudd is the one source of the love (the "gray bandit") that dwells treacherously in Dafydd's breast and has moved him to compose his famous crop of love poems.

Cywyddau, excellent, wise growth,
A lovely armful, the good crop of a skillful song-poet:
There was (matter of complaint)
No organ so unsecret as they.
The stone-house of love (of one mother, one father)
Is my breast; he accomplished my betrayal.
All the compass of the gray bandit
Was all begotten by the same one.

    I gave her (some services)
Fluent praise from my treasure,   10
Sound of harp and clock —
Too much gift, a drunken man gave it.
I, like a loving simpleton,
Sowed her praise throughout all Gwynedd.
Fertile it's flying,
Thick seed, there's a beautiful sowing!
Far-praised is the uncrude girl,
All know it, each tender, generous girl.
All were eager in my tracks,
And their "Who?" was in each street.   20
A loud paternoster
Of all those who play a sad bass-string
At every feast (marvelous lady)
Is her song, brilliant for her sake.
A tongue has made praise grow,
Beautiful is her smile, the Amen of praise,
For at the end of every prayer,
Right remembrance, she is named.
Sister is she, shining color of the sun,

To Gwgon's noble daughter.   30

    The same voice have I, where she would stand,
As the cuckoo, May's hired maid.
She manages from her grief
Just one voice in her gray cloak.
The cuckoo does not still her chatter,
She grows hoarse between crag and sea;
She sings no *cywydd* (happy oath)
Nor accent except "Cuckoo!"
It is known in Môn that I was a monks' servant
Too burdened   40
Who does (good double-sneeze)
But one work, thick of breast.

    Restless mind, honest debate,
I followed as one holding his breath.
Farewell now! without being able
Because of her to find a hiding-place or shelter.
Using to honor her
Deep materials of song for her.
She has a good portion, if she saves it,
And if it's put in good soil: 50
Seven *cywyddau* for slender Morfudd
Of straight, lively limb, and seven-times-twenty.
For love of her I'm destitute;
Let her take them, I'm without guilt.
Precious love does not ask to be paid;
She has no more claim on me.

35. *Denying that He's a Monk*

Good Morfudd of fine red cheek,
Snow-colored, aristocrat;
Immaculate, high-browed girl,
A cause of anger to the world, you carry off the prize!
Twice better are you for being respected, girl;
Praise's faithful one, tell me

(Fame's muse, land's chief light,
Lady of a golden lord) whether it was true
That you said that you do not desire, dear,
Cold sport, a man with a tonsure.   10

    O God, why, moon of pure oath,
Did you make that declaration?
If you refuse (faith's firm covenant,
He went too far) a man of religion,
For the sake of jewels, gold, and enamel,
My girl of golden forehead,
I'm content under a green birch grove
Still, sweetheart, with you, girl.
If mockery (color of summer's bright crest,
My treasure) or blasphemy at my expense,'   20
Generous Morfudd, sweetheart of blackberry-brow,
Was the reference to my gold crown,
Too serious, my noble maiden,
Is the mockery you made this long time.

    A curse for me, my faultless girl,
Brilliant, swift track of May sun,
If ever I saw
(Golden pledge) one who made a mockery,
That there was not found (so they told me,
I'd testify to the outrage) something to mock in her.   30
For this, wound-bound from battle,
I'm in pain, Morfudd, celebrated gem.
Glowing sun, portion of the salt sea,
Double the color of sunshine, you shouldn't
(Love's famed overflowing, pure white flesh)
Cast any quick mockery
(Fierce brilliance, best sort of language)
At your blessed bard in your lifetime.
There's nothing to mock, girl of slim eyebrow,
In generous Morfudd's lively poet,   40
Although the hair falls, cloak of pain,
From my skull, brilliant author.

    Your Ovid will not be perfect,

I was not a novice any month of May;
I did not wear (I did away with anger)
Either a cowl for a decent head or a habit;
I did not learn (whole violence of dispute)
On fine parchment one word of Latin.
Not gray my beard, fine weapon,
Not wider my tonsure, not less,   50
Than when we were, dear gem,
Our pain, loving each other.
You went, oh the cost and the game,
To your bed, eight fine lamps' beauty,
And your arms, liveliness of summer blossoms,
Men's ornament, around me,
And I in turn, my fond gem,
Loving you, shy, black-browed girl;
But not permissible, happy song,
All of it true, to say it right out.   60

        Hour unstained, heavy gold wealth,
For this, girl, my mute maiden,
Say, my darling, and choose
Which one you'll do, sun of the month of May,
Whether you'll be true with long, lively strength
From undenied love for me,
Or say to me, my sweetheart,
That you won't, face of desire.
If you repent loving me,
In a turmoil that was   70
(A share of it is yours while there may be fellowship),
Love God back, farewell,
But don't say, my soulmate,
A bitter word about a man with a tonsure.

36. *Discouragement*

Pleasant was my work last night
Amid the grace and the gift of late afternoon,
When a man was the same color, getting loved,
Brave in a thick blanket, as a dark bush.
A genial cock-thrush
Over my head on a green veil
Was driving (the product of memory's quest,
A known good omen) heart into me:

Thrush: "I'd know sound, good advice for you,
The long days of May; if you will, do it,   10
And sit under a birch castle,
God knows no house was better;
And under your head a pillow
Of fine feathers, the graceful plumage of trees;
And over your head, my birch tree,
A radiant fort of coverlets."

    I'm not sick, I don't want to be,
I'm not healthy, by God above;
I'm not dead, by noble Peter,
And God knows I'm not alive.   20
If I were to get one, desirable confession,
It would be a gift of grace, by Christ of heaven,
Either to die without any greeting,
Or to live a fine man in love.
There was a time, it happened,
Ah me, when I lived in health,
That Christ the high Lord could not
Rob me of summer.

37. *Loving a Highborn Girl*

Dyddgu of unshamed virtue,
My lamplight-love,
Secret wantonness indeed
Was mine up there, because of betrayal.
Lady of teeth bright as snow,
To love you was to deserve a plague.
As I am no warrior, I shall never go
To attempt the daughter of a straight-lanced lord,
Lest I be called (a man of poor office,
A familiar path) the same.   10

    Too high, say eminent ones,
I climbed, when I conveyed praise.
It is confidence that makes a climber,
He climbs bravely like a king of the woods,
Till he come, as he should,
Little by little to the treetop above.
From there it's hard
To come down lest he earn contempt.

    Sailors, when they get a wind that frees them
Where they make a course hobbling along,   20
There won't be an inch, poor trick,
From the top of a broken, bare plank,
(Oarsmen, foolish mariners)
Between them and the naked deep.
And to the shore wandering
They come, good forecasting.

    An archer who hits every trash
Besides the target and clear past,
And also a perfect hit
On the target, is it not right what he'd do?   30

    An accidental hit, sweet girl,
Would it be to get one out of a hundred;
An accidental hit, slim-browed girl,

Fair, shy jewel, for me to get you.
And because of that, famous jewel,
My hope's not bad, there's no necessity.
It's possible, girl flour-white as snow,
For me to get you, sweet, brown eyebrow.
Wholly vain to say, for whatever he could do,
That I should not have you; blessed is he who gets you!   40
Unless I get you for a song excellent
And undying, my girl of young grace,
I'll get you, gentle face,
My darling, when no one wants you.

38. *The Lady Goldsmith*

Lady goldsmith of the twig belt
Ever from the stock of birch-top,
It shall be a gain for me, a forest gift,
If I have profit, that she is so skilled.
In order to maintain the goldsmith's craft,
She went to a smithy of leaves,
Winning both praise and a greeting,
And with her hand soldered love.
By her hand, my fine gold treasure,
She excellently twisted birch;   10
And my refined lady goldsmith who does not offend me,
Gem of her lineage, purposed
To fashion a belt of tips,
Bold-privileged, from the wood of the slope:
A bit of wood that binds the waist,
Familiar craft between finger and thumb,
It's a hundred times better than a belt of fine amber,
Belt of hair from the head of a bright birch;
I'm cinctured with the tips of twigs;
It's worth all the brooches of the South.   20
Faithfully does it keep for me a long life;
I'm complete from the belt she gave.

My birch belt (it will be kept)

From the wood shall long cause desire.
It's my gain, I don't renounce it,
My life throughout the summer;
My son, my liberal brother,
My birch-bond, my girl gave it.

Display of a proper, skilled craft,
A gem of fresh birch was Morfudd's belt.   30
Splintered is my breast, cheerful stir,
Under the birch belt of a knowing girl.
Trim handiwork on good birch,
She knew how to dress the wood.
Her foresight is better than that of Jenkin
The goldsmith: she wants frequent payment.
Slim wood did she harmonize;
Blessed is the weak one who shall
(She enriched my hand for my benefit)
Be on top of the lady goldsmith.   40

39. *The Dream*

As I was (I knew hiding)
Dozing in a secret place,
I saw at the very break of dawn
A dream at dawn of day.
I saw that I was roaming
With my crowd of dogs at my hand,
And descending to a forest,
A lovely place, not a sullen oaf 's house.
I set loose without delay,
I imagined, the dogs to the wood.   10
I heard cries, voices inflamed,
Sounding often, dogs chasing.

A white hind above the clearings
I saw (I loved the chase)
And a troop of hounds on track

After her, their course exact;
Going to the slope over an unbroken height
And over two ridges and a crestline,
And back over the ridges
On the same course as a stag;   20
And her coming, having been tamed,
To my protection, and I excited;
Bare nostrils, I woke up,
Voracious, I was in the hut.

    I found a good old woman
When it was day, very gladly.
I confessed to her what I did,
Night's omen, as I saw it:

Dafydd: "By God, wise woman, if you could
Resolve this enchantment,   30
I'd match, I know a hundred wounds,
None with you. I'm without hope."

Old Woman: "A good thing, man without hope,
Is your dream, if you're a man.
The dogs, unconcealed, you saw
At your hand, if you know strong speech,
Good trackers of an unerring course,
Are your bold love-messengers.
And the white hind, a lady
You loved, color of sunny foam;   40
This is certain, she will come
To your keeping, if God keeps you."

40. *A Nod*

As I the other night,
Quite wretched, for a third of the night,
Was walking, fervently awaiting
(She was very fine) some modest girl,

Near the hall of Eiddig and his wife
(He'd shout after me if he'd known I was there),
I looked in miserable melancholy
(A sturdy fortress) all around the house.

I saw through a window's glass veil
(Men's bliss was it to see the pale beauty)   10
Lo! by my cunning I saw
The one best sweetheart living.
Bright was the form of the girl of inclined head,
And her color like Branwen ferch Llŷr.
Not daylight nor sun was
So brilliant as she.
Great is the miracle of her fair face,
So fair, she surpasses anyone living in the world.

I insisted on greeting her,
Easily she answered me.   20
We came right to the edge,
The two of us, no one knew.
There were not more than three words between us;
If there were, no one knew a word.
I didn't try to trespass on my treasure;
If I'd tried, I wouldn't have got to either.
Two sighs did we give
That broke the bond of steel between us.
Upon this, I said goodbye
To the girl who has no gentler peer.   30
One thing I'll do while I live —
Not say who she is.

41. *A Stubborn Girl*

As I was going
Over a mountain, monks of Christendom,
And my bright cloak on me,
Like a farmer, in the longing of summer,
Lo, on the moor, a limb

Of a maiden waiting for me.
I greeted her (a kind swan's mind),
Tender, prudent girl.
She answered her poet;
It's an answer of love, to my thinking.   10

    We walked together like May-girls,
And the cold one wouldn't consent.
Pliant was I for a fair girl,
She was not pliant about a kiss.
I praised her glowing eyes;
Let handsome poets praise her!
I asked, before wars come,
Whether she desired me; she was my heaven.

She: "You won't get, boy from the edge of the parish,
Any answer; I don't know yet.   20
We'll go to Llanbadarn on Sunday,
Or to the tavern, sly man;
And then in the greenwood
Or in heaven will we keep tryst.
I wouldn't want it known, lest I be blamed,
That I was amid fine birch."

Dafydd: "A plain coward am I judged by your love,
But your lover is a brave man.
Don't stand off, noble descendant,
Because of slander a woman might make.   30
I know a place of green woods
That the Other never knew
And that Eiddig will not know
While there's a veil on tree and twig.
I take my leave, maiden,
Keeper, girl-thief of the grove."

    The unkind girl wouldn't do
What she did with her word, niece of the cuckoo.
A foolish promise made me happy:
A wine-promise will be the pale girl's tryst.   40

42. *Morfudd Compared to the Sun*

I'm waiting for a girl of easy speech,
Brilliance of fine snow on an open meadow,
God sees that she's radiant,
Brighter than a brow of foam.
Color of the sounding breast of a white wave,
Light of the sun, she's modest.
She knows she deserves a love song from my mouth,
Supreme beauty of the sun in the sky.
The people's queen, with a mantle of fine fur,
She knows how to make fun of an unattractive man. 10
Fine Morfudd (alas, the vain, frail poet
Who loves her), tender, serene, lovely, fair one.
Web of gold; the shadow of a man, alas for him
Of good figure who's crying out!

　　Great is her dishonesty and her cleverness,
More than any, and she's my soul.
On one occasion, my white girl shows herself
In church and court;
Another time, girl of the whitewashed, proud,
　　　　　　　　　battlemented fort,
Bright and shining Morfudd hides,　　　　　　　20
Like the sun with rays of vital good,
Nurse of the principality of sunshine.
Praiseworthy is her fine service,
Merchant of bright, generous May.
Great is the vigil for brilliant Morfudd,
Bright, clear mirror of noble and excellent Mary.

　　To the earth, enormous edge,
The sun comes like a sprightly-hued girl,
Beautiful from the body of dawn,
A shepherdess of all the clouds.　　　　　　　30
Afterward, great, stout war, there may come
A thick cloud over her head,
When there would be (we'd know great pain)
Need of the sun that wears out eyesight.

She flees, nearly darkened
(Angry pain's mood), at night when night comes.
Brimful is the purple sky,
An image of grief, a planet place.
Far from anyone's knowing there
(She is God's ball) where she goes.   40
No hand gets to touch her,
Nor to clasp her brow.
The next day she rises again,
Burning afar from the world's roof.

Not differently (an angry portion)
Does Morfudd hide from me;
After she comes from the sky above,
Rushing low under the sky-sun,
The one of fair frown hides herself
Under the cold, evil man's lintel.   50

I pursued love in the glade
Of Penrhyn, love's dwelling-place.
Daily there's seen there
An elegant, shining girl; and nightly, her flight.
No nearer getting on hall floor
To touch hand (I've been killed)
Than will (famed, well-spending girl)
Someone's hands hold the sun.
The glowing sun has not a better, bright, glad face
Than she.   60
If there's one who's fairest this year,
The fairest (lord's kin) is our sun.

Why, for showing illicit desire,
Does not one possess the night,
And the other, splendid warmth,
Good light, color the day?
If the two faces were to appear
On a circuit about the world's four corners,
Marvel of a parchment-stiff book
In the girl's lifetime, night's coming ever.   70

43. *Morfudd's Oath*

An injury is better (fancied offense)
Than surly, boorish sulking.
Morfudd would be good to her man
At last, the color of snow's radiance.

Her oath, Luned of light,
She of good manners gave me,
By means of her ring-burdened hand,
And fervor of mind and arm,
That she will love me, lord of kindred,
If the ape loves her foster-son.   10
It's a worthy oath if not forsworn:
It's blessed I'll be if it's true.
I had no gain (hidden, full content)
Ever, since I have been given a gift,
As good as getting this from the generous one,
If it's a complete gift.
Not a gem, idle to mention,
Nor birch from the glen, nor a costume jewel.
A splendid work of Mary's high Son
By His bare hand in God's light,   20
A psalm of God, Who sealed it
A relic by His hand and His favor,
And sufficient it was, and it shall be enough
Of a knot between us both;
And deep goes and long
In the fire, the person who breaks it.

And my own upon my dear
I gave to the shy, shapely one,
A strong oath, instead of a stale one,
In her hand, color of sun,   30
As was given me through free power
In the water, by name, "Dafydd,"
A strong pang of love, God's true love,
To love her, border of snow.

Favored with grace was the pledge,
I know well, and God did it.
With her hand's form did the girl
Give a handful, and grace upon it.
Needful oath, perfect, fair, gracious,
The virtue of truth itself.   40
An oath to God by her right hand,
Lo! I swear, an oath not hollow;
A happy, proud oath, Indeg's hue,
That good oath along her beautiful hand.
A book of love shall it be in her hand,
A lord, the monarch of summer.
In cold water was ordained
The oath that Morfudd Llwyd gave.

44. *A Girl's Headdress*

Today do I, Dafydd, see
(Comfort for today will it be)
Between hair that fast drove me wild
And her brows (a king's daughter)
Placed on one forehead, a hundred pounds' worth
Of fortresses of precious stones and wrought gold.
Slim girl, too infrequently
Do I see you, most pleasant, excellent one.
See there a rare vision!
Such a forehead under a wrought-gold web!   10
By the fated Cross from the land of Eidal
And man's blood, right is the forehead.
The land's enamel, Llŷr's slayer
Is the headdress of my beloved man-hurter;
And azure pressing on cambric
On a head-seam is that which is worn.

The girl who pains me is one of Flur's vivacity,
With a fetter of good gold on her brow.
Complete sorrow is mine, Maelor's candle,
On her forehead (great her deception)   20

Is a bright frontlet, headdress causing my pain,
A gold florin, brilliant rank of joy.
A good design on fleur-de-lis leaves,
And cast-gold from the city of Paris.
She's a gem of the two commotes,
And gold of France, of the same color as the foam of a stream.
Hour of shining prime, pale face of snow,
Honor of the world's proud women.
Ah me, Son of good, chaste Mary,
How beautiful she is, and ah, that I do not prosper!   30

45. *Dyddgu*
Daughter of Ieuan ap Gruffudd ap Llywelyn

Ieuan, lord of spear-fire of worthy father,
Rightful son of Gruffudd, battle-spur,
Son of Llywelyn Llwyd, of the white wine-fort,
A ruler are you, just chief of an army:
The other night (impulse of liveliness)
I was at your house (may there be a long reward);
Despite this, till today it is not easy
(Fine hue) for me to get decent sleep.
Your gold I got, gracious and free,
Your bright wine, your cheerfulness,   10
Your fresh mead flowing for the minstrels,
Your blackhead-bragget.

Your daughter, I know she would not make love,
Fair maiden of a stone mansion.
I did not sleep nor weave verse,
Neither a full night nor part of it, plagues of tribulation.
Holy God, who'll relieve me?
Nothing enters my heart
Except her precious love;
If it were all given to me, is there need of anything more?   20
She does not love me (a plague torments me);
She does not allow me sleep, though she allows me old age.

Wonderful to the Roman Sages

How wonderful is the beauty of my slim darling,
Paler than the snow of spring;
A solitary am I from love for the gentle girl.
Pale is the forehead under twigs,
Black is the hair, chaste is the pretty girl.
Blacker is the hair (straight trees)
Than a blackbird or a clasp of jet.   30
Untrodden whiteness on gleaming flesh
Darkens the hair, the justification of praise.

    Not unlike (calm day)
Is the style of her face, says her poet,
The amiable girl who loved
The soldier once (mine is complete grief),
Peredur (of anxious watch)
Fab Efrog, brave, modest knight,
When he was looking (excellent light)
In the snow, eagle-like lord,   40
An azure veil near Esyllt's grove,
A proud path where the wild hawk had been
Killing (without anyone who'd stop him)
A blackbird (proud girl) with guilt.
Then were there accurate signs
(Does not God deserve this painting?)
In heaped-up snow matching
Her forehead, says her family;
The active blackbird's wing is
Like her eyebrow (I fostered enchantment);   50
The bird's blood after the snow
(Sun's degree) is like her cheeks.

    Such is (golden chaplet for the hair)
Dyddgu of the black, shining, lovely hair.
I was a critic once, a course for running,
Let the yonder troop of critics judge
If it's profitable, my devotion,
For me to live because of my beloved.

46. *Love Compared to a Hare*

Here's a subject, where it is there shall be
A criterion of the work of a master of hounds:
The course of a hare that comes
(Mighty confusion) out of the hedge where it was.
A gray, long ear near a green oak grove,
With a spotted cheek, fast of journey, hillock-jumping.
She's the hunting dogs' desire,
Tune of a chorus, leap of a wild dog.
A mannish hag produced on clear clay
A muscle spasm in a weak hound.   10
Short-jawed, stumpy, fed with shoots,
I know the fate of the gray one with the white trousers.
A trouserful of hemp on frost,
Pet of a thick gorse bush.
The dross of new stalks above a brook,
Liquid manure from a grassy place of wild young.
Female raider on a wing-patch of corn,
Scat, ugly, short, mad cat!
Long-travelled cat of dark-spotted cheek,
Wild, gray pouch of a swamp wood-lair.   20
Bold treasure of a rock-slope that flies in haste,
Stray of the undergrowth.
With a hill lair, with a headpiece of arrows,
A fairly wild she-kid white of limb.

      Fast from her place, on gray ice,
A push from the toe of a fur boot.
Let her be chased, on a course,
In front of men, an ember of wind,
Hopping from track to track,
From wood to lovely, bright, open field,   30
A true course along the slope
Of a flowing, red veil of bracken,
From one nook to another,
From the midst of dew to a folding of stalks.
Giddy of mind, and she loves corn,
If God allows, the earth's quick one.

She knows a fickle purpose,
A wild push, quick from her lair,
Leg of a cat, her aim the hillock-nest,
Deep fortress, she's familiar with coming there.   40
To the farmhouse, the place of shining warmth,
If she got food, she arose.

Sleepless for a lively girl,
A weak man of like form am I.
My struggle's for my soulmate,
My energy was loving my girl,
My thought when I was jealous,
My urgent aim, my passionate mind
Arose through the lore of a praise-poem
From the place where it had been for profit,   50
From the bed of love (gleaming, good girl),
From the wine-floor (adroit, lively lady).

I hunted love, vain huntsman,
To flush it, bright as the stars,
From a girl of lovely forehead (anger's speech)
Out of the square fort yonder.
What gain for me (she was not more yielding),
Pain ever without one healthy hour?
Her love ran, angry, wise girl,
God's graces, a hind's running,   60
Two-foot pace, wrath's equipment,
A thief, from her mind back to his own place.
He does not go willingly, where I set him,
From where he was binding a wound.
He does not lurk in a hidingplace;
He does not go, bound in a trap's jaws.

Land of Gwgon (great, direct burden)
Gleddyfrudd (bright his two arms),
Tonight I shall not get (sick sickening)
To sleep a wink unless I may be yonder.   70
She of the color of snow of the plain does not know
(The proud mind) a movement of love;
A harvest of fear, this warfare;

It does not go (it would come by name),
His mind's mad mood, from his district,
At the girl's demand (it was nailed there).
She of lovely color provoked long anger,
An old thief like a nightmare.

47. *Bargaining*

A girl has demanded money for secret love; Dafydd bargains her down to a
penny, then reveals that he doesn't have even that, but offers her his body as
payment, in what he regards as a beautiful mutual giving. She remains
unpersuaded, while Dafydd keeps his offer open.

The woman will not sleep with her lord,
No other man can seduce the girl.
She's not sleeping in the confines of her fort;
He does not guard my chaste girl.
She did not want less (she would not do any good thing)
Than six pounds on her oath.
I (well did I know about business)
Would give one pound to the little creature;
But that I would not give a pound all at once
To my dear girl of thoroughly fine discourse.   10
Ten shillings if she conceived
Would I give to the golden girl,
And ten shillings for trysting six times
I'd give; I would come on the journey.

On ten shillings of noble count
I lingered, and gave five.
Of these five shillings (she does not want me)
Forty pence would be enough for her.
And further (dream of a privileged mind)
If she were to take all my forty pence,   20
Too much is the wondrous, elegant girl's price
Expecting close to twenty.
Twelve pence under compulsion
Or eight as payment for my small one.

Six pence is the wage in hand,
I'd give four rather than stop.
From four to three as a fine,
And from three it goes to two.
Ah, for some money on loan!
For a penny was my gentle soul won.   30

    I can't pay, except in will,
Cash at fingertip to the girl.
If you want (may my soul gain heaven)
The body, in exchange for the body it has gained.
And it's the oath of a lad under leaves of a green bush
A curse on the man if it's me,
If he does not desire this, my bold girl,
Not according to what the girl might be owed
Will he give forever for her sake.   40
At another time when I am able
On a tryst-day, I am an obedient man.

48. *The Girls of Llanbadarn*

I'm doubled over with passion,
A plague on all the girls of the parish!
Because I didn't get (outrage of a broken tryst)
Any one of them ever,
Not a virgin of sweet promise,
Not a little girl, not a hag, not a wife.

    What obstacle, what wickedness,
What failure that they don't want me?
What harm for a girl of thin eyebrow,
Getting me in a thick, dark wood?   10
It would be no shame for her
To see me in a bed of leaves.

    At no time did I not love
(No enchantment was so clinging as this,
Passing that of men of Garwy's passion)

One or two in a day.
And despite this, I was no nearer
Getting one than the woman who is my enemy.
There was no Sunday in Llanbadarn
That I would not be, though others condemn it,   20
With my face toward the fine girl
And the nape of my neck toward the good God.
And after I had long surveyed
Over my feathers the people of my parish,
Says a bright, fresh sweetheart
To another, lively and famous for wit:

"The pale boy with a coquette's face
And his sister's hair on his head,
Adulterous is the looking
Of him with the crooked glance; he's acquainted
                                    with evil."   30

"Is it that pretense he has?"
Is the word of the other beside her.
"He'll get no answer as long as the world lasts;
To the devil with him, mad thing!"

Rough for me, the shining girl's curse,
Small recompense for dazed love.
I'll have to manage to stop
This practice (dreams of horror).
I must go like
A hermit, a wretch's office.   40
From too much looking (grim lesson)
Backwards (the picture of weakness)
It happened that I (friend of strong song)
Bent my head, without one companion.

49. *A Girl Dressing up*

Some of the girls of the lands,
This is what they do at a fair, consoling day,
Put pearls and a bright, pure ruby
On their foreheads, golden and lively,
And wear red, a girl's advantage,
And green; woe, who lacks a lover!
No arm is seen (clasp of an embrace's load)
Nor neck of a girl of slim eyebrow
Without around it (sunshine's burning hawks)
Beads, a marvelous life.   10

    Must the sun, on a costly progress,
From its place seek more color?
No more need for my very lovely sweetheart
To put a frontlet on the beautiful forehead,
Nor look there in the mirror;
Very good is the pretty one's appearance.

    The yew bow that may not be sturdy
(Count it as already two halves)
For battle, immortal gear,
With gold is its back colored;   20
And it's sold for a great price,
This bow, I know it's true.
It's not suspected (valid reminder)
That in a beautiful thing there is fault or betrayal.

    Mary! is it worse that the white wall should be
Under lime (a well-endowed sphere)
Than if one gave (expensive and deceiving the man)
A pound for the painter to come
To paint handsomely (lively intentions)
A bare place with the color of bright gold   30
And even lovelier colors
And pictures of fair shields?

Sure it is, O my body, wherever I might come,
Matching the hue of stars, I hurt.
You too, the mockings of your brother,
Well-praised girl of white teeth,
Are better in a good, gray-white petticoat
Than a countess in gold raiment.

50. *A Game of* Cnau I'm Llaw

The game of *Cnau I'm Llaw* ("Nuts in my Hand") was apparently a folk custom meant, like plucking daisy petals, to show whether one is loved. Two persons played, speaking a formulaic dialogue; one is assured that he is loved if an odd number of nuts, sent by his love, should be in the hand of the second person.

I remember a psalm from Ovid's book:
A lover's not clever
Unless he gets a friend in hand
To tell everything to.
There's one such as I would choose,
A little brother of a love poet for me;
A helper to my captive love,
An advisor on longing's knots.
She was not, dear, little woman,
Though simple, more persistent   10
(She practices hardly any deceit)
Than we two, my pretty girl.
And he also began
Making the sound of love's grief.
A rigged game, and we knew why,
For an Eigr of face we played.

Friend: "Nuts in my friendly right hand."

Dafydd: "They come for me; a gentle girl brings them."

Friend: "Peas of generous green hazel from the
                              wind-hawks' woods,

Why are they yours? They're fat nuts."   20

Dafydd: "They've been sent to me, braided strength."

Friend: "From whom?" says he. "For what reason?
Look, so that you don't refuse a gain,
Whether a gentle girl sent them."

Dafydd: "A slim young girl as pretty as fine gossamer,
Lovely Morfudd, great shall be her gift."

Friend: "Does the girl, the bards' wound, love you?"

Dafydd: "She loves me, I'm sure; I'm amorous.
If she, gem of a hundred, loves me, leave there
An odd number for joy's sake."   30

    The girl of slim eyebrow sent
Me this, there's a generous gem,
Sent the nuts, a bright omen,
Favored hazel crop, by God and Deinioel,
For a tranquil, golden song
(Beauty of a layer of snow).
A tryst in the greenwood (kind sign)
There'll be, if the sign's not a lie.
I'm a lad ascending, a choice tryst is it,
If it's a true sign, a squire of the woods.   40
If a *cywydd* (religion does not make us believe),
If an omen be true, deliverance is won!

    Flagons and forest feathers
Together, a fit crop of the woods.
Are they not husks of fat kernels,
Bright knots of hazel branches?
Fingertips once when they pressed
Through the gloves of the forest.
Not unkind was it of buttons to bear a greeting,
Samples of love.   50
A lip does not break them from gluttony,
I'm Ysgolan, no one sees them,

Nor are they broken, indeed it's forbidden,
By stone, a girl's bright gift.

　　I myself from my supply
Of nuts (the Son of Grace made them)
To her of lovely face, before the ashes of the gray earth,
Shall make payment for the fruit of the mountain pasture.

51. *His Love's Pre-eminence*

This *cywydd* opens with a triad; it is Triad 50 in *TYP* [2] (p. 129). To the
beautiful women named in this triad, Dafydd adds a fourth, a woman he has
seen in a church (the medieval equivalent of Ovid's theatre as a place for
meeting beautiful women). He invests her with mythic stature, consistent
with the splendor of the celebrated ladies with whom she is linked. At the end
of the poem, he declares that she is worth losing the world for, though prudent
heads demur.

Three women with their face like gossamer
Got in full proportion
The fine beauty, when the good state was,
That God of Heaven gave Eve.
The first of the brilliant three
Who won it (lively, fleeting gift)
Was Polixena, daughter of Priam,
A bright treasure wearing fur.
And the second was Deidameia,
Her lovely face like the light-expending summer sun.　　10
The third girl, for long a second Rhun,
Was white and slender Elen Fannog,
The one who caused commotion
And war between Greece and Troy.

　　A fourth, a noble shape of love,
Is the fine, slim, shining girl
Coming, fair and dignified,
Men's passion, to the temple, golden place,
With crowds on the bright floor

Looking at her, rare lady.   20
And me, the thought came to me to ask
Who is the pretty little thing.

   Sister is she, gay, bright moon,
Same father as the moon, to the moon;
And niece to splendid sunshine,
And her mother was the spotless dawn of day;
And from Gwynedd she has issued,
And she's a descendant of the sun in the sky.

   No woman whom I know is white,
Lime on proud stone chamber is not white,   30
A bent, pale wave is not white,
A lake's whitecaps are not white, nor snowdrift,
Not white is a truly bright face
Compared to the face of my love, by Mary!
I made a wager in my mind
(The color of wave-foam when it boils at sea)
That no believing Christian lives
Who could find fault with the girl's color;
But that she deserves a triumph of praise,
God is my pledge, she's brighter than a lamp!   40

   Let no Welshman wonder
That a girl should be saluted by that color.
With this long knife may
His heart's recess be churned
Who would think it pleasant,
While renouncing her, to gain the world.
The greater my wealth may be
And my fine, natural praise,
The more the life of my soul,
The learning I have within, would squander all at once.   50
What profit for me, gentlemen,
To leave the woman and gain goods?
No hope is there this year
For anyone older than she.

52. *Seeking Reconciliation*

The three beauties (Tegau, Dyfr, and Enid) to whom this *cywydd* likens Morfudd are named in Triad 88 (*TYP* [2], p. 215), "Three Splendid Maidens of Arthur's Court."

> Beautiful Morfudd, a golden, proud Tegau,
> Radiance of hot sun on a whitewashed fort,
> Pay for your praise before hoarding,
> The poets' deceit are you.
>
> From faith, grief grew within my round heart
> Because of how fickle you were.
> And some who call upon you, maiden,
> Say, my slender soul,
> That love of you does not abide in me, prince of pain
> (You whose brilliance is beautiful),   10
> More than foam (fair, fine girl)
> Upon water (unspoilt liveliness).
> Meager payment (spirit of a Dyfr in style),
> Twice better that you would listen
> (I'm angry to hear you talked of)
> To a man who said out of deceit
> In his haste one word of slander
> (Bright Tegau) instead of ten of praise.
> Not willingly would I speak
> About (snow shower, assuredly,   20
> Image of love, stars' color)
> Your fickleness face to face.
>
> Suppose I should, a fool's virtue,
> In drunkenness, the darkness of deceit,
> Say a mocking word,
> Between madness and fear,
> Know, by the Life of Cybi,
> Wave-color, you ought not,
> Bright gem of gold, the friend of praise,
> To refuse a minstrel reconciliation.   30
> Girl, know, under thick woods overhead,
> My mind if you refuse me.

None gets slander from my head;
Thus did the foster Son of Mary
With the blind one (undoubted report)
Upon earth, of the Jews,
Who wounded (it was a cruel story)
His breast with betrayal's sword.

Love-poet's treasure, consider also
How great, my darling, was the mercy   40
Of the pure Virgin (lovely, firm faith),
Anna's daughter (great her increase),
Fine gem, when Jesus was mocked,
The Son of holy Joseph;
She did not (she was not foolish of speech)
Hold a grudge or avenge a word.

Mortal sin, flesh's long snare,
Has no greater vanity
Than to dwell, great, terrible scorn,
In wrath, color like fair Enid.   50
Twice as fair as the sun, a good moon for long,
Calm down, honorable girl!
Do not be, your devotion's beautiful,
Surly because of a few words,
My darling, anymore towards your poet
Well-born, exiled.
My gold one, accept an apology
And compensation, where denial is impossible.
Support joy in your prayer;
Fair as fine snow, be reconciled with me.   60

53. *Morfudd's Arms*

Shape of the girl of Enid's shape,
And the slices of gold, these make passion grow in me.
Brow of clear expanse, portion of lily,
Queenly and generous hand.
A modest girl, good in humanness

And style, her nurture better than anyone's.
In a leaf-tryst, hands around neck
Led to a passion of longing
(A thing he was unfamiliar with)
And getting to clasp her lip.   10
A handsomely-grown, wine-bred, frail poet
Was I, once captive to her.

Discretion in question, there's now
(It was a gift, and God is my surety)
A knot of love, though I hide,
Between us, surely, bound am I.
A snow-white arm of shining courtesy
Of Morfudd of the sunshine-bright cheeks
Held me (bold sin was easy)
Face to face in the leaf-house nook.   20
Good was the tender, gentle one of long, white body,
Holding around me hands that love me.
Clasp of a knot of excellent love
Of a chaste, wise girl's two wrists.
Full measure it was for me, in my impetuous course,
A brave collar of secret, shy love.

A bard's smooth yoke, handsome jewel,
Less than a burden was the girl's bright arm.
Beneath an ear of the best servant of praise
A collar I can't reject,   30
The color of white lime, like encircling snow —
There's a good gift on a man's neck —
A girl put, and one knows it,
Around a poet's neck, tender, slim treasure.
It was lovely to see in bracken
A Tegau-shape strangling a man.
After getting to embrace more,
Golden lady, oh what a torque!
Craftily a magician bound me.
Long life to the girl of magical word of praise   40
Who keeps for me (a design for fine touching),
Like a nurse, my caresses.

Not a love for anyone to ridicule me for,
Image of the sun, between her hands.
Fearless, uncowardly, bold of brow
And dark am I and carefree,
With my faithful girl's two arms
Around me; is a drink of mead fine?
I was drunk, my passion,
Intoxication with a girl fresh, slim, and strong.   50
Joy of my lover without my hurting,
White-necked did a slim, gentle girl's arm make me.
Breast encirclers excellent and long,
Once they were a collar for me.

54. *The Poet's Superiority over His Rival*

The poet has mocked jealous husbands; now he is the jealous one. A rival has
entered the scene, bent plainly on mere fornication. Dafydd protests that the
woman should remember his many sacrifices of devotion, his poems, his long
walks, his rainy nights, his tears. If she gives easily to a rival what she has
denied Dafydd, she will be cursed by the poets who adore beautiful women
but can't be indifferent to a brother's hurt.

Slim girl, take my displeasure;
After summer, woe to you for the gift!
Diligent smithcraft, woe for me,
Fair maiden, to make it yours.
Alas for the man (who might come to anger)
Who mocked the jealous husband!
Alas for him who knows (a pang for one with a face
                              like candle flame,
Blue his tear) the ache of jealousy!

        I composed poetry to your face;
Costly is the office, I'm anxious.   10
My care is greater (woman's revenge)
Than that of a man in fetters
In a stone gatehouse (uncomfortable wall)
Who would slay the Pope with his bright steel,

Lest I find that the report about you (a harsh, plain denial)
Is true, bright, generous maiden.

   There is, some say, means of grief,
A brave, proud boy of splendid youth
(I am eight times an accessory) bent on loving you
At tryst, for copulation with you.   20
Though he be fine (shared knowledge of the bright one)
And a family-proud, praiseworthy peacock,
May it come (before taking him, a long danger)
To your mind (Indeg's twin)
That he will not suffer (I'm full of anger)
From rain or wind (bright color of gossamer)
What I suffered to seek you,
Naked pomp, neither here nor there,
As many times as I went on a strenuous, brave journey
To where you were.   30
He will not go wandering, pretty girl,
At night for you, color of star,
Across chains of thorns,
Simple, shy girl, as I went.
He will not stay out (no slight flood)
Under tears of the roof of a girl delightful
In memory and on the edge of an attempt
(Imprudent stroll) as I stayed.
Nor will he shed on his cheeks
This year as many flood-streams   40
Of water hot from sad and serious
(Eigr of love) as I shed.
Nor will he sing in the presence of noblemen
Till Judgment Day, of praise to you,
A hundredth part, girl of foam's color in a white petticoat,
Of the canon of song that I sang.

   Sternly you deny our trysts;
Innocent are your answers.
If you will be guilty long
With another who is too shrewd,   50
The poets of Christendom will say
To you, color of a stone-forded brook:

"Twofold trouble take you, charming girl,
When you behave (color of flood-foam,
My darling of fair, pleasing courtesies)
Badly (brilliant girl)
Towards your poet (color of froth fair and shallow) —
And your contemporary who won you!"

55. *Insisting*

The wanton girl who denied me,
Sun's brilliance, with her facile oath
(Very wrong, though it be a favor)
By stubborn words to the holy Cross,
Alas, my golden girl, that a naked member
                              of mine did not touch
Her; facile doubt
(Like Enid), a foolish, invalid oath,
Take it back!

   Yes, yes, hand, good chamberlain,
A gift to her poet, yes, low mouth;   10
Yes, breasts under a fine birch slope,
Yes, arms (she was not prodigal);
Good equipment were your feet,
Twice-fair, hidden one, yes, in the woods.
Yes, every such living thing.
A pleasant story, yes, making love.
There came from her lips a worthless vow,
Yes, yes, God knows there was nothing left.

56. *A Sweetheart's Virtues*

The girl whose cloak is purple,
For long no confession's made to the woman.
Ash went over the top of eight hearth-fires;
Hail there, dark sleep, where are you?

Hard for me to sleep one sleep
Though God Himself sang the lullaby.
I'm sleepless, a wound's the lock,
Tonight I know no slumber.
I have a good many thoughts,
Ever a fool, for something not mine,   10
A pang of rage, since I'll never get it
(It would be stupid for me to seek it),
That is (the fair one prohibits me),
Tryst with a girl who kills poets.

    It's senseless for a handsome, well-born poet
To think to get her, she's sinless.
She knows how to keep a man from a successful tryst;
Black her eyebrow, she caused me longing.
Generous about the respect I did not ask,
A miser about love's importunity.   20
Generous at home with freely served wine,
Color of seagull, niggardly of tryst.
Free with gold at her choice court,
Strict with love-meeting, modest gem.
Humbly obedient of deed in a mead-cellar,
Sluggish about a tryst, cautious, remote tryst.
Meek while playing with someone indifferent,
Proud with the haggard one who loves her.
Boldly, without wile, she keeps
Her eye on a man, she's a second Eigr.   30
A bard's perfect song, sincere,
Of good repute, of modest speech.
Face of a Dyfr, and my darling in my judgment,
Not great is her haste to a tavern.
Aloof from the face and form of men,
Of great praise, she means well.

    No one in our land
Is so proverbial as she.
There was not, there is not in our time,
Nor will there be any like her: 40
Bountiful, of a magistrate's lineage,
Feast-serving, a country's sun,

Aristocratic, blameless,
Slim of brow, beautiful girl,
Her disposition too chaste,
A gentle girl of very good manner,
Winning praise, amiable,
Shapely, intelligent, shy.

    My undoing has grown, a throng's moon,
Through one of fine growth, quiet, wise,
                        and black-browed,   50
A Tegau of beautiful wisdom,
Lovelier was that girl than anyone.

57. *The Sweetheart from Eithinfynydd*

The sweetheart from Eithinfynydd,
My beautiful soul who wants no tryst,
Of slim eyebrows, gentle glance,
Fine, golden hair, swift, wild frown,
My bliss against burdensome thinking of death,
My goddess tender and young,
My glowing mirror in gold,
My portion is she, my golden girl,
My treasure under the buttress of slopes,
My love for her grows more and more.   10

    My jewel, fine-haired, gentle girl,
My treasure who is not won on a hillside.
She does not go to the wood of the ridge above,
She loves not him who loves her, nor plays.
You can't get Morfudd to play,
She can't be got; loving Mary is she,
And loving saints, fine, lively energy,
And loving God; she'll not put her faith in me.

    The pretty girl does not know, she's a fickle one,
She does not recognize how singular she is.   20
She has no acquaintance with adultery,

My darling would want neither me nor anybody.
I myself would not want, my dear,
To live unless I got a fine, shy sweetheart.
By this have I been wounded,
Gentle Morfudd, I shall die.

58. *A Girl Mocks His Cowardice*

Dafydd: "Willowy girl of slender, fair form,
Dark of brow, who wears gold and precious stones,
Consider, Eigr of awgrim store,
Below green leaves, whether there's payment for me
(Sweet debate of clear voice),
Gem in beauty, for what I composed
To your bright color (lightsome language)
And your excellent form, eight shining hues of gossamer."

She: "I shall long do without you, Dafydd;
Love was stunned, there's talk about you,   10
That you (some knowledge of fear)
Are a coward, right name.
No one shall have me, by the Lord's favors,
You're terrible, man, but the bravest."

Dafydd: "With a cowl of fine hair, color of fine gossamer,
You're doing wrong, very polished woman.
Though I may be a friendly, elegant,
Cowardly lad in battle, too naked a breast,
No cowardly lad, where verdant woods are,
Am I at the work of Ovid's book.   20

        "And also, Eigr's equal,
Consider (there's a straight brow,
Overleaping pain) that it's never good to love
A brave man (he was cold trouble),
Lest the warrior (not an elegant acquaintance)
Be too crude.
He'll be wild and too uncivilized.

He loves war and the cold.
If he hears (earnest, tough conquest)
That there's a battle in France or Scotland,   30
Fierce venture, off on foot
An enlisted man he runs there.
Let's say he comes and escapes
From there (able to bridle a Frenchman),
He'll be scarred (an archer tramples him)
And cruel, O glittering, splendid girl.
He loves more his heavy lance yonder
And his sword (woe to one who trusts him)
And steel armor and dark shield
And army horse than a lovely girl.   40
He will not shelter you when a painful shout comes,
Nor will he chase you, except by violence out of your home.

"I with my very spirited words,
If I get you, shining color of clear gossamer,
Well do I know (I'd trim a straight song,
Come, girl) how to shelter you forever.
Say I got, tight grasp,
Same color as Deifr, two kingdoms,
Twice as bright as the sun, I'd not go for them
(Eight colors of the day) from your bright cottage."   50

59. *The Birch Hat*

Birch hat, it's good that you're kept,
Woe to Eiddig if you're a true sign!
Booty of trees, trophy of a hundred trysts,
Carved screen from the top of a forest branch.
It's brave I am, no wonder;
Mindful of your praise is he who owns you.
Trees' weaver (it's blameless),
A robe of leaves of small May stems.
Good fabric were you woven;
A store of courteous strength are you to me.   10
God praises you, free, long praise,

Roof of meadowland birch.
Garland that a bright-spoken girl gave,
Circlet from the shining, green birch tree.

A lean lad bears it, though he hide,
Fine cowl of May's mantle.
Prudent and steadfast, I keep you,
A crown against the excess of summer's fair weather.
Nurtured together in the valley, a bright, green glen,
Handsome forest birch suiting a lad.   20
Love-strength of a splendid gold girl,
Miracles and fruit of May's fine load.
Reminder against forgetting and care,
Tent above an undark brow.
Praiseworthy growth, fitting tribute of trees,
A collar from the brushwood's thick crest,
It deserves praise, fine roof of a leaf-grove;
The green wreath is grateful to be borne.
True gift of love's artful lady,
Band of hair from an elegant wood-slope.   30
A good building not fallen to ruin,
You're the work of Morfudd Llwyd and her hand.

60. *Fickleness*

Some nurse a hare at home
Until it be strong,
Long-travelled cat of dark-spotted cheek,
Wild, gray pouch of a swamp wood-lair.
Bold treasure of a rock-slope that flies in haste,
Stray of the undergrowth.
She's alien; in spite of her nurture,
To ridge and slope she climbs.

If a squirrel reaches a crest of twigs,
Worse the pay for the foster father;   10
Bold treason, in a lodging full of holes,
Unfaithful scamper, it's hardly routed with an arrow.

A wanton roebuck, with a right to gather hazel leaves,
Strong one before a hound-pack, a kind of roebuck wizard,
Wild is his rush in a freezing wind,
A very slim stag, his course very swift.
Young roebuck, he'd run as far as Yale,
Very white-tailed young beast of a bracken-lair.
Proven saying: you used to come for my sake,
Red chain, if your memory's good,   20
The leader of stags, withdrawing to the groves,
When you were once a frail young deer.

Regretted will be their taming;
Under treetops dwell the three.
Profound distress and sore pain,
They scorned the land that nursed them.

Just so, captive love, did she
In front of me, she achieved my betrayal,
With me, prudent bedfellow
(One of the color of foam), or with another   30
(Arms of the sun, that bright-fingered lamp);
Fine linen on the crystal shirt,
And a fur garment (golden her cheeks,
By gentle Mary) from the North Sea's shore.
I nursed her, despised office,
Over many a wave, from eighteen years of age;
I fashioned music and jewels
To try to pacify her.
Resourceful love; in spite of all that,
Worthless was the beloved.   40

61. *The Woodcock (I)*

Was anything (perilous occasion)
So hostile to a fine lover
As winter, coldest snow-tryst,
Long, dark, and hateful, hurling at woods?
Terrible his roaming between two towns,

Cold lad, the father of snow is he.
There was not one who did not find it hard
(Is it easy to hide anger?)
To wait in snow for her sake,
And cold snow and the frost of night.   10

    It would be easier to wait for her in a grove castle
On a summer night,
Hearing how pleasant is the tune
Of the gray cuckoo of good notes;
Unlikely in May woods
And in the condition of a tryst (if you had one),
To wander about on a sleepless errand
Under the eaves of my golden love's house!
Say that next day (strenuous hardship)
I should get her (it's doubtful she could be got)   20
In the shelter of a snug haybarn,
There'd be fear, after the winter night,
That the young man couldn't play (a fast, faulty episode)
With the pretty little woman.

    We were talking beautifully,
Industrious complaint, I and a lovely, bright gem;
It caused my bright, goodlooking girl a scare
                                (uneducated, spotted thief)
And fright
(Beak with a beak-churning stream of food),
The gray, infuriated woodcock.   30
A spotted bird of gloomy color
Of the birds of winter is he.
This is what he did (no fostering my girl),
Cocked head of a crutch, a dirty blanket:
He stoutly started his turmoil,
Bird with a blunt wing, under the bush,
And leaped till he was
In a dark hedge; he was no help to me.

    From the size of the restless racket on hoarfrost
Of the fat peasant's two wings,   40
We supposed (making an angry double-moan,

We were sad) it was Eiddig's uproar —
A rather decrepit haste between court and grove —
Wild rush, spotted tunic, needle-nose.
He wandered furiously through dung,
Long a prober of dung and frost.
Grim his loose, deceitful story,
And foolish, near a farmyard dung-field.
Neither a frequent note nor gain for me
Does he cheerfully know on a slope above,   50
Nor songs (says the fine paramour)
Through the top of the grove for a girl's sake;
He only knows to carry around (slender, threatening steel-work)
The black spear that grazes dung.
Spotted bird with sombre wing,
Briber, and his snare without warning:
May he get, bird of the red-speckled stride on a stroll,
The thick arrow-blow of a blemished exile's son!

62. *The Haycock*

Is my share of sleeplessness less
Than my profit and gain by a girl's court?
It's not easy to hide or lurk,
And how bold is the black rain.
Should the door open
At night — I wouldn't dare it,   10
Lest the girl be restrained by common command —
Is it worse in the haycock?

It's a grace for me that you're a haycock,
Funny lad, green, curly-headed, and stupid.
Good was the long-nailed rake
Yesterday that built you up on land.
I put you on, a long shelter,
Like a green cloak on song's servant.
I tried to load myself with you,
A fragile dovecote of grass.
I'll praise you steadily with my tongue,

Meadow fleece, a good place to mull praise.

From the same were you faultlessly fashioned,
Of the same sort, wide, brown hillock,   20
Of the same offense as handsome lords,
And yours will be the same downfall.
You have been cut down with brave, blue steel,
Thick, short burgess of the meadow.
Tomorrow (cheer for you is it)
From your green field, hay, you'll be dragged.
The day after tomorrow, above the tide of fine hay,
You'll be hanged, and alas for me, by Mary!

I'll entrust your body homewards
To the roof, and your soul to heaven.   30
Like an angel above the loft of the house, you'll see me
On Judgment Day
Coming to knock on the door:
"Haycock, is it time?"

63. *The Magpie's Advice*

I'm sick for a bright girl,
In a grove composing a love-charm
One day, a snatch of stout song,
The sky sweet, at the start of April,
And the nightingale on green stems,
And the handsome blackbird in a battlement of leaves —
Poet of the woods, he dwells in a woods-house —
And a thrush on a green treetop
Before the rain singing loudly
On a green coverlet golden-voiced notes;   10
And the skylark, a calm voice,
Dear, gray-cowled bird of wise speech,
Going in utter weariness
With a *cywydd* to the sky's height
(From the bare field, gentle prince,
Backwards to his chamber he climbs);

I, the poet of a tall, slim maiden,
Very cheerful in a green grove,
With the worn heart keeping remembrance,
And the soul fresh in me   20
From how fine it is to see woods
(Brisk vigor) bearing new dress,
And new shoots of wine and wheat
After pleasant rain and dew,
And green leaves on the brow of the glen,
And the thorn-bushes with fresh white points;
By Heaven! there was also
The magpie (the world's smartest bird)
Building (lovely design)
In the frowning-faced hedge's depth   30
From leaves and earthlime a proud gateway,
And her mate assisting her.

      The magpie whispered, anguished complaint,
Proud, sharp nose on the thorn-grove:

Magpie: "Great is your turbulence, vain, bitter song,
Old man, by yourself.
Better for you, by Mary of wise word,
Beside a fire, gray old man,
Than here amid dew and rain
In the green grove in cold rain."   40

Dafydd: "Hush your noise, leave me alone
A moment till it be trysting-time.
Great love for a good, faithful girl
Causes me this turbulence here."

Magpie: "Idle for you, serving lust,
Gray, abject, half-mad old man,
It's a foolish sign of love's office,
Raving for a glowing girl."

Dafydd: "You, magpie, black is your beak,
Hellish bird exceedingly fierce,   50
You too have (false visitation)

A long task and yet more work —
Your nest is like a hillock of gorse,
It shall be fat, a creel of dry, streaked wood.
You have speckled, black feathers (all are precious),
A painful face and the head of a crow,
You're motley, you have a pretty color,
You have an ugly court, you have a very hoarse voice.
And you would learn every tongue of remote, strong language,
Dappled, black wing.   60
Magpie, black is your head,
Help me if you're clever.
Give me the best advice
You may know for my great frailty."

Magpie: "I'd know the right advice for you,
Before May comes, and if you will, do it.
You don't deserve, poet, a goodlooking girl.
There's no counsel for you but one:
A very serious verse, go be a hermit,
Alas, foolish man! And love no more!"   70

        Here's my pledge, let God witness:
If I ever see the magpie's nest,
There will henceforth be in it
Neither an egg, for sure, nor a chick.

64. *The Window*

A woman denies Dafydd access through a window, unlike the case of Melwas
who got through a window to Gwenhwyfar (Guinevere), daughter of Gogfran
Gawr, in Welsh legend; Dafydd proceeds to curse the window.

    I walked within enclosures
    (A wanton song was my muttering)
    By the side (perplexing grounds)
    Of a girl's bedchamber, this was the idea.
    Good to catch sight of (brave, elegant girl),
    Through the top of the bush for a girl's sake

(Strong love is a fierce seizure),
A stout window in an oak frame.
None suffered by a window
Between fennel at night by a row of roses   10
Without sleep, as I suffered
Without lively pleasure because of a bright, holy girl.

    I asked for a kiss (lovelier her face)
From the girl through the little oak window.
Gentle jewel, it was a fault on her part,
She refused, she didn't want me.
A hindrance was the ageworn window
Where it was set to conduct the sun's light.
May I not grow old if from magic there was
A window precisely like this,   20
Except (the pleasure of two on a perilous course)
That one in Caerllion once
Through which Melwas made his way from passion
Without terrors of love
(Extreme pain, vast longing)
Once by Gogfran Gawr's daughter's house.
Although I was allowed to be while it snowed
Positioned the other side of the window from her,
I got no gain like Melwas,
The cheek languishes, what a gift!   30

    If we, I and my pretty, latticed gem,
Were face to face for nine nights,
Without modest pay, without bright stars,
Without profit between the two window posts,
More's the outrage! on both sides of the white wall,
Lip to lip, I and my slim, proud girl,
We could not, gold-gem miracle,
Get our two mouths together.
Two mouths can't manage at any time
Through a narrow, slatted wooden window   40
(My terrible death, exclusion from faith)
A kiss of peace, since it was so narrow.

    May the devil break (window den)

Its posts with a blunt hammer
(Anger's edge) and its broad shutter
And its lock and its key entirely
And whoever made it (a mastery of frustration)
And its row of hindering pillars;
Strike the bright window that keeps me from working,
And the hand that fashioned it with a saw;   50
Strike the villain that denies me union;
It hindered me in the place where the girl was.

65. *The Briar*

An unfriendly course, I loved a Tegau,
Tender association, a lament of remembrance is mine,
A goodlooking and friendly armful,
Proud generosity, not a shallow love.
I made up my mind wholly,
Memory that causes a long hindering of sleep,
A grace of meditation, a faultless intention,
To make a trip to love the pretty girl.
A penitent path to loving,
An unhappy expedition of a morning was it,   10
A good act of generosity, a kindly work,
Before anyone from my district came to know (hope is fine
Before the beginning of youth)
Where I was with my heart.

    Hard to get (golden treasure of faith)
A right of way to the manor,
To try where I'd thought
(Easy sorcery of grief during the time I know,
The profit is worse, a sort of payment on the land)
To see the girl, gentle wealth.   20
I avoided, when I heard the praise of
A golden girl's love-renown, meeting
(Good the art, secret will be
A gift poised on wisdom) with any person in the world.

I left (and I ran over there)
The people's highways and their leader.
I walked among the dwarf oaks
(It was remembered) and forts above the enclosed land,
From the fortress of the glen to the end of a beautiful
Footpath between hill and church.   30
A turn brought me, bravest lover,
To the gloom of the thick, dark wood.
There I stumbled, for a girl,
Across one of the briars.
Ensnaring near a hill, it stung me,
Accursed, the gut of a hedge,
It pulls hideously, some strip of hindrance,
A pestilential apparition.
Quick above a bank are its teeth,
An omen of shame, though thin its face.   40
It taught me hateful lameness,
Lack of success, and held me
Back at the wildwood corner;
Ensnared around both my feet.

I got (I stumbled, heavy sadness)
A fall there (difficult, swift accomplishment)
On the brow of the glen (constant pursuit)
Head over heels fast.
Woe to the vile, despised thing,
It hurt a poet (it's a mark on me)   50
As would (it earned no peace,
Sad tug) a thousand of its teeth do
(Bitter scorn, the speech is rough)
Injury to my two legs.
Weary and accursed is its burden,
Color of the idle look of blackberries.
A withe of very sturdy annoyance,
Wild pain, and a bush's strand of hair.
Hateful its work scratching the woods,
A halter on the dry hedge of a miser.   60
Leg of a tough heron under the zodiac,
Grasping, worthless branches.
A net-line that was thrown in anger,

Snare on the headland slope.
A belt's end in a gap was it,
It was a cord of the mighty valley trees.

Fire be swift, a chimney veil,
Costly, toothed cover of carven anger,
It fashioned me grim profit,
To burn it to avenge my anger.   70

66. *The Clock*

The poet dreams of loving his girl; she's in a distant town, he's a guest in a
monastery; a clock wakes him, calling his promiscuous soul (the "little angel")
back from its amorous flight. The mills, ducks, and yards would belong to the
monastic farm for which the clock tells time.

In my early style, elegant purpose,
I'm singing with ease
To the choice town near Rhiw Rheon
At the crag's end, and the round fort.
There (her good name was won in the past)
Is a girl who was acquainted with me.
Here today a greeting
Off to the home of the good woman.
Nightly, noble, prudent girl,
She greets me.   10

When a man sleeps (and fragile has it been found,
It's a dream) scarcely does he speak:
With my head on the pillow,
Yonder comes before day
(A broad likeness to the sight)
A little angel in a girl's bed.
I'd thought that I was down there
With my girl a short time ago.
Far was it between me
And her face (memory seeks it) when I awoke.   20

Woe to the dark-faced clock beside the hedge

That woke me up.
Useless be its head and its tongue
And its two ropes and its wheel
And its weights, those blunt-shaped balls,
And its yards and its hammer
And its ducks thinking it's day
And its restless mills.
Useless clock like a crazy click
Of a drunken cobbler, cursed be its shape.   30
Bowel false and deceitful,
A dog's cub chewing a bowl.
Frequent clap in the cloister,
A goblin's mill grinding at night.
Was a saddler of a crupper of scabs
Or a roof-tiler more unsteady?
Cold destruction take its cry
For leading me here from heaven!

    I was getting (a snug embrace)
Slumber from heaven at midnight,   40
In the folds of her long arms,
In Deifr's braiding amid breasts.
Will there be seen, food for sorrow,
Land's Eigr, such a vision again?

    Run again to her directly,
Dream, you won't have a difficult course.
Ask the girl beneath a gold roof,
If sleep comes to her tonight,
To give a glimpse, golden heart,
Niece of the sun, once of her.   50

67. *The Star*

I'm vexed because of a girl bright as foam,
God knows every man's thinking.
If, for her love, it comes to me
(My bright soul) to go to her land,

Far is it from my mind to deputize
A costly love-messenger to her lodging there,
Or to bribe a hag of base office,
Very gray-haired and persistent, to serve as a
                              love-messenger,
Or to bear before me fire-vessels
Or wax torches when it's late,   10
Rather than sleep at home during the day
And walk at night over to the home.
No one shall see me, no one shall recognize me
(I'm obsessed) until it's day.

    I myself shall get, without grudging,
Against going astray tonight,
Candles of Him Who owns the world
To conduct me to a gem of lively face.

    A blessing on the name of the Lord Creator
Who executed the design of the stars   20
So that nothing is brighter
Than the little, round, pure-white star.

    A light from the high heaven,
A candle of clear wit is it.
The candle's form does not vanish,
And it can't be stolen through deceit.
The wind of autumn's course does not extinguish it,
Mass-wafer of the roof of heaven.
Cowardly flood-water does not drown it,
A waiting-woman, feast-dish of the saints.   30
A robber does not reach it with his two hands,
Bottom of the bowl of the Trinity yonder.
It's not right for a man out of his sphere
To chase Mary's pearl.
It's a light in every region,
A gold-piece of yellow wrought gold.
True, round shield of the light,
An image of the sun in the bright sky is it.

    It will show me without concealment

(Golden, proud gem) where Morfudd is.   40
From wherever it may be, Christ will extinguish it
And send it, He will not be ungenerous,
Image of a dear, perfectly white loaf,
To a cloud's shadow to sleep.

68. *The Mist*

Yesterday, Thursday, a day for drinking
(It was good for me to get), a gift came to me,
An omen of great import (I'm thin on her account),
A full love, I got
A session of sweet song under the greenwood
With a girl, she allows me a tryst.

There was not, under the joyful God the Father,
May a gift be hers, one man who knew,
When it was Thursday, at break of day,
How full of gladness I was,   10
Going (seeing her fine form)
To the land where the tall, slender sweetheart was,
When there came in truth on the long moor
A mist like night;
A great roll that was a surface to the rain,
Gray ranks to block me;
A tin sieve rusting,
The dark earth's bird net;
A dim hedge in a narrow path,
A slovenly blanket in the sky.   20
A gray cowl turning the ground the same color,
A covert on every great, hollow valley.
High roofs to be seen,
A great bruise above the ridge, the land's exhalation.
Thick, gray, dunwhite, fragile fleece,
Same color as smoke, the meadow's cowl,
A hedge of rain to block progress,
Armor of an oppressive host,
It would deceive men, dark of form,

Rude cloak of earth.   30
Towers of lofty state,
Of Gwyn's Family, a province of the wind.
Its dour cheeks hide the land,
Torches reaching to the zodiac.
Darkness, a thick, ugly one,
World's blindness to waylay a bard.
A wide web of costly cambric,
It was cast abroad like rope.
Spider's web, a French-shop product,
Headland-moor of Gwyn and his Family.   40
Brindled smoke that will abound,
The smoke of a circle of May-woods.
Unsightly fog where dogs bark,
Ointment of the hags of Annwn.
Clumsily like the dew it dampens,
Land's habergeon neither clear nor dry.

    It's easier to walk at night on the moors
On a journey than in mist by day;
The stars come out from the sky
Like flames of waxen candles;   50
But there does not come, dull, promised pain,
The moon or the Lord's stars in mist.
Rudely the mist made me bound with black
Ever, it was lightless;
Denied me a path under the sky,
Dark, gray veil that hinders love-messengers,
And kept me, a swift capture,
From going to my slim-browed woman.

69. *May and January*

Welcome, graceful greenwood choir,
Summer's month of May, for longing is mine.
Strong knight of loving favor,
Green-chained master of the wild wood;
Friend of love and birds,

The lore of lovers and their kinsman;
Courier of nine-times-twenty rendezvous,
Favorer of honored meeting.
And great it is, by Mary, that he,
May, perfect month, is coming,   10
With his mind set, claiming warm respect,
On the conquest of every green glen.

    A stout shelter, dresser of highways,
He clothed every place with his green web.
When there comes after frost's war
The thick-leaved tent (meadow's strength) —
Green are (chirping is my religion)
The paths of May in April's place —
Then come on the highest point of oak
Songs of the birds' chicks;   20
And a cuckoo at each field's edge,
And a warbler, and a long, lively day;
And pale mist behind the wind
Shielding the center of the valley;
And a gay, bright sky of afternoon
Will there be, and handsome woods and green gossamer;
And hosts of birds on the trees,
And fresh leaves on tree-twigs;
And remembered will be Morfudd my golden girl,
And the thrill of seven-times-nine lovings.   30

    Not like the surly, dark month
That rebukes every one for loving;
That makes sad rain and a short day,
And wind to plunder woods;
And weakness, the fragileness of fear,
And a long cloak and hailstone-rain,
And provokes tidal flow and cold,
And in streams gray deluges,
And a full roar in rivers,
And makes day angry and wrathful,   40
And the sky heavy and widely cold
With its color veiling the moon.
May there come to him, swift sort of promise,
Double-bane for his boorishness!

70. *A Bright Night*

Hard puzzles through the year
Has God set to hinder a man.
Not a poor lover's free property
Is night, nor day, nor anything.
After tough annoyance,
Profit is no nearer, night prevents it.
Useless are the twigs of many a grove;
I'm sick for a girl of bright and gentle shape.
Generous Ovid's girl does not dare
(I'm her brother) in her own country by day.   10
Not great will be my gain, I know,
Or payment, while it's a bright night.

I know waiting under excellent, dense woods,
Weak-eyed from fear, for a tryst.
Worse than the sun is the bright moon,
Since (it was large) it was so cold,
A wide, twice-brilliant moon,
Bright fire of hard, cold weather.
Glib flattery, poor us if it stays,
Poor thief who may be watched.   20
Was anything worse, too strict a gift,
For a thief than a night bright and fair?

Tiresome on every new tip
Is a flower from the light of day.
Her order is each fortnight
(Her town under heaven is night)
To take her course from there,
Premeditated, greater and greater she goes
Until she's two halves.
The sun (brilliant night) of the stars.   30
She hurls the tide, handsome light,
Sun of the goblins is she!

Calm Eiddig from his bed,
Intent, by the light of the moon above,

Watches me in my lair under the good stems
Near him here.
Too helpful to the husband was the florin;
Towards heaven's town she climbs.
Too round was she on my course,
Rowel of a frost-wind's spur.   40
Hindrance of a frustrated lover is she,
Like the nape of a frosty loaf.
She prohibits summer's thief,
She was too bright for a journey to the girl.
Too high is her bed
(Portion of the mighty God) upon good weather above.

    She sees where I am (candle of the world)
In hiding, she ascends from the cloud.
Like an all-latticework sieve,
Her lip familiar with lightning.   50
Tramp-woman of a trail in heaven's sky,
Like a thong, a cauldron's lip.
Her chaplet as wide as the earth,
Same in color are the refuges of both wild and tame.
Power of a lamp to measure the field of bright stars,
Compass of the bright, blue sky.

    Day without sun, the false coin came,
She was angry, to drive me from my lair.
Shining form, before devout, radiant prime,
Good for me would it be if it darkened a bit.   60
For sending earnest love messengers,
No useless tale, to my golden girl's house
At night, shining, snug, and lovely,
Let God the Father darken the out-of-doors.
A beautiful rule would it be for our Lord,
By God, to render day bright
And to give night to us, it would be our portion,
Dark for us both.

71. *The Wave on the Dyfi*

Dr. Bromwich (*TI*, p. 26), following Gerald Morgan, judges this poem to be
evidence of Dafydd's knowledge of Ovid's *Amores,* from the many cor-
respondences between this appeal to a wave on the River Dyfi and Ovid's address to an Italian river (*Amores*, III, 6).

Curly-headed, cheerful, shouting wave,
Don't hinder (trusted gain) my crossing
To the land yonder, where a reward comes to me;
Don't delay me, nor stop me.
For the God of grace, the Lord of refuge,
O violence of the water, let me over Dyfi.
Turn back, home of three hundred nets;
I'm your bard, you crest the water.

Has anybody sung with a mouth
Of praise to your masterly tumult,   10
Companion of a sail, jewel of the brine,
Bend of the sea, as much as I?
There was no chief wind of the zodiac,
Nor swift rush between two hard dikes,
Nor quick-moving battle, nor stout branch,
Nor shoulder of steed or man
That I would not liken, I know anguish,
Strong, persistent wave, to your strength.
There was no organ nor harp,
Nor man's tongue of faultless praise   20
That I'd judge to be as mighty,
Green sea-swell, as your great, lovely cry.
No other word is had from me
About my soul, she of Nyf's beauty of treacherous fate,
But to call her blonde beauty
And her fair face a match to your stream.

Therefore do not hinder me,
Bright jouster of clear, rippling water,
From going (my darling judges me)
Through the birch grove yonder to Llanbadarn   30

To the girl (a fruitful, eloquent, gentle girl) who made me,
From dead, alive.
My counsel is constrained,
Friend, lady of the sea.
You're an obstacle between me and my commote;
With your nose, hold back and bridle the stream!

    If you knew, gray-cloaked wave —
You're a bright, fine love-messenger of a fish-swarm —
How great my reprimand for delay!
You're a mantle to the shore there.   40
Though for a second Indeg I came
Right to your edge, beautiful wave,
May an enemy's warring not slay me.
If you hinder me from going to her country,
Seven-times-twenty degrees of love will kill me.
Keep me not from Morfudd, my golden girl.

72. *Stronger Is He Who Seeks than He Who Keeps*

    Seeking a sweetheart am I,
Resolutely, without being silent, every day.
Keeping his lively little woman of gifted good sense
Is treacherous Eiddig.
Oppressively he of the oppressive look watches;
Stronger is he who seeks with zest and determination
Than he who keeps his fair woman
From a mischievous lad on a green glen-crest.

    It's not easy to keep a trim, excellent, fair one
From a thief gazing most cunningly.   10
The same task, while I wait,
Directing a glance, have I as a thief.
Tenaciously, that would be an admission,
He guards her, he'd be debased;
More tenaciously, a deep wound's rigor,
Do I make my attempt around the woman.
A lover, his stand avowed,

If he seeks her he loves, does not sleep;
And if she sleeps (unique marvel,
She's a fine, loving liar,   20
Grief of the watcher, the stupid early riser),
She's ungenerous (drowsy of mind).
About Morfudd, for profit as from a great gift,
A most proud gem, I am very like
The horse that from his pen sees
The oats but does not see the enclosure:
I too, without avoiding the enemy,
See the purest of women
And do not see, boldest claim,
Her dark mate (fair, bejewelled one).   30
May Mary not look upon the stiff-spoken man,
He, too, will never see me.
Not more bent will be the pupil of the eye
In a chieftain's head, a land's lord.

      Stronger, where he lifts a gray sword,
Am I than he, he took fright.
I visit freely (woman of most bright lineage)
My gold one's homes while I'm alive.
Curse me if I should avoid
Her of the radiant joy of the summer sun,   40
Armed office, a recompense for risk-taking,
Despite him who keeps her, golden, lively brow.

73. *Morfudd's Hair*

God put (I'm a good witness)
Two gold braids to enchant two parishes
(Gifts of passion, they're of gold,
Lovely chains) on a girl's head.
Golden torques and the precious harvest
Of a modest head-load's yellow fruit
(A man's load, a lock of love)
Went shining above the head-slope.
Grove of wax, nourishment of the best men,

A grove of golden flax, there's an earldom!   10
Beautiful fullness within a tape,
A long growth slaying men.
Flax of a gracious, best-loving girl,
Grove of wrought-gold, praise's ribbons.

    Proudly she carries (the smiling, slender girl)
A sheaf of broom, lovely, elegant maiden,
As a round crest, as a fine crown
Pretty and modest, woven color of gold,
As a mantle, a collar of fine hair,
As branching and bristling gold.   20
Brilliant gift, she bears red-gold
On her head of ropes of gold
To charm the ranking poets;
Her life was pleasant for the world.

    The girl received a noble gift;
Better was the quality of the fine hair
Of the bright girl than that of Cynfrig Cynin's,
Son of the curly-haired, gray, ugly, cross one.
Crude calf with a neck of scabby nape,
His skull is bare where healthy,   30
Drunken, needy, wanton beggar,
His cheek a blister of sour sweat.
Not similar (known to be jealous,
Wild and foolish) was his bald head
(Gentle and abundant was it braided)
To the grove on Morfudd Llwyd's head.

74. *Clandestine Love*

I learned to steal active love,
Noble, clandestine, and brave:
The best way through decorous words
Of managing to tell stealthy love.
Such have a schemer's fatigue
(A man's best love is stolen),

While we were in the midst of crowds,
The woman and I, idle pair,
Without anyone (friendly talking)
Guessing our responses.   10

    We had, as a result of our mutual trust,
Shared sport for a long time once.
Now with more constraint one gets
(With derision) the exchange of three words.
Wasting come upon him of wicked tongue
In a contortion of weakness, target of misfortune,
In place of casting slander
Upon us two of spotless name!
He was very glad if he got warning,
While we had fellowship in secret.   20

    I walked (I worshipped the leaves)
The golden girl's home (while leaves were fresh).
Pleasant, girl, was a single moment
Leading our life under the same birch grove.
Caressing, that was pleasanter still,
In a wood-retreat, hiding together,
Wandering together on the seashore,
Stopping together in a wooded slope,
Planting birch together, happy work,
Together braiding graceful fronds from trees.   30
Exchanging words of love with the slim girl,
Gazing together at lonely fields.
A craft without reproach is it for a girl —
Walking the woods together with a lover,
Keeping face, smiling together,
There was laughing lip to lip,
Falling together near the grove,
Together avoiding people, making complaint together,
Gentle living together, drinking mead together,
Sustaining love together, lying together,   40
Together keeping our secret love
Faithful, no more is told.

75. *Death for Eiddig*

A prayer for the death of Eiddig, the jealous husband, who has gone with a Welsh military league under the leadership of Sir Rhys ap Gruffudd, a South Wales lord, to fight with the English in France. The poet hopes that Eiddig will not return to deprive him of access to the wife Dafydd loves. Every danger of sea, storm, hunting, and warfare is invoked.

There went today in splendor
With Rhys, to guard the generous one,
A number of sworn brothers and foster brothers
And kin (mine is the eagerness of longing)
Of mine, to fight the French
(Mary bring them home!), from the South,
Noble, proud hawks, battlement-roaming,
Chiefs of brothers of battle.

The son of slander, there's a hornet
With you, if you allow, men,   10
An unloved enemy
To a girl's bard and to the world's bards.
A single eye, willer of sorrow,
And a single ear is his on a hundred hedges;
Both the trumpet of a stupid mind deceived by lying
And the chastiser of a woman, and her jailer.
How many times from heavy, calamitous death
I fled once, you remember;
Before him, the hollow quiver of elder,
And his family like reapers.   20
May there be for him in his hand, a load
Of devil's shit, him and his family!

If with his soul he goes (nature of a pig)
To the wild, gray ship on a fierce tide,
She will not long remain calm,
The shape of her sail full of brine.
May her headwear be the stream of white light,
Gascony mare of the swift channel.
She will not go, she will not sail,

Scoundrel, with the wretch in her.   30
May he be pushed, beaver's asshole,
Across the deck and overboard.
Generous wave, salt-sea's wing,
I'd owe you compensation,
Strand's niece, wonder of the sea-home,
Don't let the terrible old man come back!
Arrow-stream of the sea, ebbtide's stabbing-woman,
A feast for nine waves, may they suck him down.

From wave to wave, a quicksand bird,
If the dark, swift one goes to France,   40
As many great snares as there are,
May a springe be his downfall.
Think, you of the crafty, stout profession,
Of slaying him, do me gain,
And do not let the hollow boat
Separate me from a jewel of the South.

You, the crossbowman, trot on,
Hurler of the good woodstuff,
And throw with the short-stirruped crossbow wood
And shoot, what do you care if he sulks?   50
Stab the thief in the temple,
Fracture the phantom, may it be easy.
Pierce him, fail not at all,
Thrust through him with the crossbow a second wound.
You'll recognize, accurate-armed shooter,
His beard of straight, skimpy hairs,
A ragged beard of fennel of a heather bush,
The day is coming, it would be good to take him.
His staying over there consoles us.
Twelve catastrophes to him!   60
Not catching a poet, and this is beautiful,
May he not come home to his estate.
Jealous nostril of poisonous intent,
Unlovely face, if he tries to come,
As an enemy wills, loud cry,
The black thief, let him come home.

76. *Against Trusting in the World*

Misfortune is mine, the indignation of sadness,
A curse on him who made me fail!
Namely, that one, he doesn't hazard terror,
Eiddig the thief, a rustic Jew.
He has not left (there was no protection nearer)
Any wealth in my keeping, God prosecuted me.
Friendly, of spirited race, free,
Wealthy, and acquisitive was I.
I've said farewell to fine joy,
Mind eightfold aflame, and I'm poor at last.   10
Generosity, the custom of trifling love,
I'm guiltless, has brought me to nothing.

    Let not one handsome, upright lord set
His heart on the world, a traitor always.
Foreign slave, if he does so indeed,
World's letdown, he shall be deceived.
Wealth is an enchantment and an enemy,
It's a bitter conflict and man's betrayer.
Sometimes it comes, arrogant yonder,
Sometimes for certain it goes,   20
Like an ebb on the seashore,
After a tide of praise and food.

    The wise, carefree blackbird laughs
In a green grove, elegant mansion of song.
Fruitful soil is not plowed for her,
Seed is fresh, she does not plow.
And there's not (small, short-legged bird)
Any chatter more joyous than hers.
She's cheerful, by the Lord God,
Shaping song in a wood grove.   30
The most cheerful, most privileged of mind,
Are the minstrels, with their staffs keeping time.

    Weeping I'll be, mournful lord,
Tears of reproach, calling for a bright girl;

But Mary knows I have not (persistent word of praise)
Wept a tear for wealth,
Since there's not (pleasant custom)
A Welsh land of Welsh language
Where I don't get (may I be bright-tongued,
An energetic young man) payment for my work;   40
Among her sisters, there was not to be had
Under the sun's edge a woman like her.
Because of my candle, I have been bereft,
Morfudd (color of daylight) Llwyd.

77. *Doubting Wrongly*

Dafydd: "Comely, untrue Morfudd,
A visitation of praise, ah me, is it true
(Again with joy) that you, my dear,
Renounce your little brother,
He (I know him from his birth,
Eigr's fair niece) who does not hate you,
And that you dismiss (to have sorrow)
From your memory the poor fellow who loves you,
From fondness for too much talk,
Of one of snake sinews, or is it false evidence?"   10

Morfudd: "Not true; swearing does not avail,
Renouncing never came into my mind.
By the Man of Sorrows,
Dafydd, Who suffered,
I would more love in a wood-dale the track
(Cheerful chase) of your swift foot
Than my poor, sober husband
Or whatever belongs to his cheeks."

Dafydd: "You've brought heat and color to my cheek,
Most proud girl, very good, Morfudd.   20
Life will come (a time for versifying)
To a wise man after the bleak snow.

Let's not look for terror,
Do not in your day put up with your husband.
Do not cause dark, angry Eiddig
(One of duck lineage) to rejoice.
May I not have wealth from God above,
If you please me, if you'll be reconciled."

78. *Secret Love*

I am (cause of anger)
The thief of secret love.
The wild, shining birds of praise,
Strange in nature, make nests.
That is what they do, under the leaves
Plaited together, a weaving of twigs,
In a remote place for fear of the crowd,
From a fine sense for nursing.
In the same way, of the same character
As that, bedmate of sorrow,   10
Love made (the memory's locked in,
Foolishness) a nest in me;
And my two sides, by Jesus God,
Still hide it; it was work without gain.
Twigs they are, a fragile course,
Under a trim, handsome young man's side.
I sing, though I make complaint,
And my heart is ever a nest of desire.
Love for the bright, fair girl will not be dislodged
Nor enticed from the nest.   20

        Villain Eiddig will not come upon
This nest, the rough, naked savage,
And I, I don't care, stiff-legged giant,
If he should never come upon it.
I'm sure, unfailing poet,
Indeed, that it will never be known.
Unless she affords me (through wicked slander),
Generous event, a tender glance,

The heart's thought and a serious breast
Circuitously hide there.   30

    In whatever (undenied mutual love,
So it seemed) house I might be,
With a glance under a very thin eyebrow,
She who is the memory of a fine summer day sees me.
A venturer's vow, from wherever I might be,
I too see (I'm an angel)
Her laughter, a lover's acquisition,
And her manner with her slim eyebrow;
Trading a glance, I don't deny,
With my love, I get nothing else.   40
Her glance went (the gem of Wales)
And her love (a daring flight,
Slim, white, elegant, foam-bodied girl)
Through my breast and heart and body,
As a round arrow goes (fine, perfect armful)
Through a sheaf of dry stubble.

    Beuno of the wandering course will never,
Generous abbot, let this be known.
A sorrowful Welshman, without Welsh land
Shall I be, if it gets known.   50

79. *Morfudd and Dyddgu*

Woe for me (image of wretchedness)
Without delay, that I did not know
To love before marrying age
A gentle girl, innocent, slender, good,
Full of talent, loyal, wise,
Of delicate accomplishment, dear, beloved,
                and courteous,
Of renown like that of a landed heir,
Most passionate, dainty, truthful girl,
Round and firm, not tumultuous,
Full of gift and learning,   10

Beautiful and fair, an Indeg of glowing love,
An untilled land (I'm an ox),
A lover not changeable,
A wand of gold, bright her forehead,
As is (the expansive custom of praise)
Dyddgu of the dark, smooth eyebrow.

    Not of this sort is Morfudd,
But like this, a red ember.
Loving those who rebuke her,
A reluctant girl who'll be very stubborn;   20
Possessing (of upright respect)
A house and husband, fairest woman.

    Not more infrequent is my flight
At midnight on her account
From a man of her house under a window
Than by day, I'm a strong acrobat;
And the severe spouse, with the senseless word,
Striking hand against hand,
Gives a daily cry (easy lust)
And a shout for stealing his children's mother.   30

    Frail man, for his shout
May he go to the devil; why does he cry
(Alas, woe for him, an unceasing wail)
To God because of an enchantment on a woman?
Broad, impudent, long-shouting beast,
A fool's labor is his book of fiction.
Cowardly and strange what he did,
Crying for a slim, lively girl.
He awakens the South
With his speech, sweetheart's kite.   40
Not gifted, not beautiful,
Not sweet to hear, not lovely,
A man shouting, noisy trumpet,
A tune like a crow's for her brother.

    He was a bad one, he of the sleepless shout,
A liar, about a loan.

If I were to buy (bright, perfect idea)
A wife in my life, a treacherous step,
Bad-tempered copulator, to get an hour of silence,
A share, I'd give her to him,   50
So poorly (woe of a widow's state,
Bitter man) does he know how to play.

  In a word, I'm choosing
Dyddgu to love, if she's available.

80. *Eiddig's Three Doormen*

Three doormen (angry uproar,
It was trouble) of Eiddig's three doors,
They were arranged to give me a great fright;
Unlucky was my meeting with the three.

  First of Eiddig's porters of the doors and of
                              his abundance
In the angry mansion of stubborn hostility
Was a dog, stout, loud-mouthed, very nervous,
I'd get a mean rebuke, of a rabid sort.
And the second doorman is the angry door,
Woe who meets it, squeaky.   10
The third (I know daily penance)
That keeps me from getting any gain in the world
Is a plaguey old woman, sore, sullen,
Her day's coming, Eiddig's slave.
Though the night were as long (though heaven were won)
As ten nights, restless witch,
She shall not sleep one hour, in a bed with quick fleas,
Because the bones aren't healthy.
Soon weak, complaining of
Her thigh (bad-looking) and her hand,   20
And pain from her two elbows,
And her shoulder a bruise, and her knee.

  I came night before last, a dark, angry night,

Unlucky fellow, to Eiddig's land,
Gifted in step, sure of purpose,
To visit a fine moon of a gem.
Poet's prison, and I going
Heedlessly to the black door,
There leaped (he wanted to mark me)
A red dog from the pigsty at me,   30
He gave me a very surly challenge,
Gave me a full bite in the cloak's horse-hair.
He tore, chagrin's fortress, the man's dog,
Curse that frustrates me, the whole of my cloak.
I shoved the door (a bowl's clatter)
Of oak, it moved furiously.
It shouted like geese talking,
My woe if I dared to close it!
Burden of the muse's blush, I heard the hag
(The reward was worse) in a cranny,   40
Maintaining (wasn't it hard?)
To the man of the house above in haste,
"The heavy door is open,
It's great, giant's arm, the dog's commotion."

    I fled quickly back
To the door, and the stinking dog behind me.
I ran (I didn't stand long)
By the wall (I know I was cold)
Around the bright, shining, fair fort,
To wait for a brilliant gem.   50
I shot through the wall (a portage for throbbing)
Arrows of love to the slim girl.
She shot from her bright breast a swift
Love-greeting to me.
It was pleasing for me (love doesn't disappoint me)
At the other side of the stone wall from the slender girl.
I made complaint, expressed my anger,
I had to, before Eiddig's door.

    Though the husband was able to thwart copulation,
And his giant's hedge and his hag and his dog   60
To block me (it's proper for glue to stick)

From his mansion, Eiddig, and his home,
God is liberal in giving
A wood of trailing treetops and a field to me.

81. *Spoiling the Girl's Face*

The girl I'd call my gold maiden
And my bright, shy, radiant dear,
I intend (harsh good sense)
Through God's might to turn away from deception,
To have it in mind (the world greets me)
To finish with her (birches ask for her).
What pay was there for me from following her?
It would be a good hour to be done with the woman.

Defiled, strict chastisement,
Was the woman's color long ago.   10
I can't, the power's not mine,
No one can make the woman's color good.
I think, oh my hurt,
I know, oh my greater ache,
That the breeze and more
Spoils her cheeks utterly.
A smooth Enid, the breath of Eiddig
From his dark mouth causes the harm,
After he'd release, bad turn,
Hard husband, she was an Eigr in beauty,   20
Breath like peat smoke
Around her (why did the fair one not cleanse it?),
It's an anxiety like a fetter-bond
To leave the oaf together with the woman.

An effigy of varnished alder wood,
Bit of a lord of an Englishman's carving,
Bad custody, crouched thief,
An agitated lamp ruins it completely.
The good enough English fur
Goes bad in peat smoke.   30

Mist steals in air
From the fine sun his color completely.
A spreading oak branch, wood of a palisade,
Will wither at the edge of the sea.

    I promenaded (lighthearted attack by a strong oath)
To her homes while she was beautiful.
A slavish stewardship of love,
Only while she might be beautiful, not a patrimony.
He knows well to make her face unloved,
She was my darling.   40
It's best for wretched Eiddig,
Black dog, that the woman not be fair.
Soot from his mouth soiled
The color of my noble, lovely little one.
By God and Cadfan, there was need
Of the grace that preserves; she was very beautiful.

82. *Begging for His Life*

Sweetheart of bright, golden neck
From Môn who was once found compliant,
There's no hope for me now
In your country (girl eight times wave-white,
By St. Deinioel, a star-crossed passion)
For freehold land, because of a breach of the peace.
It's terrible that I didn't consider
Getting you would be an unwise effort.
No gift nor message was there
But my murder, the worse for my profit!   10

    I was sad not to get you, choice gift;
Sadder, eight times more thin from having you.
Woe's me that you (cost of a feast)
Wanted me when I was dear.
You were not sensible not to refrain;
Not good for me was your cruel strength.
You urged I be hanged

If I were found, you didn't want me.
It would be a wonder if the Pope of Rome were
Yours, my slim blessing!   20

Take secretly whatever you might see,
Be appeased for this, pale, splendid woman,
And accept a fine, maiden,
And withdraw your charge, gentle girl, from now on.
We were playful, a crooked clasp;
Bitter was the end of our play.

If one time, my tall, slim girl, you were
Content with me under a green birch grove,
Do not cause (lovely woman with wave-like face)
The women's jewel to hang,   30
Instead of (angry betrothed)
Executing your Eiddig.

In Mynyw, pride of Gwenhwyfar,
In Môn you earned my anger.
O my darling, I have been there;
And bitter was it for me that I was.

83. *A Journey for Love*

This poem tells of Dafydd's journeying for love in the vicinity of Bro Gynin. It
is his home territory; see *GDG*³, pp. xvi–xviii, and *Y Traethodydd,* 133 (April
1978), p. 83.

Did anyone walk for a mistress
What I walked (love's oppression)?
Frost and snow, such sort of sin,
Rain and wind for one of bright face.
I got only a visitation of fatigue;
Two feet never got more distress
To Cellïau'r Meirch
(The gain of a golden assault) across Eleirch,
Straight ahead in a wilderness

Night and day and no nearer grace.   10
O God, loud is that man's
Shout in Celli Fleddyn,
A speech for her sake,
I was making a profession of love for her.
Bysaleg stream, of low, hoarse sound,
Hollow-bubbling flood, narrow, short brook,
Very often for her sake
I would cross daily over it.
To Bwlch Meibion Dafydd I'd go, proud and free,
My pain deep.   20
And away there to Y Gamallt,
And to the slope for a fine-haired one.
Swiftly I'd go headlong
To Gafaelfwlch y Gyfylfaen,
To cast for a fur-gowned maiden
A glance at the good valley.
She turns neither here nor there
Without me furtively after.
I was diligent and quick
Along Pant Cwcwll in summer   30
And about Castell Gwgawn,
With a goosechick's stoop where he'd find reeds.
I ran past Adail Heilin,
The running of a tired, inarticulate hound.

      I stood below Ifor's court
Like a monk in a choir stall,
To seek, without the promised favor,
A meeting with fine Morfudd.
There's no hillock nor thick-set meadow
Around the valley of Nant-y-glo   40
That I don't know from my passion and excitement
Without the book, an Ovid of quick wit.
Easy for me while sounding in cupped hand,
That true target of gain, Gwern-y-Talwrn,
Where I got to see, dear bounty,
A tender woman under a sable mantle,
Where one can see forever,
Without growth of grass, without growing of trees,

Our bed's contour under good twigs,
A place of crumpled leaves like Adam's path.   50

Alas for the unrequited soul,
If from weariness, entirely without one payment,
It goes the same way wholly
That this wretched body went!

84. *A Girl's Magic*

Cinctures and chains of love
And the tongue's praise, lively girl,
And gold (I can absolve you)
In your court, I placed in your hand.
Sleeplessness, noble, bright maid, and a wound,
And tear-fatigue, face of keen joy,
My enemies, bold accusations,
A numerous throng, were the payment to me.
"A countess of snow color"
I called you, "face of fine parchment";   10
You would call me "ugly rascal"
In my presence, with cruel shame.
And a fair web (you of the color of a shower of snow)
Of silk I gave you.
You didn't give me the least
Little bit, pretty girl of white teeth.
Worse than holy men, I gained love's aching
Because of anger.

A proper woman are you, I'm Gwaeddan,
Worse and worse commerce of passion.   20
You drove me in the same way
As Gwaeddan once for his cap,
By magic and some act of obstruction
And deceiving illusion.
Because of a deceptive appearance, you are,
With many an insult, disappointing me.
A gleaming girl, of gifted nature,

Flawless deceit, you're from Dyfed.
There is no school of magic,
Nor game of deceit, captive mind,   30
Not Menw's magic, nor frequent craving,
Nor betrayal of warriors, nor splendid battle
(Awful grip, eightfold determination)
Except your magic and your word.

    Three warriors (it turns to wealth for me)
Knew magic before this —
Battle-tested, he keeps his surname,
The first, gentlest, was Menw;
And the second was (intelligence's good day)
Eiddilig Gor, a shrewd Irishman.   40
The third, near the seas of Môn,
Was Math, a ruler of golden kind, a lord of Arfon.

    I journeyed about my bardic work
At feast time, worse changing;
Seldom do you keep a tryst,
Like a war of Llwyd ap Cel Coed.

    Well do you deserve, fair girl of prudent judgment,
The silver harp, the string of deceit.
Your name's (while there may be trysting with a woman)
"The Enchantress of the Bright Harp."   50
You shall be made famous, a word of strong sense,
The oppressor, the harpist of deceit.
The harp was constructed
Of joy's excellence, you're a golden girl;
On it there's a carving of the stand of hindrance,
And an engraving of deception and sham.
Her corner (not the wild wood)
Is of the form of Virgil's art.
Her harp-pillar makes me wholly dead
From a genuine spell and sharp longing.   60
Deception is the pegs of this one
And lie and flattery and tortuousness.
Two jewels of gold are the worth
Of your hands for holding a harp-string.

Ah, the soft song, polished, fair lady,
Of learned metre that you can make!

　　Better is craft, they say, long magic,
Color of a radiant gull, than wealth.
Take, O betrayal of a throng, face of snow,
Candle of Camber's Land, from me　　　　　　　70
(Fortune's gift, gentle her honor)
A place at the feast, color of the swan.

85. *Disappointment*

Love on a fickle woman
I spent without great return.
I repented my loving
An untrue girl (she was my torment)
As I loved modest, stately
Morfudd, color of day, no concern of mine.
Morfudd, my darling, did not want
To be loved longer. Ah, what a fate!

　　I spent much (with constant aching)
Good verse on loving the girl.　　　　　　　　10
I spent rings on handsome love poets;
Woe for me, wretch!
Her face like a rushing layer of foam over a weir,
I spent what I had of gems.
I spent, not like a skillful man,
Jewelry of mine for her sake.
I frequented (I wove soundly)
Taverns of wine, God judges the truth.
I also frequented (shallow living)
Taverns of mead-horns, too hateful.　　　　　20
From passion's very striving, I had
Minstrels compose and sing her song
As far as farthest Ceri
(Fine snow's color) for her sake.

Being trustful is what happened to me;
Despite all this (she was my girl)
I got (except for care's fatigue,
Not in my agreement) no payment,
Except her going (an act of wrong-doing,
Twice as white as snow) under another man,   30
Making her (not profitable work)
Pregnant, my dear little woman.

Howsoever, to vex me,
It was done, she was bewitched,
Whether from love (to leave me,
Graceless judgment) or by force it was,
A poor cuckold do they call me,
Alas for the cry! because of a girl white as a
                                    boiling brook.
Some give (such signs)
To my hand (too great dread to my heart)   40
Sticks (it would be better to burn them)
Of green hazel; it was not for a fault of mine.
Others put (hostile purpose)
Round my brow a willow hat.

Morfudd, and not at my request,
Without an hour of love caused this;
God judge at last
True judgment between me and one whose face
                                    is gossamer.

86. *The Oath*

I love (a work of wild, bold passion)
A noble girl, Esyllt's niece;
Eye of dark color, a wild gem of golden hair,
She's full of love, a golden linnet,
Hue of Fflur and clear gossamer,
Most elegant branch of fierce white.

Some said to me (a strong love-bond),
"The best girl is getting married
This year, a girl like Luned,
A treasure of joy; sad the man who trusts her."   10

I don't dare, timid of mind
(Woe for the poet who's a faithful fool!),
To steal the girl twice as bright as summer
By force (of the same color as the thorn blossoms).
Her proud family (hawks of Gwynedd,
The best in our land, a feast-giving throng)
Would kill me for preventing
Her marriage to the man (a battle of hate).

Unless I get (soft, golden speech)
Her for me (she of the color of Mary's bright face)   20
There is (my life is hidden)
In my thoroughly grave and serious mind
(Is it lively?), by Cadfan's statue
And the Living Cross, no wish for a wife at all.

87. *Love's Husbandry*

This closely developed comparison (of the lover's experience — nurturing love
only to be denied fulfillment — with a farmer's cultivating a crop that is lost in
a summer storm) has a parallel in Guillaume de Lorris (*Roman de la Rose,* lines
3960-70). Dr. Bromwich takes this as evidence that Dafydd knew the *Roman*
and interprets the present poem as referring to Dafydd's love for Morfudd,
frustrated by her marriage to Y Bwa Bach (*TI,* pp. 30, 31).

I was in love, though I might pine,
And more or twice more am I.
Ambush of a love most gentle,
The cripple of pain, pure child of memory.
I kept love in my heart,
The deceiver, the gnawer of flesh.
It grows in my breast, it knows grieving,
The mother of betrayal,

Quicker than the growth (a most cunning creation)
Of a branch of a thick-topped planetree.   10
To seek a crop of love
Was always a property of my mind.

    Winter tilth, anxiety's torment,
I made, a payment of love's aching;
Between (sorrow's hidden food)
January's tenancy and Morfudd's love,
The intense, joyous, brave breast was plowed
With a deep spear-blow in one furrow,
And a plow with a practical, well-made frame
To plow the other breast.   20
The plowshare is in my heart,
And the coulter of love is above the slopes.
And in the right breast, swift wound,
The sowing and harrowing of a flood of passion.
And three months later (bright and choice discretion)
In springtime (a pang of sleepless deceit)
Sorrow put forth branches in me,
A grove that will kill me, dalliance of rage.
I get only trouble from passion,
No one believes how busy love is.   30

    On May Day to avoid any
Idleness in my life, of my own free will
I made an enclosure (lively attack of a rash crop)
Round about it, I'm a lonely man.
While love of this generous girl,
Disabling state, through my bosom
Was lively, beautiful, and fertile (it doesn't concern
                  me)
And ripe and prolific,
I visited (I didn't delay hiring)
Parties of reapers of pain.   40

    Heavy was the utter loss of all the grain,
Tribulation is always the world's provision.
The wind turned (a bolt's long course)
From the south of the twice pierced heart,

And there darkened (anguish for a mistress)
Two stars of love in my head,
Tear-gates of a bitter harvest,
Eyes, swimming because of love;
They had looked (a picture of flooding)
At Morfudd, gentle gold-maiden;   50
The louvers of floodwater,
Laborious, unlucky brooks.
Tonight blue water oppressed this breast,
A sad enclosing.
The pent-up sorrow is under my breast,
My eye leaves no handful dry.

    Terrible on stubble, an embrace of sadness,
Is a storm from the angry west;
And there comes on the cheeks a constant, heavy rain
From the eastern sky.   60
A strong tear for one of Eigr's color does not allow
(Spoiled crop) sleep to the eye.
O love, most deceiving seed,
After such ache, alas for you because of the thought,
That I could not, strong pain of desertion,
Harvest you between two showers.
The fine, long love collapsed;
About provisioning, I was disappointed.

88. *The Girl from Is Aeron*

Is Aeron ("Lower Aeron") designates the region south of the river Aeron in
Ceredigion.

    A New Year's gift is it to get the greeting
Of the Heart of Is Aeron and her love.
Weak is the straight, handsome, frivolous bard:
The Gossamer of Ceredigion has borne him off!
Alas for whoever bestows, fine vanity,
His love (stewardess of mead,
Sweet face, she's the moon of her region)

Like paying usury, where it does not prosper.
Woe to him who sees with keen sight
A frown on a golden, gentle maid.   10
She does not fret two tears' worth
For her lover, Eigr's form.
Woe to him who painfully sustains a pang for her
Within, like me,
A maiden's treasure, most upstanding,
Full of trouble, ever unpaid.

    Woe to him who would make against frost's war
A house on a beach, of thickest earth.
It will be an unsafe bed,
Briefly will it stay, and the surge will upset it.   20
Woe to him who loves (finely did I)
Her of lovely violence, I stained the sword of love,
Shining white her face, meadow-slope gossamer,
White color of foam, pale moon of Caron.
Perfect, unwrinkled, curse her,
She overcame my high spirits.
Of brilliant color, a generous, joyous one,
Fair, golden jewel of Aeron-land;
A veil of torques (the light of snow)
Along her makes her golden.   30

89. *Under the Eaves*

A lock was put on the door of the house;
I'm sick, my girl, hear me.
Come, be seen, fine of form,
For generous God's sake, show yourself.
Why should she prevail, the girl of false speech?
By Mary, transgression is maddening!

    Through strenuous passion, I struck
Three blows; the locked latch broke.
Wasn't it loud?
Did you hear? It was the sound of a bell.   10

Morfudd, my treasure of chaste mind,
Nurse of the lure of deceit,
My lair is at the other side of the wall from you;
I have to shout, pale girl.
Have mercy on an insomniac;
The night is dark, love's deceiver.
Recognize how painful is my lot;
Ah, the heaven's weather tonight!
Frequent are the waterfalls from the eaves
Upon my flesh, the instrument of love.   20
The rain is not greater (it's my wound)
Than the snow, I'm under it.
This shivering is not comfortable.
Pain on dead skin was not greater
Than I got through anxiety;
By the Man Who made me, there's no worse bed.
There was not in the Caer in Arfon
A jail worse than this road.

    I would not be outside all night,
I would not groan but for your sake.   30
I would surely not come to suffer
Nightly ache, if I did not love you.
I would not be under rain and snow
An hour's space except for you.
I would not renounce (I know anguish)
The whole world, unless there were you.

    Here am I through passion;
It is your grace, in the house are you.
My pure soul is there,
And my apparition is here outside.   40
Who listens long to me here will be doubting,
My gold one, that I live.
My obsession does not go away;
It has caused me madness here.

    An agreement was made with me;
Here am I, and where are you?

90. *A Lover's Affliction*

A changeable heart pined,
Love wrought betrayal in my breast.

Once was I (I know a hundred wounds)
In the time of youth (gladness was mine)
Not faint, not aching,
Subject to love's custody,
A charmer in song, not frail,
Good for the tryst, and brilliantly brave,
A fashioner of light work's effervescence,
Quite cheerful, full of language,   10
Healthy enough, free of blame,
Pleasant, nimble, goodlooking.

And now (affliction is swift)
I'm decaying, wasting away in sorrow.
Finished is the rashness that fired me,
Finished is the body (mine is grief's commotion),
Completely finished is the last of the voice,
And the exploits, I fell hard.
Finished is the inspiration for a pretty girl,
Finished is the talk about him who troubles love.   20

There does not arise in me (memory of song)
A happy plan or passion,
No consoling mention of them,
No love ever—unless a girl asks.

91. *The Frost*

Great gnashing of teeth was mine
From staggering far and wide by the stone walls
Last night in the midst of a naked wind
And frost, ah, how cold was the way!
Common is the winter storm, a slope's crop,
Near the house of her whose color is the sheen of
                    a wave.

Truly, alas for the lonely, there was
A man who might be filled with anger!
My fine jewel, from her pure, persistent memories,
Asks from the other side of the wall: 10

She: "Is it pleasant to endure the cold?
By God in Heaven, are you a man?"

Dafydd: "I was a man of the world today, by the
                              light of day,
One who had been baptized;
But now, because of my load of painful hurt,
                              I don't know,
Essence of brilliance, what I am."

    I fell across (surely of a hard nature)
Hurdles of hard, cold ice.
Into froth-foaming water (anguished reception)
I fell, I bruised all.   20
When there broke (base, astonishing form)
The round breastbone-plates of the waters,
Far was heard from the glowing ice pool
A cry and a shout, my plague was harsh.
Fatal blue webs of pain
Under a bright, dry sky.
Obvious, dull eye of the leaden ground,
Glass mirrors, great marl pits.
Very strange its form, blanket of mire,
A shining, slippery quarry.   30

    Now it's worse for me here
Because of ice than on the slope above;
The bright beaks
Of the eaves threaten my thin flesh,
Great nails, droplets of judgment,
As long as those of an iron harrow.
Straight, hollow needles when they fall,
Every one's an icicle.
Heavy hulled-oats' husks surprised me,
Leaden spears beside a wall.   40

Knives and slices of frost, surely,
Just sharpened at the moon's end,
Seething pimples, frosted spit-pestilence,
A cold morning to the ice spears!
Truly it's necessary (great shouts)
To avoid the weapons of frost's war.
Woe for me that the glancing wind
Quickly freezes the evil thistle-spears.
No better, I know, too remote a notion,
Are boots against the sharp chill   50
(A love-wound of the quick stir of numbed blood)
Than if they hadn't been on the poor feet.
I'm that great, kindly fellow who pines,
Who came from the mountain of ice,
Who's still seen, a long slumber,
With an ill look on his visage,
Because of death and wasting away,
Quite shriveled up and all ice.
A stout sliver of the harsh, brittle frost
Got to scorn me.   60
Sticking like glue, impetuously ascends
The cruel tremor, like bird-lime.

        Since I shall not get (elegant and splendid thought)
A place in the house of her of the color of lovely
                            fine snow,
According to the claim of a desolate career
(Previous fault), I must have, if it's to be had,
Great, bright sunshine, radiance of a heap of color,
And a sun that might dissolve this.

92. *Longing's Genealogy*

I was awake for one like Tegau,
My tear is bitter on her account.
For two months for the shape of the same girl
I did not sleep (love does not sleep)
A third of a night until last night,

Heavy stroke of luck, a late, heavy slumber.

When I was just getting a grip
On my sleep's edge, O my generous girl,
Love's sorrow, sad saying,
A questioner who was a fine, sturdy champion   10
Asked directly
A question of longing's spirited flamboyance:

Longing: "Where's the poet of Dyddgu of bright
                                      and beautiful hand?
What's your name? Don't sleep!
Fierce will be the love-wound's damage,
Open the door, I'm mighty!"

Dafydd: "If I open it, if I must,
To whom? Or who is speaking?"

Longing: "Some   call   me,   excellent   and   grave,
'Sleep's Infidel in Powys':   20
Longing son of Memory, son of Scheme,
Son of Woe's My Thought, son of Lust,
Son of Pain, son of Jealousy, son of Anger,
Son of Loose Glance, son of Grieving,
Son of Ardent Frailty, son of Vigor of Longing,
Son of Gwawl, son of Magic, son of Clud's Wound,
Son of Tear, son of Sleepless Illusion,
Son of Sad Mind, son of Ease Forever,
Son of Dark Sleeplessness, son of Greeting,
Son of Seth, son of Adam, son of Love.   30

"A gentleman am I of proud presumption,
Noble, banished am I,
Gravespoken penitent of Eigr's church,
Lord of the nobility of tear;
I'm the minister (bright one of a host,
Beautiful body) of proper Dyddgu,
And also (the bright girl said it herself)
The dispenser of love's cellar.
And dear, shy-mannered Dyddgu

Leaves me with you for your lifetime."   40

I welcomed him (lamented evening)
There last night,
The messenger of Dyddgu, lovely moon;
Hundredfold grief for me because of that welcome!

93. *The Rejected Lover*

Alone on a beach at night, the poet charges Morfudd with having abandoned him because of her husband's protests ("the Dark Idler's shaking"). Dafydd likens her to a plowman with a pair of oxen who depends now on one, now the other. And she is like a ball tossed from hand to hand in play. Competitors for her favors are encouraged to pursue her, as in a swimming match, but once she's gained, she lets them go.

Sadly I'd recognize your ways,
Pale patch, before tonight.
It's my mind, a moment of energy,
Frequent her deception, to debate with you.
Morfudd ferch Madawg Lawgam,
By the Pope, I know why
You left me on the beach
Solitary and haggard like this!

While I could (I did not injure song)
Take your married man's place,   10
Sin's claim, a loving magic,
Correct me, didn't you love me?
Now I'm the one who failed,
A deep wound, I'm exhausted, with no place of refuge.
Upon your breast, the strength of pain,
Good is the Dark Idler's shaking.
You exchanged me, it's a shame,
Bright, white star,
Like the fellow, false condition,
With a pair of steady oxen   20
Under the yoke

To the same mighty, well-made plow
(My coarsely gouged cheek was plowed);
Wild headland, it holds to its circuit,
Today the one, strong Lord God,
Tomorrow the other, most extravagant.

As they do, painful word of rebuke,
Playing ball, my pledged mistress,
You're favored, your shape was chased
From hand to hand, glowing form.   30
Long gifts, dear, lovely face,
This is what you want, you of the joy of modest Dyfr.

A squire of fit double-garb,
And these as tight as bark,
Swam ahead with sturdy energy
Without reward, a hard bargain.
He who might prosper in a birchwood,
If the girl wants, let him enter;
And he who did what was good, a fraternity of fear,
Let him go out deceived.   40

Whoever loves you will be sorry;
You've shed me, it was little trouble.
It's true, with a shove a barrel's cast,
When it's empty, aside.

94. *Invoking Dwynwen*

St. Dwyn (or Dwynwen, the suffix *gwen* meaning "holy") was revered in Wales
as the patron saint of lovers. A church dedicated to her stood in Môn—the
ruins are still to be seen at Llanddwyn—frequented by lover-pilgrims as late
as the eighteenth century. Dafydd imagines himself praying before her statue
near the throng of her petitioners. She was the daughter of the legendary first
king of Brycheiniog, mighty Brychan Yrth.

Dwynwen, with tear of the loveliness of frost,
Your golden statue knows well

From a choir of great, flaming wax how to relieve
Bitter, forlorn people over there.
Whoever keeps watch, holy, bright spell,
In your choir, a beautiful Indeg,
There is no sickness or depression
That can go with him from Llanddwyn.

    Your humble followers are your devout parishioners.
Sore and care-ridden am I;   10
This breast from longing for a lover
Is one swelling of desire;
Long pang from the depth of pain,
From what I know, it's a plague;
Unless I get, if I live,
Morfudd, there's an empty life!
Make me healthy, fairer praise,
From my distress and my weakness.
For a year, combine love-messenger service between
                        you and the girl
With God's graces.   20
No need, lively, golden image,
For you ever to fear sin or a snare of flesh.
God won't undo (His peace is good)
What He has done; you won't go from heaven.
No coquette this year will see you
Whispering near us.
Eiddig of angry, stubborn mind won't give
A beating to you, pure of mind.

    Come, as your repayment, hush, no one suspects
You, long of virgin company,   30
From Llanddwyn, land of resort,
To Cwm-y-gro, gem of Christendom.
God did not refuse you, easy peace,
The gift of fluent speech, the girl won't refuse you.
God calls you to a work of sure prayers,
Black her headband.
Let God, your host,
May it come to mind, hold fast the husband's hands
(Strong would be whoever could overcome him)

While he tracks me through leaves of May.   40
Dwynwen, if you'd once bring her out
Into May-woods a long, lingering day,
Her poet's gift, may all, fair one, be well with you;
Dwynwen, you were not base.
Show by your refined graces
You're not a coquette, wise Dwynwen.

For what you accomplished by way of great sacrifice
Of penance for the world and its burden;
For the religion, faith most faithful,
That you practised while you were alive;   50
For that brilliant nunhood
And virgin state of fine flesh bound;
For the soul, if necessary, for a long time to come,
Of Brychan Yrth of strong arms;
Beg, by your bleeding faith,
That the precious Virgin grant rescue!

95. *Tears of Love*

In the Welsh original, every line of this tribute to Dyddgu begins with the letter *D*, an alliterative device known in Welsh poetics as *cymeriad*.

O Dyddgu, light of brightest day,
Your patronage, by the Only Son of the Lord God,
You from the land of Mael who have Mary's cheeks,
Black eyes and eyebrows!
I dealt (it was like magic,
The pursuit of love) with you, O foster daughter.
Noble girl of good, smooth speech,
Painful is it to have to do with love.
Twice as bright as the beard of noisy, shallow water,   10
Bright image on a blue flood-veil,
May it occur to you to pay your brother
For swelling your praise with his tongue.
I brought you something better than two brooches,
A good share, well do I know that it is.

For you, one of twice the brightness of a wave,
A man's like dwarf birches decaying;
Dyfed knows that he is dead,
Of pure learning, and he's Dafydd.
Unfeeling girl, if some day I go,
Slender form, beneath slices of greenwood,   20
My tear trickles (deeply have I expressed it,
My pain is brave) down my tunic.
I'm frivolous and stubborn, I who hurl rain
Under brows, a dean of weeping.
Your poet finer than any,
Tears have skinned his face.
For love of you, pale daughter of light, I'm a man
Denied mercy, withered and tearful
(A day ever, matching fine snow,
Cunning sense, brilliant body).   30

Dyddgu, my gold one gaining distinction,
Fine girl, black is the color of your eyebrows,
An enduring gift, if you should freely endow me,
The wealth of all England, of excellent eyes,
Secret love would be made unprofitable at the
                              approach of May,
Your glance would make it unprofitable.
I deserve fortune for praise,
You deserve praise, by Mary's image.
Distress over you cannot be driven from my breast,
Gentle form of Tudor stock.   40
Fruitless is your poet's struggle,
Numerous the gems on your wide brow.
You thrust a gay spear under a wounded breast,
This does not trouble your mind.
I'm excluded from your love —
You're goodlooking — and unpaid,
Except that I (complaint is remarkably good)
May trail over you, O my desire,
Two drowsy eyes protesting,
Neglected pourers of a flood.   50

96. *Fatigue*

Love for Morfudd has been fostered by Dafydd and after nine years has
proved an intractable foster son.

Your love, beauty of Indeg,
Is like harsh shackles of joy
In me, a lad of vivacity and beauty,
Tiring me for nine years.
There has been, with regard to the benefit of
                              his foster father
After long residence, no worse a young man.
A self-indulgent lad, sad death,
A faulty foster son to him.

That, noble Morfudd,
Is what I shall have of payment, it's sorrow.   10
Whatever church you may go to,
Whether Sunday or feast day, be my dear,
I go with clasped fists, my devout girl,
To where you've gone;
And then, jewel of your clan,
A sardonic, playful tale,
I break my passionate eyes
On your limbs, my sweet beloved.

There will be that day either ten
Needles or twelve,   20
From one eyelid, despite what hindrance there is,
Love's pastorate, to the other,
So that one cannot approach the other, prudent,
                              wise girl,
Of golden form.
While my eyes (a demanding swarm)
Are horribly open,
Rain comes (you're a girl of shining face)
From the sign of the broken breast,
Two brooks streaming far and wide
From there, O my desire.   30

Reflect on this, chaste girl,
Thoughts of love's constellation,
That rain comes after sad trial
As far as the beard, well-shaped Morfudd.

Although I might be for part of a Sunday,
                              for a psalm,
In the comely choir, a lean youngster,
Not all the parishioners (an unbroken sadness)
Reject me, although I'm not goodlooking;
The law of love demands it,
Take me to yourself, girl.   40

97. *Being Forgetful*

Eve sufficiently noble,
Lady, the goddess of grace,
Your face the color of snow before Epiphany,
Vain to argue with you (frequent her deception)
That you ought not to abolish
The bond there always was between us.
It seems, girl of impetuous soul,
That you did not know me (deceit is painful).
Alas, is it drunk you were, fine gem,
Since last year, a period of magic?   10
Girl too impudent and victorious,
Think it over (the world celebrates you).
If there was (loving greeting)
One word between us, you the color of a ford's foam,
And if there was praise before, a look of change,
Fault of an accuser, let there be again!
Do not deserve satire like an ungenerous person,
And do not be a poor old maid.
Being forgetful does one no good,
Dispraise in *awdl* or *englyn*.   20
The end of being forgetful is care.
Tower of your house, put your gold-haired brow
Under a fine gold mantle;

Summon up your memory, beautiful, modest Eve.
Not steadfastness, what you did on my account,
Not good, fair Eve, is your memory.
Do not be untrue for long,
Do not dismiss from memory our passionate
                          love-making once.

98. *Choosing One of Four*

Her love a girl gave me,
Star of the region of Nant-y-seri,
An excellent girl, no false judgment,
Modest Morfudd, of large thoughts.
Though I might lose because of strange true love
My darling who once ran a straight course,
Though our exchange might be costly,
Costly was it for her husband.
Except for the displeasure (a wonderful, beautiful life)
Of God above, she's unrepentant,   10
After her lover (the scare was a betrayal,
The world's moon) swore to have done.

　　　If thereupon I loved half-heartedly
The wife of the bald merchant,
A hunchback with a pretentious retinue,
Wife of a certain chief, Robin Nordd,
Helen eager for wealth,
My treasure with the stubborn accent,
Queen (Lady of Wool)
Of a cloth court, in the vale of gorse fire,   20
There was need of a loving man there,
Too bad that I was not he!
She does not take (face like a lovely wave)
A song for nothing, she of brave honor.
Easy for me to get (full grasp,
Easier than anything) good socks;
And if I get motley, she of the whitest hue of gossamer
Will content me.

I'm not, carefree joy,
By God, without getting some payment: 30
Whether congratulations,
Or a fine poetic thought,
Or gold, though I might excuse it,
Or something, I'm amusing.
And even if my tongue be
Weaving tribute to Dyddgu,
There's for me, by God, no office
But pursuing fickleness.

A lady of royal stock, breeding owns her,
The world knows, is the fourth. 40
Neither she nor anyone else shall have from my wise,
discreet mouth
(She of the color of foam)
Either her name or the land from which she came
(She's very dear) or which one she was.

There's no woman (joy's chief)
Nor man I love so much
As the bright maid of a round, whitewashed fort;
Good evening to her, she's not grateful.
One gets a reputation for loving in vain;
I'll have — I will not spare — revenge. 50
If she knew one man's hoping,
That it was concerning her,
She'd hate it as much, the fine, fair girl with
lovely cheek,
As being hanged, splendid gift;
Greater heavy burden, my pain-foe,
I shall praise her, Nyf's color,
Lively form, and all Gwynedd
Praises her; blessed is he who wins her!

99. *A Girl's Pilgrimage*

Queen of consolation of the *cantref,*
A nun went for all the hosts of heaven
And for Non (the heart conceals it)
And for Dewi (a quiet Eigr)
From lovely Môn to the land of Mynyw;
May it be easy for her, my soul,
To seek (may the party prosper)
Forgiveness for what she said,
For killing her black and blue, sorrowful young man,
A thin, tormented penitent.   10
As compensation for the murder of the fellow bubbling
                                        with poetry,
She went (desolate longing) into outlawry.

        Resolutely did she with cheeks like red flowers flee,
My chosen one left Môn.
Lord Christ, let the enemy be generous,
Let Menai ebb and be kind.
May it be easy for her to go through to the other side
Of the flood-stream of Llyfni, a rough-hurling obstacle.
Y Traeth Mawr, a heap of great size,
Draw back, let her go through!   20
Y Bychan Draeth, narrow course,
Grant this passage to my blessed girl.
Copious prayers have been made,
Let Artro Fawr be tranquil.
I would pay the Abermaw ferry toll
To bear her yonder on the ebb-wave.
Nine waves of Dysynni, allow her of the color of wine
To fair Dewi's land;
And deep are the waves of Dyfi,
Rough water, confronting her.   30
Rheidol, grant for your honor
A road to a girl generous with mead.
Ystwyth, in compensation, grant me that this girl
Might go, strong, full water, over your breast.
Aeron bubbling loud with high-spirited love,

Let the wisely-praised girl through you.
Handsome Teifi, ocean spur,
Permit the girl to increase her grace.
Vigorously through the boundary river
May the girl go and come back.   40

    She who is my great fortune, she's in purple,
Is, if she lives, between Mynyw and the sea;
If she slew me long ago,
Easy outlawry, gently will she be accused.
Let Mary forgive, patron hand,
My humble seagull who killed me.
Certainly, and I shall exonerate her,
I too shall forgive my gold one for it.

100. *Shooting the Girl*

Spears (memory's companions)
Are thrust piercingly through me,
Faster than the arrow's course
From hands through the sheaf of rushes yonder,
Because of how genuinely fiercely
My darling rejects my praise.

    An arrow sharp-edged, wild, straight, and quite painful
Across under her round breast,
So long as it does not break, a rapid, straying course,
Either the skin or one stitch of the slip.   10
An iron hook with a handle for gripping get
Under the black-browed girl's two jaws,
So long as it does not touch, bad turn,
Excellent, thin-browed one, an eye.
Chop off her head, pillar of praise,
With a long axe at one blow.
Oppressive is he who forbids this.
Alas! Woe's me! Is the fine girl alive?
Loudly I give out my full cry,
More woe than "woe's me" or "him."   20

Great woe is mine if she die,
That radiant, fine girl, as a result of my prayer;
Though it's so difficult, a turn of heavy sorrow,
To win her, long life to her!
It would be best, a public favor,
That she should escape, she is so good.

101. *A Churlish Girl*

Terrible yearning, however long I try
(Love's a magician, I'm rash and green,
Because of the size of my desire)
To pursue the rare Southern Sun
(Color of a layer of foam on a stone bench),
She of a lively, black eyebrow escapes.
I may not have her against her will,
And the girl won't take me willingly.
I shall not be silent, if I go without payment,
More than a nightingale among twigs.   10

    May Mary and God and Mordëyrn,
And some who see my harsh fate
Cause (this is love's war)
Me, because of my love,
Either to die swiftly without delay,
Or to have the girl and live long.
Very likely, say some idiots,
That I (isn't this a lie?)
Can't rhyme a word (a face I might love)
But for the one girl, I'm a sad bardic master.   20

    Of praise for a girl, herself of a stock of nobles,
Of good song, and this is a sign,
Even some contented, respectable merchant
Would not for twenty pounds give what was sung;
There's not been given to me (she of nine graces of enamel)
The value of this, but only playing with payment.
A foolish gift, it was as if

A man with a yew bow
Were shooting, where an anchor drops,
A gull by the sea shore,   30
Without a sign of profit, without getting the arrows
Or the hard-clawed, wild, white bird.
I'm obstinate, shooting praise in vain;
Would it be worse to shoot the stars with an arrow?

If I were to compose (I know a hundred *englynion*)
For God what I composed for a woman,
Easily would He make for me, by right,
Someone dead, alive, a greater petition.
She would not do for me as much as
One bit, blessed girl of white teeth.   40
The girl prefers (she doesn't allow me easy sleep)
Her comfortable old house and her food
To being visible amid the dew of a feast,
An elegant Gweirful, the truly praised one of Gwynedd.
This girl of praise's word would not exchange
Where she is even if she were to be near Mary.
No girl born (a thrust of wandering love)
Blonde was so churlish.
If she of the color of highland snow rejects
My praise, it was true,   50
A rejection of the marketplaces,
It was a rejected song for my dear, modest one,
Wound after wound, slender, white, shining maiden,
Leaden and false, a plague on her head!

102. *The Poet's Affliction*

In Welsh, each line of this poem on Morfudd begins with the letter *H*; note
the parallel with Poem 95 to Dyddgu.

A lively, fair maiden used to enchant me,
Generous Morfudd, May's god-daughter.
She it is who shall be saluted,
I'm sick tonight for love of her.

She sowed in my breast (that will split in two)
A seed of love, cruel charm.
Pain's crop, this the penalty,
She of sunshine's lively color won't leave me alone.
An enchantress and a fair goddess,
Her speech is magic to me.   10
Easily she listens to a facile accusation
Against me, I shall not have her favor.
Peace I'd have, a gift and instruction
Today with my learned girl.
Tonight without crime I'm an innocent outlaw
From her parish and her house.
She put (a man's harsh aching)
Longing in her outlaw's breast.
Longer than the sea along the shore, abides
The girl's outlaw in his longing.   20
I've been shackled, my ribs nailed,
A shackle of sorrow I got.
Unlikely that I shall have beneath her fine gold
Peace with my spirited, wise girl;
Evil afflictions have come because of this,
More unlikely is it that I shall have long life.
She's descended from Ynyr:
Without her I shall not live.

103. *Saying Goodbye*

You know perfectly, one like Indeg,
Long live your forehead, a lovely magic
(Longing holds me, enchantment pursues me,
Your figure full of life) for enchanting a man.
Unlikely work, to seize you in a bright, snug cell,
Because you're so contrary.
Do not flee; wait, girl,
No need for haste to the court from the grove.
Hostess of the veil of birch trees,
Stay and console me, Morfudd.   10
If you were to come to the birch cell now,

My dear little girl,
You would not return (a good, fine room;
Simple payment) as you might come.
It's sad that I can't stop you;
I'm your slave, girl with the fair forehead.
It's painful that I can't (saddest love secret)
Keep you under a gold, flaxen roof.

    Destiny does not lead you from your baptism
As tryst led you among trees.   20
If I've been lost, come find me
Where you promised, moon of black eyebrows;
My bold, crafty will
Would claim revenge if you were to come,
For pursuing you without getting serious profit.
I'll get no chance, alas, Morfudd!

    Go, my desire, in full health,
And God your support, dear girl.
Go in health, mightier bounty,
Ten woes for me because of destiny!   30
Farewell, dear girl, the world's grace,
And give yourself your own greeting.

104. *The Foster Son*

This love of mine in fostership
(Arrogant, pampered foster son,
A handsome lad, great his immorality)
A slim girl with strong love bestowed.
A foster son to me today (not fitting to deny it,
Because of longing) is love.
Much wrong (a scowl of distress)
Has the foster son done me.
He wants to be borne for a girl's sake,
Wants to await her greeting.   10
Wants to wander in bracken,
Wants to be attracted by a woman.

Too great for me is my travail;
He wants to be hidden, and to be found.
A slim, fine girl knows my manner;
He wants to rage at her mutely.
I nurtured (I wasted away) love,
A foster son of the poetry of betrayal.
Fostering a fair, tame serpent
In my breast (from love of a slender, civil girl)   20
It was, for me to nurture, rejecting profit,
The slim, fair boy in my breast.

    A boy of remarkable manner (I have proof)
Is he in a summer month.
Love doesn't want to be denied,
Nor to be shown to a great crowd.
He won't turn from the heart's region,
He dwells but at my breast's summit.
He cannot cause us repose,
He doesn't stay in place after poetry.   30
He wouldn't sit if he were the Pope;
My unchaste boy will not lie down.
He will not stand, golden love of shy nature will
                                        not stand up,
For a girl's work.
I caused her praise to swell as far as Teifi,
I'm the foster father of the girl's love.
He's a difficult son (I took pains)
To nurture ever between ribs.
He's restless this year,
The son I nurtured for myself.   40
I've nurtured (I'm a handsome, passionate fellow)
A dear son of a narrow-browed, fair girl.

    Little (brilliant jewel) for me
Was the benefit for nurturing a son for her.
A curse (the fate of love)
On the girl who put him out to adoption,
Unless she pays (a throng's full care,
My dismay) for his nurture.

105. *The Mirror*

I didn't suppose (the strong attack of evil)
That my face was not handsome and good
Until I handled (a plain task)
The mirror; and there's a bad one!
The mirror told me at last
That I am not goodlooking.

Turning yellow for an Enid
Is the cheek, the blush is not great.
After the groaning, the cheek is glass
And a yellow-colored bruise all over.   10
You could almost make a razor
Of the long nose; isn't this pitiful?
Isn't it terrible that glad eyes
Should be blind auger-holes?
And the curly-topped, vain shock of hair
Falls every handful from its roots.

Great is the fate of mischief upon me;
It's either, to my thinking,
That I am a dusky quiver,
Evil in nature, or the mirror's not good.   20
If the fault is mine (I know the nature of a
                          long love),
Let me die!
If the mirror of spotted feature
Was at fault, ah me, what a life!

Blue, dark moon of round circumference,
Full of magic, like a magnet;
Of doubtful color, a charmed jewel;
Magicians fashioned it;
Dream of the swiftest kind,
Cold traitor and brother to ice.   30
Falsest, truly ungentlest lad,
Aflame be the hateful, thin mirror of twisted lip!

None made me wrinkled of face
(If it's right to believe the mirror there)
But the girl from Gwynedd;
There is it known how to spoil a face.

106. *Repentance*

Poet to Morfudd am I,
A costly office; I've composed verses for her.
By the Man Who owns today,
There's a pang in my head because of the fine girl,
And in my forehead there's a wound of care;
For a golden girl I'm dying.
When there comes, a shaking for bones,
Death and his violent bolts,
Prodigious will be the life ending,
A man's tongue will be finished.   10
May the Trinity, for reconciling complaint
And great turbulence, and the Virgin Mary
Forgive my wrong ways,
Amen, and I'll sing no more.

107. *Denial*

Great love upon a fair, wine-nourished girl
I bestowed as an arrow would go.
I shall gild every maiden
With words of praise for her sake.
Woe is me, bad is her memory yonder
Regarding me, she disfigures me.

I was once, near the face of the fine jewel,
The fond poet of a fair, slim-browed girl.
And now, though I don't quit,
After love, I'm neglected.   10
I lay down on a border of leaves

With the woman, under trees of fresh leaves.
I was a treasure, though I had no craft,
Skin to skin with the woman of skilled craft.
My girl does not wish, since I was,
Sinful sweetheart, to acknowledge me.
I shall no more get, except through force,
A young woman I once had.
The girl does not wish, despite being honored,
How brilliant she was, to see me,   20
More than if, at a summer fair, there were put
The beard and horns of a he-goat on me.

108. *The Heart*

Hail, short, round, little heart,
Of natural, unrelenting impulse,
Has there been a part more troubled
Than you, weaver's workshop of poetry?
Lady pilgrim, a breast nurtured it,
Blessed, supreme muscle of longing.
Round maiden very intense and fervent,
A heap of fresh, bright thoughts.
It will be quiet in an unjealous way;
It will fill like a little egg.   10
She it is, throne of the breast, that makes
(Strongly-known for the bubbling-out of poetry,
Wild roar) a poor, very eccentric, and very bold man
A very generous lover.

       Let the wine-spending family consider
The mead drink, how good it was;
This it is (a gift-source for long,
The boiling course of a flood) that makes a man
                              extravagantly generous.
A dirty pilgrim, with a dull, dead penis,
A cold head, without clothing for his buttocks,   20
And very brave out on the roads,
Cold face, he won't be there

Without either getting (let me steal away past him)
A wound or quickly causing an injury.
The second is in glowing frenzy
To wish with the lip shame on a beard.
The third no one knows:
A man's windings in adultery,
Desiring, lofty impulse,
To lead the modest, fair girl into hiding.   30

    That is the root of the plagues,
The title for this proud office is mine.
No greater trouble under heaven
For man nor beast, by God, than I
Loving (drawing near in lust,
Despite everyone's disapproval) the same girl,
The hope of the people, one of bright radiance,
Brilliant, slender, slant one, everybody knows who;
Beautiful, most glowing, a bower for the lively moon,
Morfudd of the lovely cheeks, surely;   40
The color of sunshine when there's a blazing sun
On a hillside, she of the happy, flashing eyes;
Generous, languid beauty, a prosperous, wine-giving
                                girl,
The sunlight and star of love.

109. *The Sigh*

A tough, ungentle sigh
Makes me not contained in my tunic.
A sigh, a chill piece of exhaling,
Broke in four parts
The breast holding it, the hill of sorrow;
Only barely does it not split me, from its too
                            violent pain.
Out of the nest-load of memories of the precious
                            breast
(Sigh of difficult passion)
Some constricted sound arises from me,

A thin sound of memory's anguish,   10
A disturbance of the breast, deception's cavity,
A skillful dame extinguishing a candle.
Shower from the whirlwind of a cry,
A mist-hedge of long brooding will it be.

It is a girl who provokes it, intense word;
It's an angry roar along the length of a man.
All suppose when I'm depressed,
If only I had been trained, that I'm a piper.
There's more breath in me
Than in the hollow of a blacksmith's bellows.   20
A sigh, edged labor,
Ahead strikes a stone from the wall.
A gust of rain to wither the cheek,
It's the autumn wind of longing's lot.
There was no wheat that wouldn't be winnowed
By this when it was stirred by bitterness.
Sorrowful is my office for a year;
Except Morfudd, no girl will comfort me.

110. *Indifference*

In the same way (it was vanity,
The chill of pain) am I loving
As the fool chasing his shadow
On pathways through green-dressed woods.
A young man's speech will be too proud;
Though he be swifter than the wind or the hawk,
An angry nature, he'll come no nearer
(This was an old judgment) to it in an afternoon
(Drunken of mind, brave and proper,
Brief the praise for him) than in the gray morning.   10
His shadow, which is silent,
Won't go from his side, suspecting him.

Of the same manners (disobedient about the tryst)
Am I as he, mine is the onset of grief;

I too am (I was a slim lad;
By Mary, this one has great magic)
Wasting weak and thin
From love for the slender, simple girl.
It presses my gray, wrinkled cheek;
Tonight no nearer (a lively target for weakness)   20
Winning the tall, slender girl's affection
Than on the first day of the long summer,
No more than the fool after the snow
Out of his sleep to catch his own shadow.

    She made me impatient,
Unlucky for me how chaste she is.
The attitude of the slim, tall girl doesn't change,
Nor her smile, for a lie or the truth,
Noble in manner, she's gentle and good,
Any more than a statue, she of the color of fine snow.   30
My maiden won't accept me,
My slim beloved won't reject me.
The slender, gentle girl won't stop me loving her,
The throng's jewel won't kill me at once.
But if the girl of decorous speech
(Image of a Tegau) sees me grieving,
I shall have, despite hiding passion,
A kiss the hour I seek it,
And cool laughter, she whose face is like fair weather,
An easy smile I'd have from this one.   40
I don't know which (slender, tall girl)
This is (white in color, indeed),
Whether mockery (it was soon got)
Because of true hurt, or great loving.

    She of the conversation of a Tegau, I'm raging,
Little good for me, sinless passion,
To endure a long illness, girl of excellent feature,
A goddess, and to die in the end.

III. *The Spear*

According to some manuscripts and some modern scholars, this is the *cywydd* that led Gruffudd Gryg to denounce Dafydd's poetry of love pangs (see Eurys Rowlands's review of the second edition of *GDG, LlC* 8, 1–2, 110). The eight poems of Dafydd's debate with Gruffudd Gryg appear below, Poems 147–54.

I saw the girl under the smooth, bright gold,
The color of a crossing's lively foam,
Excellent from one end to the other,
A fine maiden of twice the brightness of day,
Listening to the psalm of Noah's Ark
In Deinioel's choir at Bangor yesterday.
Beauty enough for the world,
Twofold ache (of Fflur's beauty) and a great betrayal,
To see the girl good, lovely, and fair,
What a gift! Profound anguish is mine.   10

   With a spear seven-edged she shot me,
And seven poems of angry eloquence.
A poisoned edge, I know I'm weakened,
It was the wish of the jealous ones of the land of Môn.
No man under the constellations' sky shall draw it out,
Within the heart it is.
A blacksmith did not hammer it,
A hand did not produce its sharpness.
Not known is either the color (good grade of song)
Or the shape of the sharp weapon that kills me.   20
Because of my worthy passion that suits me,
I went mad for Gwynedd's Candle.
Woe is me! She long caused me pain.
Blessed am I! She's like the fine color of Mary!
Tough within me is a sword of eighteen wounds,
A sober servant that wrinkles the cheek.
It hurts sorely, it ought to be paid with poison,
Whetted spear, a skewer of care.
She of Esyllt's beauty places it with anger,
A stake for the broken breastbone.   30

It's burdensome to keep it long within me,
The needle of my worn, broken breast.
The pain-producing awl of love,
Betrayal's foster brother is like a three-edged arrow.

112. *The Greeting*

Greet, do not greet, messenger,
I don't know who, the wife of a prosperous young lord,
Ask the girl I've greeted,
I don't know what to ward off an oppressive tax,
To come tomorrow morning,
I'm stupid, and I don't know where.
I'll come too, remembrance of an unbending anger,
I don't know what time in the world ever.
If she of the liberal name asks
(A suitor's agony) who made the greeting,   10
You say, going silent,
I'm changeable, "This I don't know."
If you see the girl with the beautiful eye —
Should you not see her, not a bad likeness
Is the sun's lovely, bright face at the clear hour of prime —
On your oath, don't say a thing.

113. *Sending for a Nun*

Finish with anger, busy love-messenger,
For May's sake, take a journey away to the March.
You left, you fled, by God,
I need you.
Gentle with questions, perfect in course,
You once performed well where you know.

You brought me a girl with one word,
Make me see Mary's daughters!
Of choice form, go to proud
Llanllugan where some white ones are.   10

Seek in the church and salute
The great jailer, a girl's watcher.
Say, busy assertion of minstrels,
This is the psalm, this to the jailer.
And cry how great is my complaint.
And seek nuns for me.
Saints from everywhere forbid me
The lady saints of the lovely dormitories,
Of the sprightliness of white snow on the edge
                              of gossamer,
Swallows, choir nuns,   20
All god-sisters
Of Morfudd, gentle gold-girl.

Your two feet are good equipment,
Bring a fair girl from the choir to the wood,
One who knows how, ours is the building,
And the black nun to the grove of leaves.
If I shall have, to fend off care,
From the refectory a shining, tall girl,
O friend of sixty other lovers,
Fetch the bell-ringer from the choir.   30
If that one, despite the rendering of praise
(Of the lively color of snow) doesn't come for you,
Try a snare on the abbess,
Before the summer moon, of the fine color of sunshine.

114. *The Skylark*

For brave hours the skylark
Goes up from his house each day,
The world's early riser, a boiling of gold song,
Towards the sky, April's gatekeeper.

A cry full of grace, master of rhymes,
Sweet path, handsome work is yours:
Song-making above a hazel grove,
The gentle sport of gray wings.
You have a mind, fond function,

And the top of language, to preach.   10
A strong song from the well of faith,
Deep privileges before God.
Up you go, of Cai's rightful passion,
And above you sing all songs;
A bright charm near the stars' enclosure,
A long progress of the heights.
Sufficient portion, high enough
You climbed, you have won favor.

Let every fortunate creature praise
His Creator, the radiant and pure ruler.   20
To praise God as He commands,
A thousand hear it, it's cherished, do not cease.
Image of the author of love, where are you?
Tender and fresh the voice in the brown-gray cloth.
Pure and consoling melody is yours,
Brown warbler-poet.
Cantor of God's chapel,
It will be a fair omen, skillful are you.
One of full privilege, with many an adroit song,
He of the wide cap is gray-crested.   30
Approach the familiar sky,
Singer, the land of a goose's heaven.

A man shall discover you above
Surely when day is longest.
When you come to worship,
God One and Three has given you a gift,
It's not a treetop above the world
That supports you, you have language,
But the graces of the just Father
And His many miracles and His design.   40

A teacher of praise between dawn and dusk,
Descend, God's blessing on your wings.
My handsome gray bird, if you will go,
And my privileged brother, as a love-messenger,
Take with you a greeting for the face of
                              excellent beauty

(Brilliant is her favor) of the moon of Gwynedd.
And ask one of her kisses,
To bring here to me, or two.
Admiral of the difficult sky-sea,
Go there as far as near her hall.   50
May I always be with her, and it shall be
(Eiddig's rage) one morning.

    On you there's such a fine for bitter killing
That none dares kill you.
If he should try it, bold commotion,
Terror for Eiddig, but you'll live.
A great perch for you is the sky,
Bow in hand, how distant you are.
A well-trodden pass, sad is the bowman,
He'll be clumsy in his grand scheme;   60
Heavy his wrath, turn above him,
While he goes by with his hawk.

115. *The Woodcock (II)*

Dafydd: "You tumultuous bird,
Importunate woodcock of angry style,
Say, bird of noble wing,
Where is your course? You're favored and elegant."

Woodcock: "Fast and furiously it's freezing,
I'm in flight, by my faith,
In haste from where I spent the summer,
To a shelter against winter snow.
Some bitter memory, the frost of black winter
And its snowdrift will not let me lurk."   10

Dafydd: "Bird, long life will not be granted you,
Handsome bird of long beak.
Come, don't say two words,
To where there's one I love, of Mary's color,
A rather lively place beside a slope,

A place of bright sunshine, where a song is heard,
To avoid the breeze of winter,
Through prolonged grace, to await summer.

"If there turns round you, proud of language,
A roamer, O most persistent whistler,   20
With a thick-headed bolt and a bow,
And sees you, the man, in your good lair,
Don't hide because of his voice, don't shut
Your eye under your bright crown.
Fly, hurry for fear of treachery,
And trick him in your spry, good way,
From hedge to hedge, great bother,
From grove to wilderness grove.
Neat of movement, if your foot sticks
In a snare at the edge of small trees,   30
Do not submit, you of restless leap,
To a round loop, a shriveled, bent snare.
Cut off bravely from about your talon
With your strong beak the withered, wrathful strands;
Sad of beak, he loves an old forest,
The piercer of earth's gaps.

"Descend today beside a wooded slope
Below the girl's house, her hair is beautiful,
And know, by Cybi's statue,
By the slope, whether she's faithful.   40
Observe her turning, watch and stay
There, O lonely bird."

Woodcock: "There'd be more need to warn you,
You witty, handsome boy, be quiet!
Too late (my fear is the freezing wind)
Will she be watched, shameful is the course.
It's strange how long she was growing cold;
Another, lively and shrewd, has taken her."

Dafydd: "If it's true, bird, my passion flies
In the track of love, I'm careless,   50
Then it's true what some sang (a warrant of true grace)

Once of such an affliction:
'A tree in the wood' — great longing is mine —
'Another with an axe possesses it.' "

116. *The Stag*

You, roebuck of fleeing haunch,
The flow of a cloud, with gray-white trousers,
Take this severe, polished letter,
For God of heaven, on your bare rump.
You're the swiftest leaping armful,
Messenger of a handsome poet.
By God, roebuck, there's need to ask
Some love-messenger work of you.

    With a heather lair above the white rock,
He of the very wild head grazes meadow-grass.   10
Excellent and noble petitioner,
Hillside-leaper, sharp is his antler.
Like a naked lamb, leap
To the slope, fair of head and nostril.
My rare lad, you won't be betrayed,
Dogs won't slay you, tall, handsome baron.
Target of a feat of praise, don't let a greyhound
Catch up with you after sunlight.
Do not fear a sharpened arrow,
Nor a dog after, if you can get a leap.   20
Stay away from Pali, red-legged hound,
And Iolydd, a skillful, red hound,
The hounds' cry is going to be heeded,
If they come after you to Tywyn-land.
Hide so you won't be seen,
Run over the hill to a bracken patch.
Jump below an old opening
On out to the field and stay no more.

    You're my love-messenger of generous heart
And my poet to beautiful, generous Dyddgu.   30

Make, fine of gait,
This journey to her father's house.
Go, in spite of the outrage of the champion of
                                    obstruction,
Comprehend the essence of Ovid's way.
Come at night beside the streams
Under the forest's top and its trees
With a kiss for me, the straight girl won't
                                    disappoint me,
From Dyddgu of the color of white feathers well-folded.
Go there, remarkable roebuck;
I would love, I would choose to be there.   40
No hand will flay you; be healthy and glad;
Your undercoat won't go on an old Englishman,
Nor your horns, my friend, nor your hooves,
Nor your flesh shall false Eiddig have.

     God keep you, the wise savior,
And the arm of Cynfelyn, from betrayal.
I too will bless you, if I may be atop
One of the beauty of rose-hip.

117. *The Wind*

Sky-wind of adroit course
That goes there with mighty uproar,
You're a prodigious warrior, rough of sound,
Rash one of the world, without foot, without wing.
It's strange how terribly you were put
From the sky's pantry without one foot
And how swiftly you run
Now over the slope above.
There's no need for a swift horse under you,
Nor bridge on an estuary, nor boat.   10
You will not drown, you were alerted,
You won't get stuck, you lack corners.
Of stealing nests, though you winnow leaves,
No one will accuse you; there will not arrest you

Either a swift host or the hand of a sergeant
Or a blue blade or flood or rain.
Neither officer nor retinue will catch you
In your day, winnower of treetop plumes.
No mother's son will slay you, false report,
No fire burn you, no deception weaken you.   20
No glance will see you, bare, enormous lair,
A thousand will hear you, great rain's nest;
Cloud-notary swift in nature,
Fine leaper over nine wilderness-lands.

    God's blessing are you along the earth,
Roar of the grievous breaking of the oak-top.
Dry-tempered, potent creature,
Trampler of cloud, massive in sojourning.
Shooter of empty, noisy heather-husks
On the snow regions above.   30
Tell me, faithful bead,
Your course, north-wind of the glen,
Wild tempest on the sea,
Sportive boy on the seashore.
Fluent author, you're a wizard.
Sower, you're a leaf-chaser.
Hurler, privileged laugher on the hill,
Of the white-breasted, wild-masted sea.

    You fly the lengths of the world,
Weather of the hillcrest, tonight be aloft,   40
Ah, man, and go to Uwch Aeron,
Bright and handsome, clear of tone.
Do not linger, do not spare,
Do not fear despite Y Bwa Bach
Of accusing complaint, serving poison;
Closed is the land and its fostering to me.
Woe for me, when I set pensive love
On Morfudd, my golden girl;
A girl has made me exiled.
Race aloft between where you are and the house
               of her father.   50

Knock at the door, make it open
Before daybreak to my messenger,
And seek a way to her, if it's to be had,
And grieve the voice of my sigh.
You come from the pure constellations,
Say this to my generous truelove:
"As long as I am in the world,
A faithful plaything am I."
Alas for my face without her,
If it be true she's not unfaithful.   60
Go up, you'll see a girl,
Go down, choice one of the sky.
Go to a pale, blonde girl;
Come back in health, you're the sky's bounty.

118. *The Seagull*

Surely, fair gull on the tide,
Of the same color as snow or the white moon,
Your beauty is unspotted,
A fragment like sun, gauntlet of the salt sea.
Light you are on the ocean wave,
Swift, proud, fish-eating bird.
There you'd go at anchor,
Hand in hand with me, sea lily.
Fashioned like writing paper shining in nature,
A nun atop the sea-tide are you.   10

With well-made praise for a girl, you shall
                         have praise afar,
Seek the bend of a fort and castle.
Look, seagull, whether you may see
A girl of Eigr's color on the fine fort.
Say my harmonious words.
Let her choose me, go to the girl.
She'd be by herself, dare to greet her.
Be adroit with the polished girl
For profit; say that I won't
(A refined, gentle lad) live unless I have her.   20

I love her, full assurance of joy,
Alas, men, never loved
Healthy Myrddin of flattery's lip
Or Taliesin a prettier girl!
The face of a sought-for girl under copper,
Supreme beauty very perfect and right.

    Alas, gull, if you get to see
The cheek of the loveliest girl in Christendom,
Unless I have the tenderest greeting,
The girl will be my death.   30

119. *Invitation to Dyddgu*

Shining girl of gifted nature,
Dyddgu with the black, smooth hair,
Inviting you (the melancholy hospitality of hidden
                              passion)
To Manafan meadow am I.

    No meagre invitation suits you,
It won't be a glutton's invitation to a hut.
Not the spread of a reaper's pay,
Not of corn, green, bright mixed corn,
Not part of a farmer's dinner.
Not like a Shrove Tuesday meat-bound,   10
Not an Englishman's visit with his friend,
Not the feast of a villein's son's weapon of beard.

    I don't promise, a good conclusion,
My gold one anything but a nightingale and mead;
A gray-backed nightingale of light cry
And a stout thrush of cheerful language.
A frowning thicket and a room
Of fresh birches, was there a better house?
While we're out under the leaves,
Our fine, strong birches will sustain us.   20
A loft for the birds to play,
A gentle grove, there's the way it is.

Nine trees of beautiful countenance
Are there of trees altogether;
Below, a round circle;
Above, a blue belfry.
Under them, a desirable home,
Fresh clover, heaven's manna.

A place for two, crowds worry them,
Or three for the space of the hour.   30
Where roebucks resort, the breed raised on oats,
Where a bird sings, it's a refined place.
Where blackbirds' lodgings are thick,
Where trees are bright, where hawks are nursed,
A place of new, good wood-building.
A place of frequent passion, a place of heaven here.
Place of a verdant palace, a place modest of frown,
A place near water, a cool, smokeless place.
A place where (a wild land)
A flour-beggar or a long-legged cheese-beggar is
                              not known.   40

There tonight, color of wave,
Go we two, my lovely girl.
Go if we go, pale, glad face,
My girl of eye of bright ember.

120. *A Girl and a Bird*

A lover's choicest desire,
Lord God, will there come together before very long,
If the strong praise be ready,
A pretty girl and a singing bird?
Despite learning to wait, there was not
For a loving, modest lad in gray-blue
A craft so pleasing, from the flood of my passion,
As waiting for a beloved girl
And spending a long time roaming
The depths of the growing branches of trees,   10

Like a master of hounds, a swift sportsman,
Who'd pursue a wild young beast
From one place to another, out of passion,
From grove to grove (another Enid)
And a little bird that preserves sanity for us
Praising her from beside a cloud.

Of clear voice, the fine, wild love-messenger
Golden-beaked on a branch
Would call the one like Esyllt,
On his faith, seeing the girl.   20
Pleasing, if flowing tears would permit it,
Would it be to hear out loud
The great joy of the bird of May
Under the perfect girl's fresh birch.
A brilliant knight of gifted melody,
Noble and golden on green leaves,
He'd sing a lively song
Hour by hour, great pain that it was.
He would not go (handsome lad of sweet cry,
The silver-voiced bird) from that same grove   30
(A pensive, genial, loud song)
More than a hermit (slender-branched).

It would be well-fitting in gentle birch-houses
If the bird were to come to the leafy grove,
Dwarf birches of snug bark,
A green, lovely, friendly cage.
Handsome birch, with a roof of hair the same age,
A lofty tower on the brow of the hill.
Growth without hewing by adze,
A house, it grows on one pillar.   40
A green bunch of enchanted throngs in an embrace
                              of leaves,
Whisks standing on stubble.
Dark fur, May's trimmed favorite,
A thick, green roof, God's grace be on it.

It would be a pleasing craft, by the relic,
To kiss the even-spoken girl,

And after our fine expenditure,
To gaze between us (little knots of sun)
Through the mantle of my perfect woman
At her breasts (passionate coins)   50
And to soothe today the look
Of an eye colored blue and drowsy
(The blaze of a jewel of brilliant renown)
Upon the girl who acted falsely.

121. *The Leaf-House*

Handsome poets, welcome my excellent gold-girl,
Joy of a fine land,
The goodlooking sweetheart who used to welcome me
In birches and hazels, the mantles of May,
Bright, stalwart, and proud above the end of the slope,
A good place for liking a woman's color;
Right furnishings of the wild fort,
A room is better if it grows.

       If the slender, gentle girl I love comes
To the leaf-house that God the Father made,   10
The fine trees will be a consolation,
A house free from soot today.
There's not too much work under the roof,
Not worse is the architecture of the holy God.
My friend and I have the same speech,
There in the woods may we
Hear the speech of birds,
Minstrels of the woods, a bright lady loves them;
Cywyddau (weavings of branches)
Of the chick-proprietors of the leaves;   20
A race with no bitter legend,
Chick-musicians of the fort of oaks.
Dewi will boldly endow it,
The hands of May will construct it,
And his tape is the cheerful cuckoo,
And his square is the nightingale of the trees,

And his house-timber is a long day of summer,
And his laths are the distress of the fine invalid;
And the altar of love is the grove,
Wisely, and I am his axe.   30

　　I shall not at the start of the year
Get the house for longer than this one.
It is far from my mind to give bribes
To a hag from an old, enclosed corner;
I won't try (I'll declare an injury)
By a building that I rejected.

122. *Mass of the Grove*

　　I was in a pleasant place today,
Under mantles of the fine, green hazel trees,
Listening at the start of day
To the skillful cock-thrush
Singing a polished *englyn,*
Bright prophecies and lessons.

　　A traveller from afar, judicious of nature,
Long was the journey of the gray love-messenger.
He came here from the fine county of Caer,
Because my golden girl commanded him.   10
Wordy, without one password,
There he heads, to the valley of Nentyrch.
Morfudd had sent it,
The metrical song of May's foster son.
About him there was an alb
Of flowers of the sweet boughs of May,
And his chasuble (they resembled green mantles)
Was of wings of wind.

　　By the great God, there was nothing there
But all gold as the altar's roof.   20
I heard in shining language
A long chanting, unfailing,

Reading to the parish, no excess of agitation,
The Gospel distinctly.
He raised there on a height of ash trees
A mass-wafer of a good leaf.
And a nightingale, fine, slim, eloquent,
From the corner of the grove beside him,
The valley's poetess, rang for a hundred
A sanctus bell, swift was her whistle.   30
And the elevation of the Host
To the heaven above the thicket;
And devotion to our Lord Father,
And a chalice of passion and love.
I'm content with the music,
A birch-grove in the gentle woods fostered it.

123. *The Cock-Thrush (II)*

Every May (when trysting is perfect) there is
On the tips of the branches of the wood
A brave singer on a glassy fort of hazels,
Active under green wings:
A handsome cock-thrush sings
(A gift in lieu of an organ) by law.

A long preacher in all tongues,
A prince of the forest he was;
He's a sheriff in the birchwood of May;
He'd sing in seven score tongues.   10
A decent magistrate at the end of twigs,
Steward of the involved leaf-court;
A teacher long my associate,
Linguist atop the plane tree mansion;
An honest servant on the green crest above,
A companion in the woods for me;
He's a singer of the best sort of song,
Who combines intelligence and instinct.

What is more, Christendom's Creirwy,

To go for the girl and me,   20
Confidently and proudly he flew
With beautiful sorcery;
From clearing to clearing through love,
From grove to grove for a girl's sake,
He learned the greeting and descended
Where the girl was, she was gentle.

    He spoke well my message,
He's faithful, a chief manager of profit.
He showed, foster brother of a hundred,
The truth in his letter of warranty.   30
He read a speech in meter,
Fine, lovely poetry from his house of blue glass.
He summoned me at legal length,
By roll, at summer's beginning.
I paid as forfeit (I did not desire bitterness)
A substantial tribute, a fine for contempt.
Although I know I might lose (a consequence of profit)
Fines under green trees,
A girl's love for me will not fail,
Beautiful energies, nor my complaint to her.   40
If the messenger is wisely eloquent,
He will attempt to betray her.

    O you of hidden thought, may God make
For me and handsome Dewi
A generous condition, my very cunning girl,
Regarding the messenger, sophisticated champion,
To let him stay with his beautiful cry,
A love poet from Paradise,
A magistrate, bright support of May,
Of good, wise name; there he belonged.   50

124. *Trouble in a Tavern*

I came to a choice city,
With my handsome squire after me.
Fine, lively spending, a place of abundant complaint,
I took, I was proud from my youth,
A respectable enough common lodging,
And I'd have wine.

I saw a slender, beautiful maiden
In the house, my lovely soul.
I cast my mind entirely (color of the rising sun)
On my slim beatitude.   10
I bought a roast, not for boasting,
And costly wine, for me and the girl there.
Young men like to play —
I called the girl (a shy one) to the bench.
I whispered (I was a bold, insistent man,
This is sure) two words of magic;
I made (love was not idle)
An agreement to come to the spirited girl
When the company would go
To sleep; she was a girl of black eyebrow.   20

After they slept, sad was the expedition,
Everyone but me and the girl,
I tried expertly to gain
The girl's bed; there was a surfeit.
I got, when I made a sound there,
A bad fall, there were no good successes;
It was easier to rise (rash sin)
Clumsily than very quickly.
I hit (I didn't leap healthfully)
The shin (and alas for the leg)   30
Against the side (some ostler's work)
Of a loud, stupid stool, above the ankle.
I got (it was a tale of repentance)
Up (Welshmen will love me);
I hit (too much desire is evil)

Where I was set without one easy step
(Frequent deception of a foolish effort)
My forehead on the edge of the table,
Where there was a bowl for some time loose
And a talking brass pan.   40
They fell from the table (very stout arrangement)
And the two trestles, and all the furnishings;
The pan gave a cry
After me, it was heard far off;
The bowl shouted (I was too vain a man),
And the dogs barked at me.

There were beside thick walls
Three Englishmen in a stinking bed,
Troubled about their three packs—
Hickin and Jenkin and Jack.   50
The slave with a mouth of dregs whispered,
An angry speech, to the two:

"There's a Welshman, the constant stir of trickery,
Roaming too slyly here;
He's a thief, if we allow,
Watch out, keep guard against this one."

The ostler roused up all the crowd,
And it was a monstrous story.
Scowling were they around me,
Searching round me to find me;   60
And I, ugly, unsightly pains,
Keeping silent in the dark.
I prayed, no bold face,
Secretly, like one in fear;
And by the power of true, loving prayer
And by the grace of the faithful Jesus,
I gained, a tangle of sleeplessness,
Without wage, my own old bed.
I escaped, good the saints nearby;
I pray to God for pardon.   70

125. *The Rattle Bag*

The rattle bag — stones in a pouch of dried animal's skin, attached to a
stick — was used by herdsmen in medieval Wales to frighten animals.

As I was (most fluent praise)
One day in summer
Under trees between a mountain and an open field
Waiting for my soft-spoken girl,
She came (denial's not worse)
Where she promised, a faithful moon.
We sat together, a fine subject
(Suspicious kind of thing), the girl and I,
Exchanging, before the claim's worn out,
Words with the excellent girl.   10

    As we were thus (she was shy)
Understanding each other's love,
Hiding fault, taking mead,
For an hour's space lying together,
There came (weakness bare of breeding)
With a cry (some filthy trouble)
The coarse, bursting, shrill sound of the bottom of a sack
Of a dwarf in the guise of a shepherd;
And with him, public and hateful, there was
An offensive, worn-cheeked, harsh-horned rattle bag.   20
He sounded (the sallow-bellied visitor)
The rattle bag; woe to the scabby leg!
And then before satisfaction
The fine girl got frightened; woe is me!
When she heard (wounded heart failing)
The sifting of the stones, she'd stay no longer.

    Under Christ, no sound in Christendom
(Of a hundred foul names) was so harsh.
A pouch at a stick's end resounding,
A ringing bell of round stones and gravel.   30
A *crowd* of English stones making
A trembling sound in a bullock's skin.

A cage of three thousand beetles,
A cauldron in tumult, a black scrotum.
The keeper of a meadow, as old as grass,
Dark-skinned, pregnant with splinters,
Whose accent is hateful to an old roebuck,
Devil's bell, with a stake in its haunch;
A scarred, scabby, stone-bearing gravel-womb,
May it become buckle-thongs!   40
Curse the misshapen churl,
Amen, who frightened my girl.

126. *The Goose Shed*

As I once at night
(The girl was good, alas for me because of the journey)
Had come as an end to wandering
To where the prudent, polished girl was:

She: "Have you long been by yourself?
You're a long-suffering lover."

Dafydd: "My gold one, you know that it's too long;
How could it not be long?"

    Lo, I heard a very brave man
Take a stag's leap, eyes of a lion,   10
Making an impetuous attack to pursue me
Cruelly and full of wrath,
From anger because of his brilliant wife,
A valiant, strong one, by God and the relic!
I was conscious of fleeing from him,
The gray lad was conscious of a nightmare.

She: "You're slow to get a steel spur.
Tonight wait for me myself.
Poor weapons to suffice
Are those *cywyddau* of yours."   20

I fled to a room, a closed cell,
And it was furnished for the geese.
From my chamber I said this,
"There's been no better refuge against care."
There arose an old mother goose of dented nose,
And her feathers were a shelter for her children.
She loosened her cloak around me,
A vindictive mother was she.
And the persistent, gray goose attacked me
And devastated me and cast me under her.   30
Kinswoman (badly was I corrected)
Of a dear heron, with a wide, gray paw.

My sister said to me the next day
(A slim, tall, pretty girl of wise, gentle speech)
Seven times more sorry was she than about our plight,
The two of us, or about the husband's words,
To see the old mother goose with year-old feathers
And silly, bent neck beating me.
If the governemt
Of the men of Chester and their strict customs permitted it,   40
I would do to the mother goose (an occasion of offense,
Let those who dare it warn her)
Some dishonor to her nine year-old body;
For her humor the goose will weep.

127. *The Peat Pit*

Alas for the poet (even if he might be blamed)
Who's full of worry being lost.
Dark is the night on the rough moor.
Dark, oh for a torch!
Dark over there, no good will come to me,
Dark (madness is mine) here.
Dark below, mine is a treacherous land,
It's dark in the moon's direction.

Woe is me that she, of completely good lineage,

Well-shaped, how dark it is,   10
Does not know that I am (all her praise is mine)
In thick darkness out of doors.
These regions are trackless;
I know well that I wouldn't, even by day,
Be able to give directions
Either to a town, or here, or there,
Much less, the crueller the comfort,
Now that it's night, without light or stars.
It's not wise for a poet from another land,
Nor is it good against wrong or treachery,   20
If I'm found in the same country as my enemy
Who confines me, I and my dark, gray horse.
It would be no wiser, more difficult there,
For us to be found, fleeing,
In a peat pool after tender courtesy,
Drowned, my horse and I.
A danger on a moor is a depth nearby;
Who can do anything more in a peat pit?

     It's a fishpond for Gwyn ap Nudd,
Woe to us that we suffer it!   30
A pit between heath and ravine,
The place of fiends and their children.
The water I'd not drink willingly,
It is their privilege and their bath.
Lake of bitter wine, an auburn flow,
Refuge where pigs washed themselves.
I entirely fouled my socks
Of kersey from Chester in the hollow bog.
A surge where there's no freedom for a net,
Stagnant water, I was not honored in it.   40
I don't know why, but for dishonor,
I should go with my horse to the peat pit!

     A curse on the boor (he didn't triumph)
Who dug it; it was at a great heat.
I'll be slow to give, if I reach land,
My blessing on the peat-land.

128. *Insulting his Servant*

On the Feast of St. Peter, I was looking
In Rhosyr, a place of many fine men,
At the clothing of people with gold treasure,
And at Môn's throng beside the sea.
There was there (she is Gwynedd's sun,
In pomp of fire, of Enid's sort)
A girl delicate, round of neck, pale, and wise,
And she was superior and good and well-bred;
And my lovely, elegant girl was of the same form
At the fair as Mary's living image;   10
And the world, because of her fine, pale face,
After her, her color like snow;
It was a marvel for the crowds,
A gift from heaven, the sort of woman she was.
I too, from my wound and my sleeplessness,
Always watching to get the sweetheart.
There was no lad who was more wanton
In his frank intention and small discretion.
Facing the lovely armful
At a distance I would indeed be   20
Until she went (of profound gentility)
To the bright, clearly-lit stone gallery.

　　　Twenty turned about in my direction
Of my fellow carousers around me.
Costly for the nobleman who desires it,
I tasted the wine, a fine chief-steward,
Bought (the work was not satisfying)
On the spur two full gallons.

Dafydd: "Go, boy, from my bright sphere,
Take this to the fair girl of a moment ago.   30
Run to her ear and whisper
To her royal form and swear
That she's the girl in Gwynedd
I love the most, by the Man Who rules.

"Go to her chamber;
Say, 'Hail, fine girl!
Of keen, right breed, here's a gift
For you, my dear, fair girl.' "

She: "Is not the city public?
Why did we not know you, boy?   40
Very foolish is it, a rude thought,
If it be so, to ask who gave it."

Servant: "Dafydd, a poet of fine love,
A dark, gray man, and I am his love-messenger.
His praise has gone forth in Gwynedd;
Hear it; it's like the sound of a bell."

She: "Get up, by the Five Wounds!
And beat him! Where are all of you?"

    She took the bright wine from the city
And poured it on my servant's hair!   50
A dishonor was that to me;
Mary's curse on my bold, high-hearted treasure.
If she deliberately disgraced me
There, an experience of anguish,
Azure and caddis her cloak,
May her foolish lip lack wine!
If I knew it, firm beam,
Madog Hir would have her, my darling.
Reluctantly would Einion Dot, a coarse, bold host,
Make her one of an alehouse.   60

    She shall see (beauty of a lively seagull)
Her ear wholly with her eye
Now when I ever send
To the girl out of sorts with love
A spoonful of lukewarm water
As a gift, whether she's pretty or plain.

129. *Dawn*

I groaned aloud,
Night before last it was a long night;
Night before last, shy, bright, pretty girl,
One night was a week, my darling;
But a short night, says the critic,
Does the fair girl cause without one word of denial:

    Last night I was in a fierce mood
(A fine Nyf) with heaven's candle,
Insisting on pay for sleeplessness,
Great was my respect beside a sweetheart.   10
When my grasp was strongest,
And my state best, dark her eyebrow,
A sheet above, restless appetite,
By the true God, lo, daybreak.

She: "Get up," said the pretty girl with the shining veil,
"Hide this. There's the quick signal.
Forlorn tear of your kinsfolk,
Go to the devil; do you see the day below?"

Dafydd: "Tall maiden, good, stately, slim, pure,
This is not true; it's better: 20
The moon that the Lord God gave
And stars that are around her:
This, if I give a positive name,
Is what's thought to be dawn."

She: "A fine speech; if that's true,
Why is the crow singing above?"

Dafydd: "Insects are trying
(They disturb her sleep) to kill her."

She: "Dogs are crying in the town there,
And others are hitting back."   30

Dafydd: "Believe my denial exactly,
It's a disturbance dogs make at night."

She: "Stop your excuse, servant of song;
A shallow mind says pain is far off,
While taking a journey, like booty,
Of danger in your day; it's forenoon.
For Christ's sake, get up quietly,
And open the heavy door over there.
Very heavy are the steps of the two feet,
The dogs are very eager; run to the woods."   40

Dafydd: "Alas! the grove isn't far,
And I'm quicker than a dog.
Unless a knowing one sees me, I won't be caught,
If God grants, on this ground."

She: "Tell me, good, busy poet,
For God's sake, if you'll come here."

Dafydd: "I shall come, I'm your nightingale,
Surely, my girl, if night comes."

130. *The Echo Stone*

Few fierce stones
Have the same practice (cold-boiling witch)
As this hollow, blubber-lipped stone,
A bitch of clumsy labors.
It says more without stopping,
On the brow of the glen after rain,
Than loud Myrddin fab Saith Gudyn,
Great in wrath, the sorrowful man.

    It's close to me and defrauding me,
While hunting around it   10
And waiting for a girl below the field,
Under a generous, trailing wood-grove.
She seeking me for our feast;
I, too, seeking a well-loved gem,
Like the two horned oxen, old and bold,
"What is it that you want?"

Each calls to the other;
Getting together, it's a good world,
The girl and I, hope is mine,
In the shadow of the sad stone of the crag.   20

    Wise buffoon, however low
We might talk, a powerful pledge,
Answer and retort
In its language would it also make, hollowly.
The girl lost color, slender, golden image,
Took fright because of its cry,
Deceitful and loose, flees then,
And what girl would not do well to flee?
Stark destruction, surely, twice-doubled,
On the windpipe of the hoarse crag-ravine!   30
Heap that bleats like a bugler,
Bare cairn like a great hewn fort.
There's either a fiend in it,
Old, unsightly cupboard,
Or dogs in the hollow rock
Of the sound of chattering or noise of basins.
Cry of a nightmare killing a poor old goose;
Wail of a strong bitch under a crooked chest.
A loud witch shouting hoarsely
From the stone to provoke fear.   40
A noted lady of wrath, rather forbidding,
She hindered me where the girl was.
Prevented an invitation to a lad—
Curse her for hindering him!

131. *Yesterday*

A sinless day was the day before yesterday,
God was good to Dafydd yesterday.
Not of the same kind (gift's law) was
The day before yesterday as beautiful yesterday.
It's bad that (too naked a kind of target)
The day before yesterday is a brother to wise yesterday.

O great, fair, excellent Mary of the day before yesterday,
Will there be such a day as yesterday?
O splendid God of chaste law,
Will there come to me a yesterday in my lifetime?   10
I give (better than the day before yesterday)
A hundred greetings to yesterday!

    Yesterday old Dafydd (the pain of hidden love)
Was avenged with new love.
After my wound (I am blind)
I'm tough like a withe from an apple tree
That bends easily (affliction's touch)
And will not break after a strong blow.
There is in me (faint memory of a smile)
The soul of a shivery old cat;   20
Let the wood-gray body be wounded, beaten,
Whatever be at it, it will live.
A slow walker am I, wise in love's affliction,
Along an acre where another runs,
And a master upon the bright girl of graceful accomplishment,
Despite pain, where the game is best.

    Better far (a fine proverb of flooding love)
Is discretion than gold (I am a wayfarer).
O God, is indiscretion strength for me?
And do they know what is discretion?   30
Better is labor (a swimmer of love)
Than malice (I'm brave).
Morfudd would be good to her man
At last, the color of snow's radiance.
I did right to praise her;
If it was not right, my soul to the devil!
Good-evening to the girl of bright greeting,
And good-day because she was not in earnest.
She whom I almost subdued
Is aha! the wife of Y Bwa Bach.   40

132. *Carousing*

I paid for drink like one who pays with the lip,
Paying steadily, a golden out-pouring.
I paid easily and cheerfully,
Strong payment, by the light of Christ.
Payment (no small, sour drink)
For costly wine for my golden-haired woman.
Excellently was I able (I merited peace;
A good work, generous, long, and natural,
Decent, well-taught love) to give a fitting crop
Of the vines of France for one of the white look
                of a stream.   10

    If we were on Easter Day in Gascony
(It shall be soon), the sweet girl and I,
It would be fine if our drink
(For one bright of body) were of claret for us.
According to the judgment of the taverner
(Long does he love me and will be slow to hate me),
The fourth good day of verse
Was today, at my invitation.
I said then, a false reproach,
"A pity it was not a third of a day."   20
My two marks will cause a woman to drink,
A woman of complete gift.
For the sake of the fair girl, there was seen on
                top of the table
The pouring of wine mightily.
The circuit is long, the neighborhood a desert,
But confident is the beloved who drinks the wine.
Easily do I drink, most lavish expenditure,
Easily does he drink who sees his spirited girl.

133. *A Kiss*

Greetings (lively double-champion,
It would deserve praise) to today forever,
Excelling (holy journey)
Yesterday or the day before yesterday of feeble journey.
Not similar was (a French countenance)
Yesterday's consolation to that of today.
Not the same poetry (it's changeable)
Has today as yesterday (good, lively payment).
Yes, God the Father, will there come a day
As bright as today's spirited day?   10
Today I got a lively gift,
A challenge to yesterday, tardy is its gift.

    I got the value, it made me laugh,
Of a hundred shillings and a mark, a mantle for a lip,
The girl's kiss, I am constant,
Elegant Luned, a bright light.
A pretty and gentle New Year's gift,
Hear, by Mary, a lock on the lip.
It keeps within me the love of the prosperous girl,
A sign of great affliction, a knot upon love.   20
Memory comes within me to sustain it,
The great generosity of a girl's love.
The crown (for the mouth's rule)
Of Caerfyrddin about my lip.
A refined pax for the lip of earnest love,
A handsome knot between a slim poet and a girl.
No one will perceive its nature,
The meeting of two breaths, it's good.
I got, and what wealth,
The wise, fine girl's lip-treasure.   30
I'm strong from getting it as an eyebrow's target,
The treasure of a lip bright, kind, and deeply praised.
I'll cry its praise, rich discourse,
I trembled at the pure breath.
A love knot of double setting,
The encircling fort of the wholly excellent lip.

Although I got (a twin encounter without violence)
A crop of praise, this on my lip,
It's a treasure for me, of the three fragrances of honey,
Threefold woe for me if Tyrel shall get it,   40
And if he shall get also (a fragile beauty,
Always a wanton) the caresses of great repute.
It would be no less (I shall have her frown)
An evil than Luned's fist against me!

She sealed and gave order for
(I was simple) my praise for her.
No more will a word of praise come from my tongue
For a girl (it causes a surging of love)
Except what may come, awesome face of a gull,
On my faith, for fair Luned.   50
The beloved breath of love's pain,
O God, will there any more come in my life
Such a day, a fine sunshine day,
With my glad girl for me as today?

134. *Newborough*

Greetings, long of beautiful form,
Newborough town, home of true hope,
With her lovely, fair temple and her blue-gray towers
And her wine and her people and her warriors
And her beer and her mead and her love
And her generous women
And her wealth for free.

A snug corner is Rhosyr,
A field for men to play;
A bower for the country forestalling departure,
The town there is heaven's cousin.   10
A prosperous assembly of the sincere and the generous,
A habitation, Môn's burial-place for mead.
Of towns, the equal of heaven,
A castle and a mead-cell for me.

The pathways of our fame, a royal place,
A great host from everywhere praises it.
A fruitful place to sing for gain,
Where a woman is faithful, where wealth's to be had.
Where poets are fluent, where tables are free,
It's a place for me, on my oath!   20
The chief tower of praise, a free, lively circuit,
It is, under heaven, the chief town for giving.
An open pantry of the best,
A hearth, a sparkler for poets.
Money for feeding the Five Ages,
To me, far-reaching is their discretion and their morality.
An orchard of praise for the drinks,
The Cauldron of Rebirth of every generous lord.
The honor of every commoner in a city,
The headland of shining, fresh mead-drink.   30

135. *Stealing a Girl*

A thief in a graceless infatuation
Was I the other night, I wanted a girl;
Completely did the region's pretty one above compel me,
A girl's thief by stealth there.
A poet weak from infatuation with a fair girl,
Woe to the thief reckless because of his charmed sleep!
With regard to the way (better than wrought gold)
In which I had her, alas for anxiety!

After getting (poetry will lament it)
Wine and mead (a gentle, pale gem),   10
They were drunk, petty, jealous men
(Mine the excellent pain), boys and men.
They slept, after making a row,
Absurd people.
Scattered, wandering tumult, like a sullen crowd,
A great mob like a family of pigs.
Great was the proprietor's misfortune
(They were drunk) from this course.

The white-toothed girl was not drunk;
I'm not feeble; she drank no drink.   20
If I was drunk, I know what was had,
Drunk with love, say those who know it.
Although the quiet pair lowered
The lit candle of flaming wax,
A long story, a poet of bright lineage,
She of the color of lively foam would not sleep,
My girl, I too would not sleep,
However great was my drunkenness.
This is what I was thinking, to try to get her
Out of the evil bed to the branches yonder.   30
Though it be difficult (the husband's rough anger)
To get her away from her thin husband,
Of May's beauty, I stole her,
By Mary's living statue, I was valiant.
The men did not know that she,
The region's moon-beauty, was there;
If they knew, it would be no great thing,
For a fine woman once, to rip my head off.
If the girl went with the same purpose
To a carousal with them,   40
Her parents, unattractive people,
Would keep the girl from a tryst with her poet.
Long must we, nightingales of the night,
The long sleep of Maelgwn, wait for her.

136. *The Gray Friar's Advice*

Yesterday at Mass I heard
A golden *englyn* of an angel from heaven,
And the recital of serious subjects,
And a round construction, and Christ's *awdl.*

The disciple of Mary's Son taught me;
He spoke like this, easy praise:

"Dafydd, from a somewhat sober mind,

Of incomparable song, good expression,
Impose on the inspiration of your mouth
God's patronage, and do not speak what is false.   10
From the woods, unfortunate threefold longing,
Or leaves there's nothing but fickleness.
Stop being with girls,
Try for Mary's sake to hate mead.
Not worth a green bean would be treetops
Or a tavern, but the Lord's language."

Dafydd: "By the Man Who owns today,
There's a pang in my head because of the fine girl,
And in my forehead there's a wound of care;
For a golden girl I'm dying."   20

137. *The Poet and the Gray Friar*

Dafydd has been to confession, where he played accuser and self-apologist, not penitent. He is in love, he confessed, but his girl is killing him by not returning his love. The Friar's response is to advise continence and to denounce licentious poets; to that, Dafydd responds with a spirited defense of his profession.

Ah me, that the famous girl
With her court in the grove does not know
The conversation of the mouse-gray friar
About her today.

I went to the friar
To confess my sin;
I acknowledged to him, indeed,
That I was a kind of poet;
And that I had always loved
A girl of white face and black eyebrow;   10
And that from my murderer I have not had
Profit with regard to a lady or favor;
But have been loving her long and steadily,
And pining greatly from her love,

And carrying her praise throughout Wales,
And being without her in spite of that,
And longing to feel her
In my bed between me and the wall.

    The friar said to me then,
"I would give you good counsel,   20
If you've loved a face of foam,
Paper-pale, a long spell till now,
Ease the pain of the day to come;
It's profit for your soul to stop
And to be quiet with the *cywyddau*
And to use your beads.
It was not for a *cywydd* nor an *englyn*
That God purchased the soul of man.
There's nothing in your poetry, wandering minstrels,
But rigmarole and empty sounds   30
And goading men and women
To sin and falseness.
Not good is the sensual praise
That may lead the soul to the devil."

    I in turn answered the friar
For every word that he said:
"God is not so cruel
As old men say.
God won't damn the soul of a gentle man
For loving a wife or a maid.   40
Three things are loved throughout the world:
A woman and good weather and health.

    "A woman is the loveliest flower
In heaven except God Himself.
Of a woman was every person born
Of all peoples, except three.
And therefore it's not strange
To love girls and women.
From heaven has delight been won
And from hell, every sadness.   50

"Poetry makes happier
The old and young, sick and well.
It's as necessary for me to compose poetry
As it is for you to preach,
And it's as right for me to solicit gifts for poetry
As it is for you to beg.
Are not the hymns and the sequences
Englynion and *odlau?*
And *cywyddau* to holy God
Are the psalms of the Prophet David.   60

        "Not on one food and seasoning
Does God feed man.
A time was given for food,
And a time for prayer,
And a time for preaching,
And a time for entertainment.
Poetry is sung at every feast
To amuse girls,
And the pater in church
To seek the land of Paradise.   70

        "Truth did Ystudfach say,
Celebrating with his poets:
'Cheerful face, his house is full,
Sad face, evil dwells there.'
Although some love holiness,
Others love diversion.
There are few who know a sweet *cywydd,*
But everyone knows his pater.
And therefore, legal friar,
It's not poetry that is the greatest sin.   80

        "When it's as good for everyone
To hear a pater with the harp
As for Gwynedd girls
To hear a *cywydd* of wantonness,
I shall sing, by my hand,
The pater forever without stopping.
Till then, shame on Dafydd
If he sing any pater but a *cywydd.*"

138. *The Black Friar's Warning*

Profitably I'm thinking
Of the patriarch's command yonder.
God knows (sense will sound out)
How to understand the black friars.
These are (faith false in manner)
The length of the whole world rashly
(Stupid monks, contemporaries)
Ever two by two under the yoke.

    There did I get surly nonsense
From the friar with the coarse mouth,   10
Trying (not a generous connection)
To contaminate me with his impudence.
This is how
The friar with the ponderous, brass tongue counselled:

Friar: "Consider when you may see the man,
How swiftly he turns to soil.
Surely does his image go
Into the earth unprofitably."

Dafydd: "Though the great turf turn
To an ugly spectacle, red-black friar,   20
Noble, glowing flesh will turn,
Proud beauty, only the same color as the elegant lime."

Friar: "Your love for the slim, bright girl,
Golden-haired, with the long, lively hair,
This will cause you to go to the hot-skin cauldron,
And there's no getting you ever from the cauldron of pain."

    Then I said to him,
"Black friar, yes, insect, be still!
It's an unworthy work for you,
To grieve a man instead of being silent.   30
Despite your persistence and your perjury
And your terrible words and your discourteous noise,

Shame on me if Dafydd should refuse
Ten of those beauties in one day!"

139. *Morfudd Grown Old*

May God give life and grace unstinted
(Crow of loose virtue) to the friar with long horse's hair.
They would not merit peace who might blaspheme
The friar of the shadow of the form
Of a lord whom Rome might honor,
Naked of foot, a man with hair like a nest of thorns.
The robe that wanders the world is a net,
A sort of crossbar, a blessing of the spirit.

    A mass-priest musician of wise word,
He sings well, kite of the pure God.   10
Great is the chartered privilege of his house,
Ram from the roof of heaven.
Fluent from his mouth of eloquence,
Life from his lip, magician to Mary.
He said, praise of tough discernment,
About the color of the woman who's seldom false:

    "Do thou take, dear first of a hundred,
A shirt of cambric and crystal.
Wear — do not strip for a week —
A vest for the pampered, sleek, long flesh.   20
I was noble, a second tale of Deirdre;
It will be darker, and twofold sorrow for me!"

    Gray, bald friar-man of skillful praise,
Thus the black friar regarding the girl's beauty.
Were I Pope, I would not be done
With Morfudd while I was a foolish boy.
Now, resentment's accusations,
The Creator has disfigured her,
Till sound rectitude has not
One gray lock of hair less bright,   30

Betrayal of a feast, a persecutor of beauty;
The girl's color does not fare like good gold.
Queen of the land of sleeplessness,
Men's betrayal because of beauty and face,
She was abundant, life is one sleeplessness,
She's a dream; how swift is a lifetime!
A twig-broom on an earth of malt,
A light-gray, half-hollow elder tree.

Tonight I'll not get, sick wounding,
To sleep a wink if I'm not there.   40
It's a blow of the girl's love,
An old thief like a nightmare.
Magical was she fashioned,
Gray, larcenous enchantress.
Old rod of an Irish mangonel,
Cold summer-place; she was once beautiful.

140. *A Fortress against Envy*

The envy, you weak Britons,
Of Caesar's nation, presumptuous people,
Plagued it, if consummated,
And made it worse than it was.
A bond of envy and obstruction
And jealous of nature
Is it to begrudge intentionally
A good man his gift and his praise.
He'll have trouble, Lord God of heaven,
From the rabble of envy.   10
I am begrudged,
By the Cross, more than anyone,
I'm a young man under strong constraint
By cold people, I know of what parish.
Some powerful ones of gentle vision
Give, increase advantage to me.
And the wretches speak out,
Alas for strength, and do wrong.

God gave, a nature habitually protective,
A fortress to keep me, the fine strength of the breast,   20
As good, against fear of a man's revenge
Against his enemy, as Calais.
Retreat does not profit (pure heart,
Citadel of Troy) a loved unfortunate one.
The high, secret, steel sting
Of the breast, the belly's Tower of Babylon:
The strength of one strong man
Would keep the castle, a cell of song,
Against the men that talk,
While a store lasted, through good conduct;   30
With hope as a wall
From gentle Angharad's love;
And a catapult-stone of pleasantry,
Against either scorn or great humbling;
And a coat of mail of smooth fold
Of constant peace of the true God my Father;
A brown eye is the watchman
At the tower battlement upon fine proud ones.
An interpreter, who is praised over there,
Is the lively ear of the governor;   40
And the harbor sentry (no concern of mine at my tryst)
Is the tongue by God's grace;
The buildings outside are
The hands and feet, they are firm.

God the Father, You own it,
Put provisions in your tower.
Don't allow a man's interior to be empty and reviled,
Lest it be captured.
Try to keep it from villains,
O choir of the land of saints near sky and stars.   50
Threaten (hateful gathering)
The threateners of the lively, polished lad.
We know as we pass
(Cold command) which ones they are.

Though the anchor-strong sea might come
Through mighty King Edward's rear,

A living poet to the bright, beautiful, open-handed girl
Is he, and so may he be.

141. *His Shadow*

Yesterday I was under the best of leaves
Waiting for a girl, one like Elen,
And avoiding rain beneath the green cloak
Of the birch, like a foolish boy.
Lo, I saw some figure
Standing unhandsomely by itself.
I fled across there,
Like a gentle fellow,
And against the plague I crossed
My body with saints' charms.   10

Dafydd: "Say, and stop being silent,
You're a man here, who you are."

Shadow: "I am, leave off your questioning,
Your own remarkable shadow.
Be quiet, for Mary's sake, don't obstruct a benefit,
For me to tell my message.
I come, a good custom,
At your side nakedly here
To show, jewel of shy complaint,
What sort of thing you are; there's a bewitching
                              carries you off."   20

Dafydd: "No (a generous man), hideous wretch,
I'm not that, fiend's body!
Same shape as a hunchbacked goat,
You're more like, ghastly likeness,
An apparition full of longing
Than a man of proper form.
A herdsman in motley, bickering,
Legs of a hag on a black stilt.
Shepherd of goblins of filthy omen,

Bogeyman in the form of a bald monk.   30
Herdsman playing *griors,*
A grown heron grazing bog reeds.
Crane casting its full spread,
Forts of a ghost at the edge of the corn.
The face of a doltish pilgrim,
Black friar of a man in an old rag.
Body-shape rolled in hemp,
Where have you been, old barnyard post?"

Shadow: "Many a day, if I were to reproach you,
With you, alas for you that I know you!"   40

Dafydd: "What other blemish on me
Do you know, neck of a pitcher,
But what every sensible man
In the whole world knows? Devil's dung to you!
I haven't reviled my commote,
I haven't struck, I know, a crooked blow,
I haven't flung at hens with a sling of stones,
I haven't frightened any little ones.
I don't resist my talent,
I haven't hindered the wife of a foreigner."   50

Shadow: "By my faith, if I were to speak out
To some that don't know what I know
(A strict moment before breaking off persuasion),
By my faith, you'd be in the gallows."

Dafydd: "Take care (yours is the painful trap)
That you don't confess for a long time what you know,
While it's mine, more than if there were
A stitch on the edge of the mouth."

142. *The Song*

I learned a song of paradise
With my hands, at the end of a bench;
And the learning, a man's way,
Gilded the harp somewhat.
Here's the song that on my bench
From amid a tryst, in knots,
Of a noble heiress deserving praise,
I composed with love's prick.

 The girls of the lands are saying
About me, and this will be my favor: 10

 "This is a tune of obvious nature,
And a simpleton is the man who offers it."

 Out of my poor pretence, I put into sol-fa
An easy psalm, rich is my privilege,
And a melody with the loving song,
The young men say,
A lucky, winning note from sweet, skillful excitement
Gets me praise, it's the poets' tune.
The singing voice of a bright, happy bird,
This is the music handsome poets want.   20

 Woe is me that (great is the desire)
Dyddgu does not hear this poet's song.
If she lives, she'll hear beneath the perch
The familiar song of a nightingale in gray tunic,
In accord with the teaching of Hildr under the
        harp's top string;
Too much music, a drunken man sang it;
The labored cry of a string, the voice of a clock,
A plaintive echo, in the style of an Englishman's
        psalter.
Neither a witty piper of France
Nor a chief poet made such a symphonic song.   30

 Let his lip be profitless
And his *cywydd* and his ten nails

Who might sing a song of praise
(God won't chide, nor will harp music)
Of a good, shining, bright, glad-eyed girl,
And who's getting to sing this song!

143. *The Sword*

Long are you, gray form,
By God, sword, along the thigh.
Your blade does not allow (a daring, handsome lord)
Shame to its companion.
I keep you at my right side,
God keep your keeper!
My treasure, you are bright,
I'm a master, and you are my strength.
My sweetheart's husband who does not love my life,
Fierce his obstruction, craftsman of conspiracy,   10
Taciturn, famous, base,
Gross is his evil, foolish of frown, like an ox,
Sometimes he's silent, good soul,
And sometimes he threatens me.
While I own you, strong, passionate lord,
In spite of his threat, mighty weapon,
A curse be on his bed,
And scorched be your master if he should flee,
Neither on horseback, a disgrace to imagine,
Nor on foot because of the husband yonder,   20
Unless, because of two angry words, he inflicts on me
Punishment in your day (Eiddig's aversion).
Battle-bite to put an enemy to flight,
Cyrseus, a two-lipped shearer of a man.
You're the finest hand-staff;
You've thrown off rust, you're a flint.
Treasure of the crows of battle of swift-moving encounter;
Let the men of Deira flee; hard are the two edges.
Edge of a field of lightning-fire,
I keep you in your latticed sheath.   30
You're sharp for me against an enemy,
Elegant, bright, keen-grooved sword.

Sharp, strong weapon, here is my gold oath,
Where I lay hand and commission on you:
Lest there be in a grove's castle
Some kite of the night to hinder us,
Boy's pomp of a lighted, twirling stick,
Run, steel, like a wheel of fire.
Do not hide, Cuhelyn's shield,
In my hand if the man comes.   40
Brave wheel, of bright setting,
War are you, lucky metal.
This guards me from rascals,
Most needed sword, descendant of Hawt-y-Clŷr.

Outlawed I'll be during the long feast
In the woods, I and my shy girl.
It is not discourteous for me to plunder,
If a girl, not love of wealth, commands.
Some of the family will exonerate me;
Broad is my track beside the houses of my gold one.   50
I'm no fugitive, I'm Ovid,
The heart of a lover is proud.

144. *The Ruin*

Dafydd: "You, broken hut of gaping bottom,
Between moorland and meadow,
Woe to them that saw you, as they supposed,
A pleasant feast once,
And who see you today with broken top,
Under a roof of laths, a shattered, broken house;
And also by your happy wall
There was a day, a rebuke for pain,
In you when it was merrier
Than you are, scabby roof-frame,   10
When I saw (brightly did I bear praise)
In your corner a lovely one there,
A maiden she was, well-born and gentle,
Of lively shape, lying together,

And each one's arm, embrace of a girl's bounty,
A knot around the other,
The arm of a tall, slender girl (the edge of
                                broken, fine snow)
Under the ear of praise's best servant;
And my arm too, foolish tricks,
Under the left ear of the gentle, fair girl.   20
Joy with pleasure among your green trees,
But today is not the day."

Ruin: "Lament is mine (the bewitched speech of a
                                refuge)
Because of the course that the wild wind made.
A storm from the bosom of the east
Did injury along the wall of stones.
The sigh of the wind, a way of anger,
From the south has unroofed me."

Dafydd: "Is it the wind that late caused havoc?
It winnowed well your roof last night.   30
Roughly it shattered your laths;
A dread enchanter is the world always.
Your corner (mine is open double-woe)
Was my bed, not the lair of pigs.
Yesterday you were in fine condition
Snug above my gentle darling,
Easy encounter; today you are,
By Peter, without beam or under-thatch.
Various subject for frequent madness,
Is this the shattered hut of a kind of deception?"   40

Ruin: "Some time ago the family went,
Dafydd, under the Cross; their custom was good."

145. *Loving in the Winter*

Alas for him who may love, barren and snowy,
Except in summer, appalling is the demand,
After one night because of a pretty girl
Whom I had, my memory of love,
In the winter, I say it in anger,
Dark and bare after Christmas,
With snow, the sign is cold,
And frost and the fluent icicles.

In good humor (judgment's great wait)
I came drunk from the tavern   10
To try (great was my terror)
To see the blonde, loving girl,
Through the wood of the glen, love will not let me down,
The other side of a stone wall from a slim girl.
Bad for me, drops of a wave,
Was the steady cheese-dish from the eaves.
And when I came (I sensed a gift,
It was dangerous) beside the wall,
Thick beneath the cold rooftop
Was a very wet icicle of the freezing moon.   20

Expertly into my mouth it trickles,
The pomp of cold whistles of an ice-sheathe.
Bright rake of a frosty claw,
Delicate harrow-teeth of the ice.
Materials of wrath,
Like a grove of tender leaves, Eiddig's Paris candles,
Cold tears, memorable daggers of ice,
All of dark ice.
The nape of my neck knew (angry tune)
The pain of the blue spindles.   30

I made a sign, knocking
Gently on a window with my hand.
The husband heard more quickly at sleep-time
Than his woman, he was severe.
He nudged the slim moon-girl

With his cold elbow;
He supposed through someone's plot there's
An intent one seeking money.
The stupid blockhead got up
From his own bed, plague's breath.   40
A coward was the graceless, enraged fellow.
The villain shouted after me.
He brought upon my head, hazardous journey,
A crowd of all the hateful in the town.
He put a candle of Mary of the chaste rendezvous
At the furrow in my footstep,
Cried out, I know a hundred cries,
"Here is his track, and it's sharp!"

Then I fled, violence most brave,
Along the black ridge and the ice   50
To go to the sweetest birch grove
And my shelter in summer, at a run.
I imagined there was (praise for a blessing)
The leaf-meadow with the lovely roof,
And gentle birds who loved me,
And a girl I had seen in May.

There was no such place,
There's anguish, except a wood-grove;
Not a sign of love, nor caring,
Nor the girl I had seen, nor the leaves.   60
The vast, naked winter winnowed,
Green fabric, the leaves down.

Therefore I'm asking for May,
And thawing-weather that wouldn't make me cold.
I'm a man who doesn't love winter plowing
During a long salute to summer.

146. *Waiting in Vain*

I was fine in choosing, yesterday I made,
Monday, a date with a girl.
Where I saw a girl the color of the foam of an
                                    ebb-tide's surge
On Sunday, she'd promised
To come to the requested rendezvous —
Where the cheerful girl did not come.

    With many a glance (happy girl,
The fair one is modest and graceful)
One summer I cast out in haste
(She was above) toward the district of hers   10
(A tranquil mind above the seashore)
To where she was; she would deceive a man.
She of noble inspiration is a virgin;
And a disgrace for me, Amen,
If I were to deceive (easily she denied me)
Her, and there is no easy way.
From the morning (a girl of bright amber)
Till forenoon under the beautiful hedge;
From forenoon (a poet's ransom)
Till midday, two periods;   20
From midday that's affirmed
Till an afternoon that lasts long;
From afternoon (simple enough talk)
Until the night, crude longing.
It's a long vigil for me to wait for her,
Handsome, golden lady, at the edge of the moor.

    If I were, by the dear Pope,
In the grove (a senseless course)
For as long as the man was (condition of a flock,
A gasp of sorrow) with the load of sticks,   30
Pale and gentle her face,
Woe is me, I would see no one!

The Verse Debate Between Dafydd ap Gwilym and Gruffudd Gryg

147. *Gruffudd's First* Cywydd

A wonder for sad Dafydd
Son of Gwilym Gam, blameless man,
A very bold fellow, sorrow's bedmate,
Spears have paralyzed him a hundred times.
The ill-bred fellow is also
Fostering song, faint and in bondage.
Prolonged (weak occupation) is his cry,
By the Mother of God, he says there's
A pitiful agony upon a Welshman;
Amazing that he's alive!   10
Everywhere, cheek of some passion,
Mary hears that his wound is great.

    Spears the number of the stars are
Ravaging Dafydd's whole body.
Woe is me if sharp spears
Are in the chief poet.
Not the spear of a tumult amid a thousand,
Not the pang of St. Anthony's fire, but the pang of
                              a weak one.
Not a spear in the back,
Not a radical disease, but baseness.   20
Not an assaulting spear, nor a wrathful one,
Not a spear of strength, but a spear of frustration.

    There are weapons (master of the webs of song)
Firmly in his breast.
It's ten years ago today
That Dafydd said, fine of song,
That there were in him perhaps a hundred
Weapons, blows of steel,
Arrows, the memory of sadness's frustrations,
And thoroughly was he afflicted.   30

A powerful revulsion possessed him,
In men's judgment, because of these spears.

A great lie, poet of betrayal,
Did Dafydd tell, of nonsense.
If Arthur, great support of a wall,
Who used to make a swift rout on a throng,
It's true, if all the spears were
Present in a hundred wounds
(He waged wild war),
The truth is he'd not live one month;   40
Much less, a slender boy is the fine lad,
Love's minister, he's weak.
Ah me, if a Welshman from Môn stabbed him
With a spear (wouldn't that be a grief for him?)
With his golden hand on its shaft,
Under his broken breast sorely,
If he'd be for a full hour in the morning
Alive (his color is pitiful) —
To say nothing of going faint (no sweet discretion)
Because of many spears!   50

His oaths are the death of him;
His color has been slain by weapons.
By my faith, the wise, amusing boy,
Though he be boastful, accomplished, and cultured,
The clever man from another land would make
Complaint (by a sad arrow is his steep betrayal).
Danger of death for him (from the serious trial)
Because of the weapons of Morfudd.

148. *Dafydd's First* Cywydd

Gruffudd Gryg (having a worthless, empty muse,
Trembling, head aching,
With the output in song of a one year-old girl)
Is silly (same growth as a goose-chick).
A *cywydd* of pretended praise, lacking generous favor,

Is not of less dignity that a eulogy.
Perfect in form, a sincere cry
Is the fine *cywydd* of Ovid, alas for it!
One hates it, another sang it,
Bad reputation, another satirized it.   10

    A harp on whose pillar no hands have been put,
Bright column of rain,
A girl will not forbid if it
Is a companion to a *cywydd*.
It will be expressive if three strings are to be had,
A singer of music; an idiot has played it:
In a tavern of unruly beer
A tinker plays it beside the belly of a narrow tankard.
He throws it away, this is disgusting,
Old dog-dung, may he be hated.   20

    An old parchment book, a work of broken lip,
That might be cast away into the dung
(Untidy at its baptism
Is its verse of pen and hand)
Will be sought again with its soiled leaves
And its wage of love (without the same basis).

    Bile and hate we had judged it
To blame poetry where no wrong was.
Why does the poet over there pain me
In order to depose me from my office —   30
Gruffudd of sad behavior
Son of a Gwynedd father, Cynwrig?
A man lacking the amiability of a man of Gwynedd,
He has distorted with his mouth all the world's poetry.
No work is there, where mead is long,
For the singer of the songs of Gwynedd
But to cut (peevish his slander,
It's a great burden) the path in front of him.

    No poet here sings to fine weather
A *cywydd* with his ten nails   40
That Gruffudd, solemn in fear, does not sing

(Complaining look) a *cywydd* like him.
Everyone would make a strong building
If wood could be had and men's health;
It's easier to get, where wood is poor,
Long expedition, a carpenter than material.
If he wants poetry, golden, gentle hammer-blow,
Let him go to the woods to cut matter.
Not very skillful, aptly nicknamed,
Is the praise-poet of remarkable renown   50
Who needs a vain thread
For the material of his hollow *cywydd*.
With his hand on a well-finished handrail,
The old fawn, he runs slowly.
Let the poet sing to the other goodlooking girl
A *cywydd* made out of his own old wood.

    I give (I aim backwards)
A warning to the very foolish Gruffudd,
The darling of every fair, a strong one will obstruct him,
Boasting's stammering book, the echo-stone of poets: —   60
Let the son of stuttering pay
(A payment for poetry) a portion of his work to me.

149. *Gruffudd's Second* Cywydd

He's wild, I don't know whether it's better for me
To see Dafydd fab Gwilym,
With his grimly deceiving hand of illicit gain;
Handsome Dafydd is like Gwenwlydd.
Good in my presence, a ready shoulder,
And bad in my absence, and reckless.
Dafydd told the men of the South
In his false *cywydd*
That there was nothing of mine in my poetry
Except for his teaching; he was the bardic master.   10
He told a lie, by Dewi!
And let me be tested whenever it's desired.
He swore that I do with my tongue

(The best of men) nothing but distort poetry.
It's obvious that I would not wish, as a speaker,
Ever to distort a word of praise.
Simple is his course, his accusations are numerous,
Dafydd is fond of his own voice.
Every immodest bird in the cosy birches
Is fond of how lovely his voice is.   20

    May cold misfortune (through a musical turn of words)
Come to that man of us two,
And wasting on his tongue
Wherever he be, who would make merchandise of poetry.
Though my tongue may be impeded, eager energy,
In a swelling of anger,
There's no like achievement except through fervor;
Not stammering, by Mary, is a word of the poetry.

    A hobby horse in every playground
Was excellent, its appearance perfect.   30
Come nearer: — it has two dull legs of stakes,
Tossing stiffly.
Surely, no apparition
Of a poor wooden thing was worse now.

    Second is the organ in Bangor;
Some will play it because of the choir's roaring.
The year, in pursuit of the solemn cry,
A silly, expensive trip, that it came to the town,
Everyone in the parish would give an offering from his coffer
For what the leaden thing played.   40

    The noise of his constant anger spread abroad,
The third is thick-bearded Dafydd.
Beloved in Gwynedd, they said, when new
Was his *cywydd* once.
Now his *cywydd* is more shrivelled,
His wood-craft has gone into the shade.

    Why, with twisted Welsh,
Does the son of fair Ardudfyl not see

Who he is, an angry, doubly-wounded cry.
And who am I? I am beloved.   50
If it were most pleasing for Dafydd
To have open warfare without hiding
(The country's coward will be the roar of some),
He was a base man not to warn me,
To keep me from being taken in a seizure of indignation
By stealth, as a hundred have been taken.
He attacked me (he scorned favor,
The briber of song) without warning.

No one would give, if I wouldn't give,
A wood star for his sulking.   60

150. *Dafydd's Second* Cywydd

The scribe of the parish, his craft restrains it,
Careful are his tears, rather stuttering Gruffudd,
A model, gloomy man, for me,
He sings well, of trustworthy recollection.
Fine conversation, if he wants,
And a kind word he might have;
And if he doesn't want, false constraint,
Whatever I want, I shall also do.
God knows that I, of bright, strong voice,
Have not denied a word I said,   10
That there was no need (destiny of peace)
For a pattern of his poetry; he's a simple man.

The testimony is here, where the target is,
Lengthy prohibition, in his poetry itself.
It's a fact that in our presence
Long-backed Tudur ap Cyfnerth sang
To me both of the wooden horse (bright-toothed deer)
And about the organ (saints' concert)
A song some time before the age of crying,
Earlier than he sang, stubborn cub.   20
Why should he go (pure of custom,

Radiant in strength) for paying the cost of poetry
(Bold, brave servant) to lodge long
With Tudur (excellent man)?

    Let the lad be willing to acknowledge him
(Brave humility) a pattern for poetry,
And not insist, unconcealed gift,
On satire clearly to be avoided.
It's absurd for a fine, active boy
To send very unfriendly gifts   30
From Môn, accusations that are pressed,
To me as far as Pryderi's land.
The name of my country is Bro Gadell,
Renowned are its men (this is better).
A blow from his tongue is swelling;
Hempen stuff, if he's angry at me,
Let's come together (he was a fine favorite)
Hand to hand between our two courageous hosts.
Let's test each other if we're chief poets
With two lovely, poetry-hurling tongues,   40
And two hostile songs, fine to mention,
And two vigorous bodies,
And a strong thrust on good, handsome feet;
And he who'd depart from the war, let him depart.

    May he permit me, and furious the encounter;
A halter for me if I should leave off.
A blow from the copious poetry of plagiarism
Does not pass by his father cheaply.
If he's not sulking, strong cry,
No contention, I'm glad;   50
If he's sulking, where the Gascony stallion chases him,
Gwyn ap Nudd take me if I care!

151. *Gruffudd's Third* Cywydd

Dafydd, isn't it regrettable
That the anger grew which was
(Slander has been cast, a powerful reproach,
By the great God) between you and me?
You believed it, transparent, trivial testimony.
It's a belief the poets are going to hear of.
For me, double grief in my mind
If I bother to seek satisfaction for anger.
Great is that mind of yours up there,
Greater is your taunt against me,   10
And little did you wish
For me of strong, powerful, daring song.

Your desire to fight is obvious;
My grace is ample, and I'm modest about rank.
May I not wait in my passion in summer
And get my girl, if I retreat
For one poet, dangerous fool,
A foot or an inch in the world.

Great is your talk of satisfaction,
You used to say that you were brave.   20
Choose, Dafydd, either tell
Me what you want or be silent,
) Either a contest, man of wide scowl,
For distinction; or open fighting;
Or contending back and forth
Over a fire, arrogant, dark man.

If you've grown angry, if you're surly,
If your follies are numerous, your hypocrisy
                          simple-minded,
Place here (tramping through the world)
Your displeasure, O dark madman.   30
There's payment, I'd warrant,
The width of your torn and gaping cowl,
Tenfold success in the presence of a host,
Contending with you over your language.

It is unknown that I shall not prevail,
Either with body or with song, I'm diligent.

    Let's come together, we're impetuous men,
With two swords excellently sharp.
Having the first name for learning, let us two test
Who is the warrior in battle, who is best.   40
Dafydd, if one dares to come
With slender sword, if you wish fame,
And two tongues, the fragile poetry of terror,
And two steel blades in our hands,
God will judge between two passions,
Come to the attack, you auger of song!
Let it go to the devil, everlasting journey,
The cursed heart that retreats.

    I reckon you very unhappy, Dafydd,
That Dyddgu laments the day.   50
I am not sad, may I despise flight,
Gweirful is happy from my errant course.
Alas for Dyddgu, chaste, wise girl;
Blessed is Gweirful, she will see no fault.

    I am a lion of authority, you're a calf.
The eagle's chick am I, you're the hen's chick.
And I am brave and terrible,
With a gentleman's magnificence in hardship.
And a chief song is mine,
And "stammerer" they call me and "strong."   60
And I don't care (great, new passion)
Ever after, what I might do.

    If without interference I strike
A man's teeth with my sword's edge,
Very little favor
Will be won from me for a prayer.
Difficult for a solitary poet
To deal with an angry, mighty man.
Capable good sense with poetry comes from the head;
Beware, I am not Rhys Meigen.   70

152. *Dafydd's Third* Cywydd

Gruffudd Gryg readying scorn,
Grouse of the lying, crude song,
Shame on your beard in Arfon,
And upon your lip shame in Môn.
I'm wise (God has been good to you)
While spinning in my throat (protecting you).
Escaping strangely from the wandering poets
Are you, fat, unprofitable food for lice.
Very persistent enemy of poets,
Rule your reckless pride.   10
With ready, brilliant, impudent intention,
Bridle, end your deception.
Ask for refuge, you were perverse,
Restrain your boasting, dark bastard.

Denying the couplet, spiderly web,
Woe for you that you cannot do it confidently,
About the two chicks (doubtful enough)
Of eagle and hen (a very foolish man);
A speech of wrong and crooked pride,
Your song is rough, dark, bent man.   20

Your journey to the joyful court is immodest,
Man of no profit, you're called to be
The thorn of song, pitiful-looking fellow,
Or the gorse-bush of the language of Gwynedd.
And if one who keeps step should play
With you on sea-surge and land,
An oppressive journey, you will do
Nothing better there than curse.

Everyone will be bold under the lively wood of the thicket
In another's absence, rude-faced fear.   30
Wherever I might hear (without the discipline of active love)
A coarse word of your poetry, bold, raucous man,
I shall repay, slightest impediment,
Three times as much poetry to you, Gruffudd.

I'll not have the same opinion
(If I fault this, may I not exist in the summer),
Neither fear of you (you did not fashion a greeting)
Nor loving you, until you deserve love.

    I shall go to Gwynedd of my many feasts
In spite of you, frail, dark man;   40
Even if your judgment is firm against me,
I shall have jewels and gold in Môn.
As for you, from the place where you're distrusted,
If you come to the land of the South,
You'll be (a mate to judgment's anger)
The badger in a bag, strengthless arm.
I'm as good (a venture of your bright custom)
In your country as you in your lifetime;
I'm better than you (fault is at odds with you,
My claim is persistent) in my own country.   50

    Weary trouble is it for you, Gruffudd,
Violent trial, if the game gets serious.
I well know, of gentle, fine kinship with Menw,
To allege that you are not of the same name
As Rhys Meigen of the bellows-anus,
Snare of lard, without a pure mind.
The way you were, there was no praise;
Avoid being (your boast is vain)
A dead, crooked Rhys (habit of impediment)
Who was killed with poetry, shape like a neck of wax.   60
You too, well did I come,
Shall have satire; I was a carpenter of grief.

153. *Gruffudd's Fourth* Cywydd

Gweirful, lady of wisest intention,
Alas, cultured acquaintance, that I
Must for some time
Delay your praise; you're a lady.
Ample for you is the word of praise from my tongue,

And how much I loved you, by Mary!
He'd hit a corner, there's a bad angel
Obstructing song, a laxness in hiding.
Weak Dafydd fab Gwilym
Does not allow, from hatred towards me,   10
The satirizing of an indispensable person,
Nor the composition of poetry, more than a sea-current.
Do not grow angry, bright color of a beautiful night,
Gweirful, for your true poet's sake.
While I am engaged in satire,
Goodbye; I shall be a quiet one.

Tudur Goch, mangy, angry poet,
Son of Iorwerth, belly of a wick's tallow,
I mourn that because of distress I may not,
Cub of dung, sing to you.   20
Debility take your bitter, surly poetry;
You're evil; farewell, Tudur.

Dafydd, weaver of poetry,
Must do reparation for what he said.
Harmony of a nightingale in a park,
He makes sport of the great injury.
Not gracious to anyone, he is not blamelessly,
By the Pope's hand, his mother's son.
I am not of the same father, though I be a poet,
Nor of the same mother as the poet of derision.   30

For the sake of honor he devotes himself to
Contending in Môn with me.
I have seven companions
In Aberffraw in Môn
(Frequent for me is a proven gift)
For every one of Dafydd's, and more.
A vain poet like Dafydd has great need of poetry,
Being inspired by rage.
Challenges to fight before confessing,
His tongue of upstart poetry.   40
Well did he imagine he'd get, reasonable grasp,
The corner of a cudgel on a weak, unreasonable man.

I shall be without fear of the poet from the South,
I shall not be silent, though he's silent.
My poetry shall I set against my enemy,
Because I was not very shallow,
And my amusing song under the glass-green birches,
And my good sense and my strong confidence.

    With regard to pedigree, O my hope,
With regard to reconciliation, a woman's strength,   50
Let request be made, remote garden,
To Ardudfyl who sees better.
She knows how to avoid perjury,
Her husband am I from Môn.
If he was my son, public remembrance,
He's not descended from me at all.
Badly does the suppliant respect,
The poet Dafydd, his father.

154. *Dafydd's Fourth* Cywydd

A crossbow is the word-commanding Gruffudd,
And a bow of craft, though he be thick-tongued.
He's shooting (woe's invitation)
Every target, he does not grant shelter to the Pope;
And scarcely (color of the blush of aloes)
Does he hit one (it's a blemish),
Yet he conducts the poetry of opposition;
The tribute is dispraise for no one.
If it be without me (the passion of one remembrance,
Memory of a birch-tryst), song is miserable.   10
It would be less shame for him
To check my hand (avenging my pain)
Than to reproach me (swift wrath)
With how sad I was; he deserved my anger.

    If there were forks (not a weak total attack)
Under the brows of the vigorous man,
A tongue having the nature of a chieftain

(Feeble lord) and of a poisoned spear
Can stir up the indignation
In his breast and take away his privilege.   20
If the lad with the frowning smile has got
New status in sustaining the muse,
I may yet see him in the rear;
Love's novice is negligent.

Let bare-cheeked Gruffudd consider
(And the tip of his tongue is lead)
That by himself he will not go unimpeded
(Poor man of one-third of the word,
A feeble guide) but will press as a blind man
Across thistles yonder.   30
He can, dusky quiver,
Cold cheek, get the fill of an ox-horn.
I do not desire (I shall not join deceit)
Reconciliation with an angry madman.

It would be easier in Gwynedd to assign
The dark man as father to Bleddyn
Than him sailing the sea
From the country of Môn as father to me.
I'm a man not perjured
Who was with a lady of Môn;   40
There was conceived then, pestilent course,
A stuttering son, not in good shape,
Gruffudd with lifeless-colored cheeks,
The shape of a dog, son of Mald y Cwd.
A servant to the lepers of Uwch-Conwy,
I know, I know; how should I not know who?

Roof of flax-hemp, of dark passion,
Tudur Goch, be still with the song.
Lenten name for ribaldry,
Wretch of shame, was there a worse lip?   50
Very great hatred, lord of terror,
Anus of a goose, withdraw from between me and the man.

Supplemental Poems

Compositions of Doubtful Authorship

Poems I–XXII are *englynion*. Some of the notes are from manuscript sources; I put my translations of these notes in quotation marks. A few texts are corrupt, marked here by ellipsis dots.

I. O lively poet, over there is a girl like a beautiful garden, a girl in small hazels, of a generous manner with wealth, a radiant, pure girl of the profound language of seven saints.

II. You're a wrinkled thief and frowning, Gwgan, your eye has darkened, unsavoury sack of a hasty wolf, dead, black dog, let me be.

III. *"Englyn* to Ifor Hael's Mother"

Good fortune, brilliant girl of gossamer body in a fort, Angharad ferch Morgan, red-gold in color, hand of silver gift, altogether best girl, color of fine snow!

IV. Excellent Jesus, redemption of the pure, eternal wood, in our presence is our prayer forever, Jesus is in memory: "Son of God, Jesus, Father!" every night and day.

V. I made a bad face when I saw, all seven men are worthless, a straight wood-score in my purse; lively is the bright wine for minstrels, but bitter pain without profit when it's to be paid for.

"Dafydd ap Gwilym composed this for the friends who had drawn the score from his purse under his head and added it

and judged the wood-score in his purse to correspond to the
value of the wine he had drunk."

VI. A splendid plate of silver, and it sent to the table, and a
place for the poets to sing, wrought gold after the devasta-
tion, silver as boars for dark drinking horns.

VII. Morfudd, beautiful, pale day of the holy God, is worthy of
praise: I shall not stop following you until there come on a
holly tree or from alder berries fresh white wine.

VIII. Great is the branching of an oak, great are the woods of the
world, great is it to be skillful, very great is the depth of the
open sea, greater is my plea for Morfudd.

IX. I'll not be done with Morfudd, fond, loving limb, though
the Pope of Rome command, lively color of cheeks like the
rising sun, till the honey comes from the stones.

In one manuscript, the following *englyn,* ascribed to Gruffudd Gryg,
precedes the above:

For fear of the stout, long law, Dafydd, O guilty man, and
the Bwa, keen butcher, it's best for you, for fear of a harsh
appointed day, to practice being done with Morfudd.

X. Let me be silent while I be silent, shining sphere of the sun,
generous, amiable Morfudd, God knows that there's an
hour of silence for your courtly servant, but weeping gray
rain.

In some manuscripts the following *englyn* precedes the above:

What are you doing here, my severe lion? A summery
place, a strange place is your nest.

Tending a tryst among trees of good stock, waiting ever for the same girl.

XI. No tear fell more frail than yours, lively shape of bright radiance, of vehement force from beauty's portion, in the degree of tears on a fairer cheek.

The poets exercised themselves in *cynghanedd* by composing nonsense verses; the following surreal *englyn* appears to be an example:

XII. Gruel of heated battle of hot limbs on a pathway, toad of a castle of myriads, empty, spacious son of a dry, sullen sack, fine belly, fine wood, empty virgin.

This *englyn* is a computation: Christ was carried in the divinely anointed womb of Mary a total of 276 days:

XIII. Sixteen nights, a worthy anointing, of carrying and two hundred and sixty in all was Christ, the Steward-King, in the womb of the fair Virgin.

XIV. In a girl's haunches on a slope of Llangollen did I spill before contention; beer and mead was had today and on her lip, the taste of fine wine.

XV. A hubbub of unmannerly folk are you, I know your custom, to put the blameless poet of sweet speech, good his lineage and his honor, to turning the spit.

XVI. "Englyn that Dafydd sang to his mother's cat that she called Heilin." "The first *englyn* that Dafydd ap Gwilym made."

Ten sharp claws were bred for Heilin, he leaps hedge and roof; happy are you at good meat; pull Gray Mouse from the ceiling.

The following also appears to be a tribute to a cat:

XVII.   There's a fellow, a pusher, among us, grasping, anxiety of
birds and fish, a blade will not kill him, trained in song,
dropping praise, he will not drown; he did not burn, he will
not burn.

This *englyn* with its note occurs in a manuscript containing a
vocabulary by Thomas Wiliams, under the word for white bread
(*coesed*):

XVIII.   "And so Dafydd ap Gwilym made the *englyn* below when he
was set at the lowest end of the table with a loaf of red crust
in front of him, and at the highest end of the table, a fair
white loaf."

Bare, round, tender loaf, come from there to the men
below! Bad is the custom of fine white bread for some of the
minstrels who do not run.

XIX.   Rhys Meigen addressing Dafydd as if he were a servant:

Get up, your cloak is of hemp, descendant of Ifor ap
Llywarch, for Mary's sake, give hay to the horses, if you
won't give hay, give oats.

Dafydd's response:

If to the thin, gray bay with his rump in pieces, a thief of
hay of every valley, long the hair of his flank, the empty hay
will choke him as he pulls it.

XX.   "Gwilym Gam baking barley at a kiln above Melin y Prior
in a wet harvest, said to Dafydd ap Gwilym the *englyn*
below, and did not believe that he was father to him until
the youth answered him, because the boy was dull, without
showing his inclination to compose verse."

"Dafydd's father ordering him to bring gorse to bake barley at a wet harvest:"

Hurry, do it, bring gorse inside; it's turning bad weather; drive the sheep from the sprouts, *hoi, hoi!* Turn the calves from the flax.

"Dafydd's answer to his father:"

We two are spoiling the grain at the oven without warming it; bad weather won't permit having dinner, green barley doesn't bake in the rain.

"Dafydd, because his father hit him because the fire does not kindle, sings to him:"

Soot of the soot-frame reaching the stars, carpenter of the bier of hell, a Judas-face baking, Gwilym Gam has been with his mother.

XXI. "The conversation between Dafydd ap Gwilym and the old woman about the way to make oatcake:"

Dafydd: Open the door, for love of Mary, tomorrow I'm going to my country; here I am an orphan, of good word, under your father's house.

Old Woman: I won't open all summer for this speech; you'll have to wait for me to let you in until you give, as a loan, an answer to my face for this: How do you make, you plunderer, very crisp bread from city oats?

Dafydd: Get oxen and a wagon, as a favor, get a plowman, a worker, and a servant.

And plow land and fallow it roughly and sow it and harrow it and marl it well and seal it there strongly, may grace attend his hands, and get rain for it and weed it green.

And get reapers, soldiers from the battle when it fails them
. . . men from my parish, and carry it to my house and
thresh the dark oats from the stack and after threshing it,
bake it dry.

From the kiln to the mill, from the sack to the hopper, and
then hull it in high comfort; winnow all the grain on a
February chill, put the mill [stone] on top of it and grind it
thick.

And roast it, unleavened, baked without salt, and fire
under its slate-pale, green tip; and the lazy lad will eat it as
bread without any care, its taste good.

Farewell to you, old woman and kindred of your bearing
. . . till I come again to seek you in this quest, till you get a
petticoat from the crow's cuirass, till wool come through the
blue rock.

XXII. "A Stag"

Yesterday I saw a horn as long as a rod and on it nine
branches, a proud husband with a harrow on his head and
[his] bald wife from the yellow crag.

Elegies

I. By IOLO GOCH

Cywydd: "Magical yesterday was the life of Dafydd ap Gwilym Gam, high-spirited man, if his day were longer, of woven *awdl*, good passion, the knot of poetry. He fashioned praise by the tape; there's good usage for a man. Mine the intention, I shall sing an elegy for love of the man. He was the jewel of the shires and their plowshare, the land's plaything and its beauty, the pattern of gaiety and its mode, my deliverance because of fine gift; hawk of the girls of Deheubarth, without him, I know, dismiss them as offscouring; every fine warbler's *cywydd*, because he went, is most sorrowful."

Poet: "You dog, be quiet, *cywydd*! The world's not good, nor will it last long. While Dafydd of skillful song lived, you were respected and happy; and therefore after him, it won't be fitting to ask for you. Hurl whatever's woven of praise and its double point [the *cywydd* couplet] onto the loft. The architect of languages has departed; but if he were alive he'd be everyone's teacher. Awesome my complaint, from heavy fright; awesome was his learning. And he was the tailor of love for a girl, and the harp of court and family, and the treasurer of minstrels and their praise, and a harpoon of battle and debate; and wretched without mediation and an outrage was it to destroy the man, the roof-beam of poets; and sorrowful is the world, and he will not arise again. A powerful, brave, acute teacher of gleaming cry was he, and a monarch; he's gone to heaven."

II. By Madog Benfras

The poets' wealth, he was a brave man, did God Jesus choose. Pain was intense when the lord of the universe took the chief, the lord of poetry, architect of the white fort of wine-song, the chief of bardic mastery, peacock of poetry, harbor of song, home of worth, parliament of the minstrels' poetry and praise, chief serpent of war, the architect of fortune, bannered spear, peacock of ensealed praise, lord of pure red cloak, orchard of song, red spear of ash, capital of song, head of battle's turn, heartache's pantry, brush of love, the prince of excellent praise, leader and standard and feat, chieftain of earnest verse-craft, a head for men, fuller of praise.

Great the mourning because he was brought to his day; orphaned is song because of Dafydd. May Mary and God Jesus of choice word forgive Dafydd ap Gwilym for youth and wantonness, obstinacy in great love, love's offspring, spear-leader of youth, the prop of praise; alas, not to hear him! A lord of battle was he and a spear-errant, the sworn-brother of good praise, extinguishing battle. Weaver of song, good was he, after him, he was every praise, after my bold brother with broken spear, he was worthy, woe is me for what I know of long weariness, no fine man will restrain me, and of heartache for the chief of poets. The steward of love with respect to gold and renown, of great secrecy, praise of maidens, song's praise-word, a soldier sang it, the mill of praise and tribute; great on my cheek, a slayer is the flood, is tear's measure — wanton, merry man, same liveliness as Aneirin, pattern of generous song — for the fellowship of wine.

Summer's empty on account of Dafydd, the carpenters' square of poetry, squire of woods. Good teacher of poets, more wonderful than any man who was, God's my surety. Alas that it might not be long, woodland gift, the lifetime of Dafydd, nightingale of Dyfed. He gave a summons like Taliesin, a roll of praise, very generous with wine. Lord of longing, he was not old, now we must, after inspiration's net, *awdl*'s birdhouse, a poet successful in praise, abandon song like un-tilled land; from praise of twenty girls' love, love has become forfeit-land.

He was delightful, a tear has drowned both my cheeks; it hinders my gain. Surely Dafydd was the most loving man of the men at the woodland's edge. With an *awdl* of competitive praise, he was not poor, a peacock certainly, a proverb. God of heaven bore off the target's lord, good gift of song-tailoring, Dafydd, maidens' toy, pro-foundest in praise, a two-edged sword.

Dafydd, his day has come, doctor of praise, bitterness hears it; good, wise hawk of Deheubarth, fine in my memory, he will not go without me.

III. By Gruffudd Gryg

Dafydd ap Gwilym, for me there was dismay that he was not handsomely on high in the land of Deheubarth and that there was battle between me and the golden poet.

Alas for the poets, because of their hawk of a master-poet, and alas for the world because of the splendid man; alas for me too, by the relics of Christendom, an assault of deep pain over Dyfed's peacock. I'd prefer fair-featured satire from Dafydd's head, a poet's mind, shining strength of praise, to composing for me by some other there not intelligent. I'm a disciple, he taught me, *cywydd*-teacher, fluent, bold author.

Before his death there was a quarrel between me and him, it was bitter. Whoever, generous and faultless, overflow of song, was in the wrong, the living God of heaven forgave today the chief poet of beautiful nurture. I too, poetry's webs, give pardon for what he said. A long time he was in the right, and I formerly in the wrong; I was pleading for a lie; lord of love, he is for the truth.

King of sun and bright moon, there was a cry both terrible and sad because of the bearing away of Dafydd ap Gwilym, surely a blameless man, a renovator of poetry like the two confluences of the Cai, a fine lord of strong verse, bard of the degree of chief poet, a whetted cutting-blade; man of gem-word, of Taliesin's renown, worthy magistrate, the soul of wine; Merlin's whelp, excellent great-gentle one, the chair of poetry, mighty his memory; retentive of mind, large his passion, an evangelist, counsel of song; a tone-string that will be lamented, pillar of the songs of the South-land.

One gains from his head every eloquence, his graceful praise like Cynddelw. Sprightly, handsome man, a liberal Aneirin, a generous servant who dispensed wine; defender with steel weapon, brave and terrible, in the path of war, where there was need. On the battlefield of song he was a joyous man, and wise he was when it was demanded. Like Trahaearn would I judge him, or like Llywarch of long renown was this man, or Casnodyn, profound man, or most ardent Adam Fras.

Wisely did Mary's foster-son, under a glass chancel, take the man of poetry's word, and leave Bleddyn the knave, wretched vagabond, a bent sickle. Christ of choice estate did justly, getting a sure choice of the two, mastery was got, a generous man, to bear away the best. God has chosen a court poet and rejected the company of the hateful one.

Every *cantref* is now sadder, and heaven is now nine times merrier.

IV. By Gruffudd Gryg: The Yew Tree Above Dafydd's Grave

Yew tree for the best lad, near the wall of Ystrad Fflur and its mansion, good was God to you, bliss of trees, to grow you as a house for Dafydd. Holy Dafydd prophesied of you, before you were grown against sadness; after your growing, Dafydd fashioned you, because of his youth was it, to dedicate you as a house of green leaves, a house and every grove bearing leaves; a hidden castle of the dead against snow-wind, as good as the branching tree before.

He's beneath you speechless, the bond of the grave, he did not go with my consent, hive of the angels of the worlds, he was brave, in a tomb was he; and the supremacy of song, his nature equal to it; and alas for Dyddgu when he became mute.

Her young court poet made her brow flourish while he was alive; you too, choice branches, make a return of fidelity to a lord. Gently guard his tomb, a triple grave is like a good aunt. Don't go a step, do not learn to refuse, yew tree, from the grave.

No flock of goats shall foul you, do not waste away, your growth is in your father's land. Fire shall not burn you, hospitable in nature, nor carpenter cut you, nor love wound you, nor shoemaker strip you, in a man's day, of your cloak in your own ground; nor, too, will churl or fuel-gatherer cut you, lest you be of a fearful mind, with an axe, lest they be blamed, your load is green, from off your trunk. Leaves are the roof, yours is a good place, God honor your miracles!

V. Two anonymous elegiac *englynion*:

Dafydd, fine, brave poet, is it here that you were put under green wood, under a green tree, lively, handsome yew tree? When you were buried, song was hidden.

Green tree, thick yew, home of the Nightingale of the Teifi, Dafydd is near; in the earth is complete poetry; unprofitable for us is every day and night.

Notes

Bibliographical Note

Glossary

Index of Titles

Index of First Lines

ABBREVIATIONS

BDG   *Barddoniaeth Dafydd ab Gwilym* (the 1789 edition by Owen Jones and William Owen). No. 6 in my bibliographical note above.

DG   Rachel Bromwich, *Dafydd ap Gwilym* (Writers of Wales Series, 1974). No. 39.

DGG   *Cywyddau Dafydd ap Gwilym a'i Gyfoeswyr* (edited by Ifor Williams and Thomas Roberts, 1914; 1935). No. 7.

GDG   *Gwaith Dafydd ap Gwilym* (Thomas Parry's edition; superscript 1 is 1952; 2 is 1963; 3 is 1979). No. 8.

LlC   *Llên Cymru*. A journal of Welsh literary scholarship and criticism published by the University of Wales Press.

PW   *Poetry Wales*. A quarterly in Welsh and English, published with the support of the Welsh Arts Council.

TI   Rachel Bromwich, *Tradition and Innovation in the Poetry of Dafydd ap Gwilym* (1967). No. 34.

TYP   Rachel Bromwich, *Trioedd Ynys Prydein* (1961; 1978). No. 28.

Notes

1.4.   Dr. Parry (*GDG* ³, p. 434, note to Poem 3) gives this traditional division of the Five Ages of the world before Christ: (1) from the Creation to the Flood; (2) from the Flood to Abraham; (3) from Abraham to David; (4) from David to the Captivity; (5) from the Captivity to the Coming of Christ.

2.27.   The burning bush in which God appeared to Moses is a symbol for the devout soul: blazing but not consumed.

4.5.   A monastic community? A chapel?

4.48.   That is, His passing from the world to the grave.

6.1.   *Aur*, the Welsh word for "gold," often means figuratively "handsome" or "excellent"; so it is used in this and many other of Dafydd's poems.

6.37.   A Marcher lord, Fulke Fitz Warine, cited for heroic qualities by Welsh bards (*GDG* ³, p. 438).

7.10.   *Hael*, "generous"; Rhydderch, like Nudd, was noted for generosity; such allusions indicate that Dafydd was familiar with those indexes of Welsh tradition, the "Welsh Triads." For Rhydderch, see Triad 2 ("Three Generous Men of the Island of Britain") in *TYP* ², p. 5, and the note, pp. 504, 505. Ifor Williams (*DGG* ¹, p. 219) observes that Dafydd kept his promise: Ifor Hael became famous through Dafydd's praise, being known by the epithet Dafydd gave him and serving in his turn as a model of generosity for later poets to cite.

7.24.   That is, notes Ifor Williams, the epithet *hael*.

8.9.   Literally, "psalm of Solomon."

8.41.   Board game or games, resembling backgammon and chess, for which the rules have been lost.

9.34.   Rheged was an ancient northern Welsh kingdom; here it is emblematic of generosity; Taliesin wrote bardic eulogies to the sixth-century king of Rheged, Urien.

9.47.   A wooded spot near Gwernyclepa, Ifor's home.

10.34.   Dafydd would wish to continue receiving from Ifor the kind of patronage Taliesin received from Urien.

11.18.   Thought of the happy life he's lost saddens Dafydd.

11.26.   Nest's generosity (which the poet contemplates in her death) matched that of the loving saints who sustained her.

12.1.   Literally, "Book of Donatus," that is, grammar; Dr. Parry's note to this line suggests the interpretation "rule" or "custom." Dr. Bromwich reads "Book of Donatus" as referring to the bardic uncle himself (*DG*, p. 21).

12.35. Gwri Golden Hair is the name given Pryderi, hero-prince of Dyf-
        ed, by his foster parents, in "Pwyll," *Mabinogion*, p. 20; Pryderi's
        wife was named Cigfa.

13.2.   The "Land of Énchantment" is Dyfed. A tale of an enchantment
        cast upon Dyfed is "Manawydan Son of Llŷr," *Mabinogion*, pp.
        41–54.

13.118. An obscure reference, this may simply mean "like a Parisian
        aristocrat."

13.130. The family's ancient home-parish by the sea, where Llywelyn was
        buried; known in English as St. Dogmael's.

14.12. The poet's longing for the hospitality of Ieuan's court is greater
        even than his longing for a girl's greeting.

14.35. Ieuan, the "battle-door," has a shield with lattice-like ornamenta-
        tion; "door" is used several times in this poem as a figure for
        defender or *lord*.

15.40. Bleddyn was an inferior poet, now unknown, also referred to in
        Poem 154; Cynddelw Brydydd Mawr was a celebrated Welsh
        poet of the twelfth century; Hywel resembles the latter, as he also
        resembles (from the other contrasting pairs) these instances of
        power, discipline, and quality: hawk, lucid minstrel, elders,
        wheat, wine, peacock's feather-fleece. The final stanza of the
        poem continues this strategy of compliment, distinguishing
        Hywel from meek folk and likening him to that legendary type of
        generosity, Rhydderch.

16.56. Literally, grief's weaving.

16.70. Angharad was a native of Buellt, a Welsh land east of
        Ceredigion.

17.14. Llywelyn Fychan gave the cry for the now silent Rhydderch, his
        sworn-brother.

17.16. Amlyn and Emig were legendary friends; the story was translated
        into Welsh from the French romance of *Amis et Amiles*.

17.20. Dafydd's comparison is triadic: Three great cries— Amlyn's cry
        for Emig; A lover's cry for his beloved; Llywelyn's cry for Rhyd-
        derch.

18.16. Without the nightingale, slain by the wild archer.

19.27. *Couples*: joined rafters that support a roof; *couple* has the same
        meaning in lines 28 and 43, as well as in Poem 128, line 57;
        figuratively, *couple* (the Welsh is *cwpl*, a borrowing from Middle
        English) may mean "strong person" or "support."

21.2.   Gwalchmai is the Welsh name for the courteous Arthurian
        knight, Gawain.

21.37. Conjectural for *cecyrdlai*.

22.25. The fox races away in front of any hunter's horns.

23.12. The fresh leaves.

23.16. The leaf-florins are uncut (literally, "without angle"), like coins
        that are intact, none of their precious metal having been clipped
        away. See Gwyn Thomas's endorsement of this reading proposed
        by D. J. Bowen (*PW* 8: 4, 32). The gloss for *diongl* ("without
        angle") in *GDG* is *esmwyth, rhwydd* ("comfortable; easy, generous").

25.30.	That is, in the woods.
27.6.	For the cauldron of rebirth, see "Branwen Daughter of Llŷr," *Mabinogion*, p. 37.
27.49.	*you*: the sun.
29.23.	"Robert" and "Hywel Fychan" are unknown; the context indicates that Robert was an artist (outdone by God, the maker of holly) and Hywel, a love poet who celebrated groves like this one.
31.4.	Conferring woven birch is a sign of love in Dafydd's poems: another wreath in Poem 32 (the girl substitutes a garland of peacock feathers); a belt in Poem 38; a hat in Poem 59.
31.6.	*Chwaer*, "sister," often means, as here, the woman who is loved.
31.32.	Madog would provide lovers a narrow strip of forest ground.
31.53.	*He*: Iorwerth.
32.32.	In the Middle Ages, Virgil had a popular reputation as a magician.
34.14.	Compare Poem 142.
34.30.	Perhaps a reference to the daughter of the last king of Ceredigion.
34.33.	*She*: the cuckoo.
34.42.	Two sneezes were evidently thought to be a sign of good luck. Dafydd has been burdened by the love that fills his breast and moves him to sing. The reference to being a servant of monks is obscure. Was Dafydd once a novice? Or is he likening himself to a lowly member of a religious house devoted to one task?
35.42.	Note these other references to Dafydd's hair: in Poem 48 he is said to have his sister's hair on his head (D. J. Bowen speculates that *sister* here means his love, the blonde Morfudd); in Poem 105, his hair is falling out (as in the present poem); in Poem 63, the magpie calls him *gray*.
35.43.	That is, Dafydd is not going to follow the Gospel counsels of perfection (such as voluntary poverty) which monks vowed to observe.
37.10.	Lest he be called a warrior. Yet his courtship calls for daring and perseverance. He is like an animal that has climbed so high in a tree that it's hard for him to come down; like sailors whose vessel provides slender safety at sea yet conveys them to the shore; like an archer whose many misses are compensated for by one bull's eye.
37.36.	That compels his failure.
37.39.	*he*: her jealous keeper.
38.38.	*the weak one*: Dafydd himself.
43.4.	The same couplet appears in Poem 131, lines 33, 34.
43.48.	Dr. Parry discusses the surname "Llwyd" in an article on Dafydd ap Gwilym in *Yorkshire Celtic Studies* 5, pp. 25, 26, arguing that Llwyd may indeed have been the family name of Morfudd's father, Madog Lawgam (*Lawgam* is an epithet, meaning "crooked hand"). The name "Morfudd Llwyd" appears in three other poems: Poems 59, 73, and 76. Dr. Parry acknowledges the possibility that Dafydd might have been called "Dafydd Llwyd"

(*GDG* ³, pp. xxxii, xxxiii) and notes the consequent suggestion by
D. J. Bowen that Dafydd's calling his love "Morfudd Llwyd"
could be a sharing of surname as in a pretended marriage.

44.11. A religious treasure, not identified.

45.52. Compare the account in the tale of Peredur in the *Mabinogion* (p.
199); in the *Mabinogion*, it is a duck, not a blackbird, that has
been killed.

46.22. These two couplets also occur in Poem 60, lines 3–6.

46.66. Dafydd compares love in various aspects to the behaviour of the
hare, which he has described in the first 42 lines of the poem. In
lines 43–52, he likens his own restless love-aspirations to the
rapid darting of the hare. Then, in lines 53–66, he likens himself
to a hunter attempting to flush out the girl's love, which eludes
him like a stricken hind.

46.68. Ceredigion.

46.78. The same line occurs in Poem 139, line 42 (a poem on
Morfudd). Is this another of the Morfudd poems localized in the
Bro Gynin region (cf. Poems 42, 83, 98)? The poet's "mad mood"
is fixed on his *bro*, his district (line 75), nailed there, in obedience
to his beloved's demand, though she is not moved by love herself.
Their love is a shared life, but now it is not shared. To express
this paradoxical disruption, Dafydd uses animal images: the hind
in flight (Morfudd's coldness driving love from her mind?); an
animal nursing a wound and being unwillingly dislodged; an
animal not lurking in a covert (a lover not trysting?); an animal
trapped.

50.4. Perhaps a reference to the passage in *Remedia Amoris* (lines
579–608) that recommends that lovers avoid solitude and seek the
company of friends.

50.21. The stems of the hazel nuts have been woven together.

51.3. Dr. Bromwich (*TYP* ², p. 130) translates this as "the chance was
fortunate," but I take the parenthesis as referring to Eve's condition before the Fall; a parallel reference would make Adam in
Paradise a patron of lovers: in Poem 24, "Summer" (lines 29–34),
the jealous husband (Eiddig) is "Adam's bastard son," contrasted
with "Ovid's man," whose portion is summer; and summer is
called "paradise" (line 15).

51.11. Rhun is a man's name and so does not fit the context; Dr. Parry
(*GDG* ³, p. 487) suggests it is a scribe's correction to produce
cynghanedd; it is the middle element in *cynghanedd sain*, one syllable
that must (if the line is to have *cynghanedd*) begin with *rh* and end
with *un*; obviously, nothing else would serve the metrical purpose.

51.12. *Bannawg* means "famous" as well as "horned"; Dr. Bromwich
translates the term as "magnificent," but there was a tradition
(noted by Dr. Bromwich and Dr. Parry) that Helen had a mark
between her eyebrows which made her "horned"; this second
meaning (as Dr. Bromwich comments, *TYP* ², p. 343) also suggests the horns of cuckoldry that Helen's famous amour was to
confer on Menelaus.

51.28.   This genealogy may be compared with Poem 92, "Longing's Genealogy," as a playing with the Welsh tradition of genealogical identification.

52.16.   *a man*: Dafydd, who has, he says, carelessly charged Morfudd with fickleness, when he should have been praising her; he urges her not to be angry but to be as forgiving as Jesus and Mary, as Dafydd imitates Jesus' patience.

54.14.   Saunders Lewis, the Welsh critic, poet, and dramatist, has suggested that this may be a reference to Cola di Rienzi, who was held in the papal prison at Avignon under sentence of death from August to December of 1352, when he was pardoned and released (cited by Dr. Parry, *GDG* ³, p. xxxv).

54.41.   I have reversed lines 40 and 41, for a clearer sequence in translation.

56.3.   Eight nights have passed.

58.3.   "With a supply of awgrim stones," the Arabic device for counting; or "of known wealth" (in Welsh, *awgrym* came to mean a sign or suggestion).

60.6.   These two couplets also occur in Poem 46, lines 19–22.

60.20.   *Red chain*: an ornamental chain, perhaps suggesting the linking of lovers.

60.22.   Compare Wyatt's "They Flee From Me."

60.24.   Hare, squirrel, and roebuck, all of them instances of tamed animals that may flee from their masters, as the girl has fled from the poet.

63.6.   *Bwlch dail*, "a gap of leaves"; Ifor Williams explains this as a treetop with a gap in the leaves like a notched battlement (*DGG* ¹, p. 211).

67.12.   That is, to the girl's home.

68.32.   *Gwyn's Family*: the *tylwyth teg*, the fairies of Welsh folklore; see also line 40, and these references in other poems to the leader of the *tylwyth teg*, Gwyn ap Nudd: 26.40; 127.29; 150.52.

69.15.   "Frost's war" is winter, a frequent kenning in Dafydd's poetry.

70.25.   *Her*: the moon's.

70.38.   *she*: the moon, the "florin" of the preceding line.

70.54.   Because the moon casts the same light on house and woods.

71.24.   *Nyf* (a word meaning "snow") is apparently here a woman's name.

71.43.   May he be spared drowning.

72.22.   She, who would be ungenerous to sleep while her lover's near, sleeps little, while her dull, drowsy husband keeps watch.

72.34.   Than Dafydd's eye as he attends fixedly to the girl.

73.27.   *Cynfrig Cynin*: Morfudd's husband.

75.65.   That is, dead.

76.43.   "Candle," like "soul" and "gem," is a common figure for the beloved.

77.10.   The reference of the first phrase (in the Welsh it is simply *sinews* [of a] *snake*) is obscure; it could apply to one who told Morfudd that Dafydd was untrue to her.

78.47.   Beuno is an early saint of North Wales, credited with restoring the decapitated St. Winifred to life; the Jesuits built a college named for him near St. Asaph, for their theological students; Gerard Manley Hopkins studied there, learned Welsh, and wrote a dramatic fragment on Beuno's miraculous healing of Winifred: no.152 in *The Poems of Gerard Manley Hopkins,* Fourth Edition, ed. W. H. Gardner and N. H. MacKenzie (London: Oxford University Press, 1970), pp. 187–93. Beuno's "wandering course" took him to many sites where he founded churches still associated with his name.

80.44.   Dr. Parry concurs with Ifor Williams that the phrase, "giant's arm," is some sort of oath; could it be a kenning for the heavy door, like "giant's hedge" in line 60?

82.30.   *The women's jewel*: Dafydd.

83.12.   Dafydd's own shout.

83.54.   From the following sources, one can identify, at least conjecturally, most of the places named in this poem: *GDG* [3], pp. xv-xviii, xxvi, xxvii; *DG*, pp. 17, 18; *Y Traethodydd*, 133, 84–88; Ordnance Survey one-inch map, Aberystwyth, Sheet 127. Whatever doubts remain, it seems clear that the scene is the vicinity of Bro Gynin (though Bro Gynin is not named in the poem). Beginning with Bro Gynin, then, and taking the other place-names as they occur in the poem, these appear to be the stages of the journey described in Poem 83:

Bro Gynin. The poet's birthplace, a mile and a half from Penrhyncoch; four miles from the outskirts of the town of Aberystwyth and the parish church of Llanbadarn; at an elevaton of about 250 feet. It is beside a ford over the River Stewy (where a modern road crosses the stream), on the south bank, some 4 1/2 miles from the point at which the waters of the stream enter the ocean at Clarach Bay.

Celliau'r Meirch. Perhaps the same as Llety'r Meirch or March, a small farm about a mile across open country from Bro Gynin, and half a mile from Elerch. *Meirch* is the plural of *march,* "horse, stallion." *Celliau* means "groves." *Llety* means "lodging."

Eleirch. An earlier form of Elerch, which is the name of a village northeast of Bro Gynin, about 1 3/4 miles distant by modern road. Elerch is at an elevation of about 600 feet. The summit of Pumlumon (2468 feet), the highest point in Cardiganshire, is some 6 1/2 miles due east of Elerch. Elerch stands near the upper course of the River Leri.

Celli Fleddyn. Unidentified.

Bysaleg stream. This is the Stewy (which the poet says he would cross daily), flowing past Bro Gynin from its source on a mountain whose 1435-foot summit is about 2 1/2 miles east of Bro Gynin.

Bwlch Meibion Dafydd. A pass on the ridge between Bro Gynin and Elerch ("Pass of the Sons of David"). Elevation about 650 feet.

Y Gamallt. Dr. Parry speculates that this may be a version of the name *Y Warallt*, a place located about a mile from Bro Gynin. *Gafaelfwlch y Gyfylfaen.* Perhaps a version of the name Bwlch y Maen ("Pass of the Stone"). *Gafael* means "to hold, to grasp"; *cyfyl* means "vicinity." Bwlch y Maen is located about 1 1/2 miles east of Elerch, toward the summit of Pumlumon.

Pant Cwcwll. David Jenkins suggests that the town of Talybont may be the place referred to as *Pant Cwcwll.* The name *Tal pant Cwcwll* occurs in a charter of the monastery of Strata Florida, dated 1336, which also names Castelham or Broncastellan (near Penrhyncoch) in this region (which is still called *Tirymynach*, "Monk's Land"). Talybont is a village on the River Leri, about three miles downstream from Elerch. It is also on the main route from Aberystwyth northward to the River Dyfi and Merionethshire.

Castell Gwgawn. Also named in the Strata Florida charter of 1336, as being on the northern border of the parish of Llanbadarn.

Adail Heilin. *Adail* means "building" or "dwelling-place." Heilin is a personal name. A crown document notes land belonging to a certain Heylin in the commote of Genau'r Glyn, north of Tirymynach.

Ifor's court. Not identified.

Nant-y-glo. Perhaps the farmstead now known as Cwm-y-glo. *Nant* means "brook," *cwm* means "valley" or "glen." Cwm-y-gro, named in Poem 94, line 32, as Morfudd's home, may be the same place. Cwm-y-glo is half a mile east of Bro Gynin.

Gwern-y-Talwrn. Dr. Bromwich suggests that Gwern-y-Talwrn may be Pen-y-talwrn near Ponterwyd. *Gwern* means "alder-grove" or "marsh." *Pen* means "head, top, end." *Talwrn* means "spot" or "field."

The identifiable sites from Celliau'r Meirch through Adail Heilin indicate that the poet's route has been northwards. The sequence of names is not quite in a direct path. Eleirch, for example, is named before the stream and pass that lie between it and Bro Gynin. We can only conjecturally reconstruct an itinerary from these places Dafydd names as part of his love-quest; sometimes his language indicates repeated or habitual movements (as his daily crossing Bysaleg for her sake). But to proceed: after having crossed the stream Bysaleg and the ridge north of Bro Gynin, Dafydd may have climbed east to Bwlch-y-Maen, where higher ground let him "cast for a fur-gowned maiden / A glance at the good valley." He may then have proceeded northwest to the commote of Genau'r Glyn (less than three miles from Bro Gynin as the crow flies, over four miles by way of Elerch and Talybont). After the unidentified "Ifor's court," the two remaining sites would take Dafydd back south: Cwm-y-glo, half a mile east of Bro Gynin, and Pen-y-talwrn, further east and south, near Ponterwyd, over five miles from Bro Gynin. Ponterwyd is at an elevation of about 800 feet; the road there from Bro Gynin ascends to above 1000 feet. Dafydd's "true target of gain" is this last high place, where once — though not on this particular journey — he embraced Morfudd

In poem 98, line 2, Morfudd's region is said to be Nant-y-seri, which Dr. Parry observes may be the modern Cwmseiri just north of Cwm-y-glo and half a mile east of Bro Gynin. Dr. Bromwich notes (*DG,* p. 18) that Morfudd may have lived at Cwm-y-glo before her marriage.

Cwmbwa, a farm about half a mile south of Bro Gynin, may have taken its name from Y Bwa Bach, Morfudd's husband. The neighborhood of Bro Gynin, therefore, was probably Morfudd's home both before and after her marriage. Even allowing for the gaps in our knowledge, then, these place-names demonstrate that Bro Gynin and its environs, within a radius of four or five miles, constituted the scene of the central drama of Dafydd's poems, his love for Morfudd. In Poem 117, he says that he has been exiled from this district of Uwch Aeron by the hostility of Y Bwa Bach. When he made the excursion of Poem 83, Morfudd must have been unmarried; the jealous husband is not named in the poem. Dafydd, I take it, was still living at his birthplace-home. Though his journey is without fulfillment, he travels ground that he knows well, and with happy memories and hopes. His pain may be deep, but he goes shouting, headlong, "proud and free." Even the images connoting furtiveness and fatigue — the goosechick stooping among reeds, the hound out of voice from running, the monk standing at watch in a choir stall — are yet of creatures in an environment that is home to them.

The poet has hiked at least fifteen miles, crossing streams and mountain passes, beside farms and through villages, as well as over wilderness terrain; he has been alone, yet his instinct is for company. He is sad, yet his self-awareness is comic; he is weary, yet exhilirated. No wonder Morfudd could not forget *him,* so that after her marriage to Y Bwa Bach, Dafydd could quote her as saying (Poem 77, lines 15, 16) that she would love — more than she loves her sober husband — the track of Dafydd's swift foot.

84.19.   Gwaeddan is a character in a now lost legend.

84.28.   Dyfed is known as "Gwlad yr Hud": the Land of Enchantment.

84.31.   Menw is recruited as an enchanter by Arthur in "Culhwch and Olwen" (*Mabinogion,* p. 108).

84.37.   See *TYP* [2], p. 457, where Menw's full name is translated "Little Son of Three Cries," agreeing with the bird-shape taken by Menw. In line 50 of this poem, Dafydd will confer a name on his enchantress.

84.40.   Eiddilig Gor is an obscure figure; the name may mean "Frail Dwarf."

84.42.   Math is the title character in "Math Son of Mathonwy" (*Mabinogion*, pp. 55-75). See *TYP* [2], p. 55, for a discussion of Dafydd's triad of enchanters.

84.46.   A war of illusions and vanishings; in "Manawydan Son of Llŷr"
           (*Mabinogion,* pp. 41–54), Llwyd ap Cel Coed casts an enchant-
           ment on all of Dyfed.
84.48.   A silver harp was awarded at medieval *eisteddfodau;* one was kept
           at St. Dogmael's Abbey in Dyfed (D. J. Bowen, *LlC* 8: 1–2,
           p. 4).
84.58.   Virgil's art (in medieval tradition) was magic.
84.72.   This poem provides a good example of rhetorical structure in the
           poetry of Dafydd ap Gwilym. The following outline may suggest
           how Dafydd builds the poem, with specific development, with
           example, with allusions, with extended comparison, with ironic
           logic.

I. (1–18) The poet has been generous to the woman, but she has
been ungenerous to him.
   A. (1–8) He has given her praise and gold; in return, he has
gained only sleeplessness, hurt, exhaustion from tears, and hostile
accusations.
   B. (9–12) He has called her a countess of fair complexion; she
has called him, in his presence, an ugly rascal.
   C. (13–18) He has given her silk; she has given him nothing at
all, so that he has experienced a hermit's lonely frustration.
II. (19–28) She has teased and deceived him.
He is like Gwaeddan (a character in some lost story), who was
tormented about his cap.
III. (29–46) Of the legendary sorcerers who have deceived war-
riors, none is her equal.
   A. (29–42) Among her predecessors are the notable sorcerers
named as a Welsh triad: Menw, Eiddilig Gor, and Math.
   B. (43–46) She wars against him with magical deceptions, like
Llwyd ap Cel Coed in the tale of Manawydan Son of Llŷr.
IV. (47–72) At feasts, though she has not kept tryst with him, the
poet praises her.
   A. (47–66) For the art of her enticing illusions, she deserves
the prize of a silver harp.
The poet awards her a title to match those of the legendary
sorcerers: "The Enchantress of the Bright Harp." The material of
which her harp is constructed is joy, but carved on the harp is
her resistance to love and her dishonesty. She does not go to the
wild woods but stays in a magician's corner. The pillar of her
harp casts a spell on the poet, and its pegs are flattering lies.
How beautifully she plays! Her performing hands are worth
treasure; her songs are expertly crafted.
   B. (67–72) What can he do but exclaim that she should take a
place at the feast, for she is the light of all Wales.

The poem illustrates the magic it describes: Dafydd begins with a
complaint at his impoverishment through love, but as he dwells

upon the frustrating charms of his enchantress, he can only
— helplessly — salute her gracious craft, which is better than
wealth.

85.44. Hazel sticks and a willow hat were marks of scorn conferred on unsuccessful lovers (see *GDG*³, p. 511).

91.5. Snow.

91.22. Likening the ice to plate-armor.

91.31. Unlike *GDG*, I begin a new paragraph with this line.

91.53. Apparently a reference to a Welsh Rip Van Winkle.

92.10. In the Welsh text, this is line 12; I have changed the order of these lines for easier reading in translation.

92.26. Gwawl son of Clud is a character in "Pwyll Prince of Dyfed," *Mabinogion,* pp. 13–16; a bold and intrusive suitor.

93.5. "Morfudd daughter of Madawg Lawgam." *Lawgam* is not a surname but an epithet meaning "crooked hand." For the possibility that Morfudd's family name was Llwyd, see my note to line 48 of Poem 43.

94.32. *Cwm-y-gro*: perhaps the modern Cwm-y-glo, near Bro Gynin (see *GDG*³, p. xvii).

95.2. That is, grant your patronage.

95.3. She (whose cheeks are like the Virgin's) comes from Maelienydd.

95.10. Likening Dyddgu's brilliance to a waterfall.

95.20. Beneath the leaves.

95.29. Dyddgu is always a day — a pun, since the first element of her name (*dydd*) means "day" in Welsh.

95.40. She belongs to the princely line of Deheubarth (*GDG*³, p. xxv).

96.24. The needles prop his eyes open and so he has to weep.

96.28. The signs of the zodiac were thought to influence the weather; here Dafydd conceives of a zodiacal configuration associated with heartbreak which provokes the storm of his tears.

98.2. Perhaps the same as Cwmseiri, which is near Bro Gynin (*GDG*³, p. xxvii).

98.16. "Robin Nordd" is probably a diminutive form of the name of an Aberystwyth burgess, Robert le Northern (*GDG*³, p. xvi). The name is Anglo-Norman; Dafydd satirizes this non-Welsh merchant who prospers in an English borough in Wales. The "cloth court" where Helen presides could be Robin's warehouse.

98.47. Evidently Morfudd; a round, white fort is often identified as the home of Dafydd's love. Perhaps the fort referred to is the house of Y Bwa Bach at Cwmbwa, a farm noted on early maps as *Ummabowa* (cf. David Jenkins, "Dafydd ap Gwilym yn ei Fro," *Y Traethodydd* 133: 85). In Poem 42, line 19, Morfudd is called "girl of the whitewashed, proud, battlemented fort," and the poet says he has pursued love "in the glade of Penrhyn, love's dwelling-place" (line 52). Penrhyn may be Penrhyncoch, which is near Cwmbwa. See the note to Poem 83, for further discussion of Dafydd's *bro*.

99.1. A *cantref* is a "hundred," a region of governmental administration;

it is a division of a *gwlad* or state and contains two or more smaller units called "commotes" (*cymydau*).

102.27. Perhaps a reference to Ynyr Nannau (see *GDG* [3], pp. 524 and xxxi, xxxii); the mansion "Nannau" stands just to the north of Dolgellau.

106.4. Or "spear."

106.6. These two couplets (lines 3–6) appear also in Poem 136, lines 17–20.

106.7. "Shaking" is conjectural for *osgel*.

108.25. Effect of drunkenness, the first effect being to send the man in disarray out onto the roads, the second, to embolden him to insult another man, and the third, to provoke lust.

111.6. The cathedral at Bangor is dedicated to St. Deinioel.

111.11. See my note to line 4 of Poem 147.

114.57. Taking *sercl* ("circle") to mean *sky*, where the skylark can hover, as though miraculously supported by God.

114.58. How far the bird flies from an archer with bow in hand; the "well-trodden pass" of the next line is the bird's oft-travelled escape route, the sky.

119.12. A celebration of reaching manhood?

119.37. That is, nicely shaded.

121.14. Than that of a manmade building.

121.25. *his*: May's.

121.32. *the house*: a house where in winter he has met resistance; he prefers the summer leaf-house.

122.9. Dr. Parry, following Ifor Williams, takes this to be the county of Caerfyrddin (Carmarthenshire). R. Geraint Gruffydd argues in *Ysgrifau Beirniadol* 10 (1977), 183, that the reference is to the earldom of Caerlleon Gawr, that is, the earldom of Chester. Dr. Gruffydd proposes a variant reading for lines 7–12; the following is a translation of his proposed text:

> A traveller from afar of judicious nature, / The gray love-messenger travelled long: / He came here from the fine county of Caerlleon, / Because my golden girl commanded him, / To Ceirio (until one gets a warrant), / And the place he heads for is the head of a valley.

That is, Dr. Gruffydd suggests, the bird has been sent by Morfudd from Chester to Ceirio, one of the poet's haunts in north Ceredigion; this is the only means she has for greeting him until they can securely come together again.

123.19. This line is missing its first three syllables; the fragment that remains is this: *mwy Creirwy cred*: more/ Creirwy/ Christendom. Creirwy was a pattern for beauty; see *TYP* [2], p. 311. Dr. Parry notes that the first half of line 19 is not legible in his manuscript source.

125.31. *crowd*: the ancient stringed instrument.

128.1. The principal feast of St. Peter is observed on June 29.

128.2. For another poem on Rhosyr, see Poem 134.

128.39. Responding to the servant.

128.47. Addressing her own attendants.

128.57. *beam*: literally, *cwpl*, joined rafters supporting a roof; figuratively, strong person or support.

128.60. Madog Hir ("Tall Madog") and Einion Dot ("Giddy Einion") are characters in lost Welsh story; it would appear from the epithets and context that Madog Hir was a large warrior and Einion Dot an aggressive drinker; Dafydd wishes that the haughty lady fall into the hands of the first and be scorned by the second.

131.34. This couplet also appears in Poem 43, lines 3, 4.

132.28. A variant of a proverb, *Hawdd yf a wŷl ei wely*, "Easily does he drink who sees his bed."

133.40. In *GDG* ³, pp. xxxiv, xxxv, Dr. Parry accepts the argument of D. J. Bowen in the *Bulletin of the Board of Celtic Studies* 25, 28, that this is a reference to Jean Tyrel, the feudal lord of Poix, who won a lawsuit against Edward III in 1359.

134.7. The town's old name; it was changed to Newborough in 1305. Poem 128 is also set in Rhosyr.

134.24. *Buarth baban*: a lighted stick twirled to amuse children.

135.44. The ruler Maelgwn Gwynedd died of the plague in the sixth century; a proverb speaks of his long sleep in the grave.

136.18. *pang*: or "spear."

136.20. The same two couplets appear in Poem 106, lines 3-6.

137.43. The reference is doubtless to the Virgin Mary.

137.46. Dr. Parry notes Ifor Williams' suggestion that the exceptions not born of woman are Adam, Eve, and Melchisedek (*GDG* ³, p. 540).

137.74. Ystudfach is a bard known only by his name; the quotation is a Welsh proverb.

139.22. The friar recommends sober attire and renunciation of the flesh to Morfudd by reminding her of the Irish heroine Deirdre, whose infidelity had tragic consequences; Morfudd's splendor will similarly darken in death. The friar appears to speak in Morfudd's person, imagining her future state. Joseph Clancy takes lines 21 and 22 as quoting Deirdre. In an essay in *50 o Gywyddau Dafydd ap Gwilym* (Swansea, 1980), pp. 87-8, Gwyn Thomas suggests that in these lines the black friar is comparing the darkening of Morfudd's flesh through mortal decay to the darkening — that is, soiling — of a small, fine shirt Dafydd might wear for a week; in line 21, Dr. Thomas would read *fun* instead of *fûm* ("woman" in place of "I was"), so that the sense of lines 21-2 would be:
Noble girl (a second tale of Deirdre), / She will be darker [than the soiled shirt], alas!

139.23. Since he has long hair, the friar's baldness must be either his tonsure or a tonsure-like bald spot.

139.37. A malthouse floor. Lines 37 and 38 liken Morfudd in age to a broom or an old, small tree.

139.42. The same line concludes Poem 46.

139.45.   Dr. Parry comments (*PW* 8: 4, 40): "The mangonel was an engine used at sieges to hurl heavy stones, and consisted of a wooden frame, attached to which was a flexible beam which could be bent and then suddenly released. Morfudd was bent like this beam, and the comparison implies not only the appearance of the crooked old woman, but also the menace and the viciousness of the bent beam."

140.58.   Dr. Parry cites (*GDG* ³, pp. xxxiii, xxxiv) the argument of Saunders Lewis (*LlC*, 2, 202) that this is an allusion to the year-long seige by Edward III of the port of Calais, in 1346-7.

141.31.   Presumably a game.

141.45.   A commote is a local district of government smaller than a *cantref* or "hundred." Dafydd's native commote was named Perfedd.

142.36.   This poem may be compared with Poem 34, as an ironic description of the poet's profuse music; though it be profitless, he perseveres.

143.4.   The sword's companion is the poet.

145.16.   That is, the drops falling.

145.57.   Literally, "no place of the same age."

146.30.   The "man with the load of sticks" is the man in the moon.

146.32.   Though the poet were to wait outdoors like sheep all night, his girl would not come to him.

147.4.   Poem 111 tells of the implanting of one such spear. In Welsh, the word *gwayw* can mean both "spear" and "pain" or "pang," and the plural *gwewyr* can mean "pains" or "anguish" as well as "spears." This permits a punning not possible in English. In lines 13-22 of the present poem, Gruffudd plays freely with the word; the reader of an English translation should keep both senses in mind when reading "spear" or "pang."

147.30.   In Poem 96, addressed to Morfudd, Dafydd says love has been afflicting him for nine years.

147.50.   Gruffudd wonders how Dafydd could survive an attack of a hundred spears; that would down even Arthur. Dafydd, who could not survive one such blow, must be exaggerating his case. The reference to Môn may be a taunting reminder that Gruffudd, who with this poem is thrusting at Dafydd, is himself from Môn.

147.55.   *man from another land*: Dafydd, who is from the South of Wales (the North-South dividing line for Wales being the river Dyfi).

148.6.   Dafydd defends not just himself but the *cywydd*, the form he stamped with his genius; the *cywydd* is a vehicle for fiction ("pretended praise") as deserving of honor for its artistry and feeling as a non-fictional praise-poem.

148.11.   Which has not yet been played.

148.20.   Not the *cywydd* but he who sings the *cywydd* may merit blame; like a harp which charms a girl when it accompanies a *cywydd*, but which a tavern drunkard may play upon and then throw away as if it were excrement.

148.26.   An old book that someone might toss on a dung heap may be sought by another who prizes its hand-inscribed verses despite its soiled leaves (untidily "baptized" with dirt), for the sake of its wage of love (the love its verses express, based on the poet's art, not the worn pages).

148.38. Gruffudd is an unoriginal poet who can only follow in the footsteps of others.

148.49. *Cryg*: hoarse; stammerer.

148.55. The one like Dafydd's Dyddgu; Gruffudd will address his fourth *cywydd* in this debate to a woman named Gweirful.

149.4. *Gwenwlydd*: the Welsh form of the name of Ganelon, the traitor at Roncesvalles where Roland was ambushed.

149.48. Ardudfyl is Dafydd's mother.

149.60. In Welsh, this is a proverbial expression for indifference.

150.33. Land of Cadell; Cadell, son of Rhodri Mawr, was a ruler in South Wales.

151.26. Gruffudd proposes three ways of resolving their dispute: poetic competition (which is what this *ymryson*—a verse debate—amounts to); physical combat; or trial by fire.

151.52. *Gweirful*: Gruffudd's beloved.

152.46. *badger in a bag*: a rough sport that figures in "Pwyll," the first of the *Mabinogion* tales: a victim in a bag is cudgelled.

153.58. Gruffudd pretends to be the husband of Dafydd's mother, Ardudfyl; Dafydd is no true son to him—that is, Dafydd is a bastard.

154.14. The debate began with Gruffudd's mockery of Dafydd's lovelorn poetry. Dafydd's defense is that his sadness has found expression in imaginative poetry of distinction: If it be without me (the passion of one remembrance, / Memory of a birch-tryst), song is miserable.

Gruffudd would subsequently affirm the same, in his elegy on Dafydd, which concludes that after the death of the master poet: "Every *cantref* is now sadder, and heaven is now nine times merrier."

154.20. Evidently an allusion to the confrontation with the giant Ysbaddaden in "Culhwch and Olwen" in the *Mabinogion*. The eyes of the giant are held open with forks; when provoked, he hurls a spear which is caught and thrown back at him, wounding him. An appropriate allusion for this debate on the spears of love, in which the poets hurl one another's lines at each other.

154.36 *Bleddyn*: another inferior poet. It is worth noting that Gruffudd and Dafydd (for all their exchange of insults) deferentially rank one another above these lesser poets.

Bibliographical Note

In this note, I list a selection of works dealing with Dafydd ap Gwilym or with matters of Welsh literature, language, and history that are relevant to the study of his poetry. But Dafydd ap Gwilym can be understood and properly appreciated only within the larger context of European literature. By way of acknowledging this important fact, I shall name just one book which, though it does not discuss Dafydd ap Gwilym, casts critical light upon his work: Peter Dronke's *The Medieval Lyric* (London: Cambridge University Press, 1968; 1977). Its extensive bibliography (supplemented in the second edition) provides a survey of scholarship and criticism in the field, while the author's sensitive explorations of individual poems reflect the attention being paid by a widening circle of modern readers to the riches of medieval lyric.

In June, 1972, Dr. Dronke participated in a University of Wales colloquium at Gregynog on the theme, "Dafydd ap Gwilym a Barddoniaeth Serch yr Oesoedd Canol," that is, "Dafydd ap Gwilym and the Love Poetry of the Middle Ages." In his paper on courtly love and love in the *fabliau,* Dr. Dronke expresses admiration for the variety of the poems of Dafydd ap Gwilym, noting that they illustrate nearly the whole range of the courtly lyric of Europe and also include pieces that resemble *fabliaux.* Further, Dr. Dronke observes, all of Dafydd's poems have a personal stamp, some of them being distinctive inventions not matched elsewhere in European lyric. Peter Dronke's paper (with those of other participants in the colloquium) was later published, in Welsh translation, in a volume edited by John Rowlands, titled, *Dafydd ap Gwilym a Chanu Serch Yr Oesoedd Canol* (Cardiff: University of Wales Press, 1975).

I group the following titles in five categories: Bibliographies; Editions; Language and History; Criticism; Translations. The works are listed by date of publication and in some cases by distinction of topic. With a few exceptions, I limit myself to recent publications likely to be still in print or available in academic libraries. I give particular attention to books written for the English reader; and I use English terms and place-names in giving bibliographical information on Welsh titles. Readers interested in purchasing any of the Welsh books I mention may address inquiries to these offices:

For University of Wales Press publications:

> University of Wales Press
> 6, Gwennyth Street
> Cathays
> Cardiff CF2 4YD
> Wales, U.K.

For information on other Welsh publishers:

> Welsh Books Council
> Queen's Square
> Aberystwyth, Dyfed
> Wales, U.K.

Bibliographies

1. The list of abbreviations for manuscripts, books, and journals given in Thomas Parry's *Gwaith Dafydd ap Gwilym* indicates the primary sources for texts and notes in that edition. It appears on pages xlix–lv in *GDG*[3]. The manuscripts used by Dr. Parry are listed on pages xlii–xlv. In the first edition of *GDG* (pp. lxxiii–cxc), there is a full discussion of the manuscripts and printed editions of Dafydd's work, introduced by a penetrating analysis of the features of style, language, and versification that Dr. Parry regards as marking the authentic work of Dafydd ap Gwilym.

2. R. Geraint Gruffydd. "Contemporary Scholarship in the Work of Dafydd ap Gwilym," *Poetry Wales*, 8, no. 4 (Spring 1973): 56–64. A discussion of translations and textual, historical, and critical studies that were published between 1952 (the year of *GDG*[1]) and 1973.

3. Rachel Bromwich. *Medieval Celtic Literature: A Select Bibliography.* Toronto: University of Toronto Press, 1974. Here are listed general scholarly sources such as bibliographies, textual and critical series, grammars and dictionaries, together with more specialized works.

The entries, topically arranged, are often accompanied with critical and descriptive comments. The scholars represented are indexed, helping one to learn the nature and extent of each scholar's activity in the field.

4. Thomas Parry and Merfyn Morgan. *Llyfryddiaeth Llenyddiaeth Gymraeg*. Cardiff: University of Wales Press, 1976. A comprehensive bibliography of Welsh literature. The entries on Dafydd ap Gwilym run from no. 1674 through no. 1754. In addition to Welsh titles, English translations and commentaries are listed, as well as work by continental scholars.

Editions

5. Thomas Parry, ed. *Peniarth 49*. Cardiff: University of Wales Press, 1929. This is a diplomatic edition (number 6 in a series) of an extensive manuscript collection of poems of Dafydd ap Gwilym, made by Dr. John Davies of Mallwyd in the sixteenth century. In his introduction to *GDG*[1] (p. cxii), Dr. Parry describes *Peniarth 49* as "y bwysicaf yn wir o'r casgliadau mawr," that is, "indeed the most important of the major [manuscript] collections" of Dafydd's work.

6. BARDDONIAETH | DAFYDD AB GWILYM | O GRYNHOAD OWEN JONES, | A WILLIAM OWEN. . . . LLUNDAIN. . . MDCCLXXXIX. This volume ("The Poetry of Dafydd ab Gwilym collected by Owen Jones and William Owen"), published in London in 1789, is the first printed collection of the poet's work. The editors' names sometimes appear in commentaries as Owain Myfyr (or Owen Jones of Llanfihangel Glyn Myfyr) and William Owen-Pughe. Besides the Welsh text of 246 poems, they give, in English, an introduction and glossary of allusions, a gesture reflecting their intention of bringing Dafydd's work before an international audience. The introduction begins, "Of Dafydd ab Gwilym, whose Poems are now for the first time offered to the public . . ." Edward Williams (better known by his bardic name of Iolo Morgannwg) assisted the editors, supplying them with doubtful traditions regarding the poet's life, together with "additional" poems, skillfully forged by him in imitation of Dafydd. A second edition of *BDG* was issued in 1873, edited by the bard Cynddelw and published in Liverpool; this second edition contains some translations of poems into English.

7. Ifor Williams and Thomas Roberts, eds. *Cywyddau Dafydd ap Gwilym a'i Gyfoeswyr*. 2d rev. ed. Bangor, 1935. A selective anthology

of works of Dafydd and his contemporaries, ascribing to Dafydd some poems excluded from the canon of *GDG*. Though long out of print and now superseded by *GDG*, this first modern critical edition of poems by Dafydd ap Gwilym merits attention; Sir Ifor Williams's introduction to Dafydd — demonstrating the poet's European context — and his notes on the poems are vigorous and illuminating.

8. Thomas Parry, ed. *Gwaith Dafydd ap Gwilym*. Cardiff: University of Wales Press, 1952; 1963; 1979. The first edition lists the poems previously attributed to Dafydd which Dr. Parry rejects from the canon, with reasons for their exclusion (pp. clxx–cxc). This list (and the preceding analysis of Dafydd's style and of the manuscript tradition, noted above in no. 1) was omitted from the later editions. Otherwise, the later editions differ only in some brief additions and alterations. The page numbers for the poems are the same in all three editions, as is the numbering of the poems and of their lines. The manuscript sources are identified in the introduction, and variant readings are given after each poem. The notes are extensive and are followed by an indexed glossary of rare or difficult terms and forms. Though scholars continue their scrutiny of both canon and texts, this magistral edition has established a standard text for the poems of Dafydd ap Gwilym.

9. D. J. Bowen, ed. *Barddoniaeth yr Uchelwyr: Detholiad.* Cardiff: University of Wales Press, 1959. Professor Bowen has assembled in this volume five poems from *GDG*, together with 35 poems by Dafydd's contemporaries, from various other sources, including manuscripts and the earlier collection by Ifor Willimas and Thomas Roberts (no. 7 above). Texts of some of the popular *cywyddau* once ascribed to Dafydd ap Gwilym but excluded from Dr. Parry's canon are included here as anonymous poems. With notes and indexed glossary.

10. Dafydd ap Gwilym. *Cywydd y Gal.* Edited by "G. T." Talybont: Y Lolfa, n.d. This pamphlet, issued in the 1970's (on fine Welsh paper from Holywell, with an illustration by Elwyn Ioan), presents the text of one of the poems traditionally ascribed to Dafydd but not included in *GDG*. In his note on the poem in *GDG*[1] (no. 113 in the list of excluded poems, p. clxxxiii), Dr. Parry observes that, though ascribed to another author in some manuscripts, there is better testimony for Dafydd's authorship, and that this is a well-crafted poem. It has the same theme as one of Ovid's (*Amores,* III, 7), the complaint at temporary impotence. Its publication by Y Lolfa is a

mark of the interest being taken in publishing some of the poems of uncertain authenticity. Dr. Parry's standards for accepting poems into the Dafydd ap Gwilym canon were conservative enough that it is indeed possible that some of the 177 excluded poems are authentic.

11. Rachel Bromwich, ed. and trans. *Dafydd ap Gwilym: A Selection of Poems*. Llandysul, Dyfed: Gwasg Gomer (Gomer Press). Scheduled for publication in 1981. Dr. Bromwich, one of the participants in the 1972 Gregynog colloquium and a leading authority on Dafydd ap Gwilym, has informed me that this volume will contain fifty-six of the poems, in Welsh texts from *GDG* and facing translations, with full notes and introduction.

Language and History

12. *Geiriadur Prifysgol Cymru: A Dictionary of the Welsh Language*. Cardiff: University of Wales Press, 1950–1967 (and continuing in serial publication; the latest supplement — 1980 — carries the definitions through the word *hwyr*). Until his death, the general editor was R. J. Thomas; the 1976 supplement names his successor, Gareth A. Bevan. An historical dictionary, on the model of the *OED*, in Welsh, but with parallel English definitions; the dated citations include many lines from Dafydd ap Gwilym.

13. *Y Geiriadur Mawr: The Complete Welsh-English, English-Welsh Dictionary*. H. Meurig Evans and W. O. Thomas; Stephen J. Williams, consulting editor. Llandybie: Christopher Davies; and Llandysul: Gwasg Gomer. First edition, 1958; sixth edition, 1975. Not so complete as its title indicates, but valuable since it includes definitions for obsolete terms such as occur in Dafydd's poems.

14. Stephen J. Williams. *Elfennau Gramadeg Cymraeg*. Cardiff: University of Wales Press, 1960. The language of Dafydd ap Gwilym is early Modern Welsh, though some of the older forms of Middle Welsh persisted through his century. As a result, one needs in studying his poetry both a standard modern grammar such as that of Professor Williams, and also a grammar of Middle Welsh.

15. D. Simon Evans. *A Grammar of Middle Welsh*. The Dublin Institute for Advanced Studies, 1970. This authoritative grammar is the author's English translation of his original work in Welsh (*Gramadeg Cymraeg Canol*, University of Wales Press, 1951), with additional material on language and sources.

16. Thomas Parry. *A History of Welsh Literature*. Translated from the

Welsh by H. Idris Bell. Oxford: At the Clarendon Press, 1955. The Welsh original (*Hanes Llenyddiaeth Gymraeg hyd 1900*) was first published by the University of Wales Press in 1945 (revised edition, 1953; reprinted 1964). Chapter 5 — the only chapter devoted to but one author — is "Dafydd ap Gwilym." The translator (whose services to Welsh studies have been considerable, including some translations of Dafydd's poems, noted below) adds to this chapter a brief appendix on "*Cynghanedd* and the Welsh Metrical System."

17. Gwyn Williams. *An Introduction to Welsh Poetry: From the Beginnings to the Sixteenth Century.* London: Faber and Faber, 1953. Both Joseph P. Clancy and Rolfe Humphries (in volumes of translation I discuss below) testify that this book stimulated their interest in the poetry of medieval Wales. Chapter 5, "The Fourteenth Century," discusses Dafydd's work against the background of his age and the work of his Welsh contemporaries. Appendix A (pp. 232–47) is on "Welsh Versification," an account of the twenty-four official meters of late medieval tradition and the principal patterns of *cynghanedd*.

18. John Morris-Jones. *Cerdd Dafod: sef Celfyddyd Barddoniaeth Gymraeg ("Welsh Poetic Art").* Oxford University Press, 1925; 1930; 1959. A classic (and now out of print) treatment of Welsh poetics, especially important for its extended exposition of *cynghanedd*.

19. Alan Lloyd Roberts. *Anghenion y Gynghanedd.* Cardiff: University of Wales Press, 1973. This Welsh school text deals with *cynghanedd* in a step-by-step manner, with many illustrations and exercises, not only for the reader but also for the aspiring writer of Welsh poetry with *cynghanedd*. Both the persistence of Welsh tradition and the modernity of Dafydd ap Gwilym are reflected in the fact that Dafydd is one of the more frequently quoted poets in this contemporary manual.

20. Eurys I. Rowlands, ed. *Poems of the Cywyddwyr.* The Dublin Institute for Advanced Studies, 1976. No poems by Dafydd ap Gwilym are included in this anthology (the twenty-five poems are from the period of about 1375–1525), but it is of value to the student of Dafydd on many counts — especially the student whose first language is English. The introduction and notes are in English, and there is a full Welsh-English vocabulary. The introduction includes discussions of the bardic order; the *cywydd*; and the varieties of *cynghanedd*, with several closely analyzed examples.

21. John Edward Lloyd. *A History of Wales from the Earliest Times to the Edwardian Conquest.* Two volumes. London: Longmans, Green,

1911–1954. Though later historians are subjecting its findings to revision, this remains a work of careful scholarship that shows a reader the sweep of early Welsh history and recounts its struggles with epic clarity and grandeur.

22. Glanmor Williams. *The Welsh Church from Conquest to Reformation.* Cardiff: University of Wales Press, 1962. This work provides a continuation, in effect, of J. E. Lloyd's *History.* Despite its focus on the church, the book treats vernacular literature (including Dafydd ap Gwilym) with some detail.

23. Rees Davies, "Cymru yn Oes Dafydd ap Gwilym," *Taliesin,* 28: 5–23. This is a reprint of one of the papers from the 1972 Gregynog colloquium. Dr. Davies' essay demonstrates the political disunity of Wales following the English Conquest of 1282, the mixing of loyalties in an epoch of change. Dafydd's family — serving the English government yet jealously preserving Welsh culture — is a signal instance of this phenomenon.

24. A. D. Carr. "The World of Dafydd ap Gwilym," *Poetry Wales,* 8:4, 3–16. A sketch of social conditions in fourteenth century Wales, focussing on the class of the *uchelwyr,* the "noblemen," that is, the esquires or landholding freemen, to which Dafydd belonged. The oppressions of Edward the Third's government, engaged in French and Scottish wars, were to alienate the *uchelwyr,* some of whom served with the French against the English and some of whom would later join in the rebellion of Owain Glyndŵr. Though Dafydd was not a political poet, his bitter references to war, violence, taxation — even when he is speaking figuratively — reflect a world where these were bitter realities. The beggars, the wretches, the non-men of his poems (some he jibes at, some he likens himself to) correspond to the bondsmen who were the most taxed of the populace and the most devastated by plague. We should realize that when Dafydd calls down a plague on the unfriendly women of his parish who make him feel outcast, he is not just hurling a word at them: he is wishing them Black Death.

25. R. T. Jenkins and J. E. Lloyd. *A Dictionary of Welsh Biography.* London: Honourable Society of Cymmrodorion, 1959. A reference work providing biographical information on (among a host of other Welsh persons) Dafydd ap Gwilym and historical figures mentioned by him or associated with him.

26. S. Baring-Gould. *The Lives of the Saints.* New York: Longmans, Green, 1898. This edition has a Volume 16 with observations on

obscure Welsh saints not included in the main calendar of saints comprising the rest of the set.

27. William Rees. *An Historical Atlas of Wales: From Early to Modern Times.* London: Faber and Faber, 1951; 1972.

28. Rachel Bromwich, ed. and trans. *Trioedd Ynys Prydein: The Welsh Triads.* Cardiff: University of Wales Press, 1961; second edition, 1978. The triads dealt with in this work comprise an index to narrative traditions of the ancient Britons and of their medieval Welsh descendants. Since allusion to these traditions is a frequent device of the poets, the reader of Dafydd ap Gwilym will welcome this volume as a virtual dictionary of Welsh legend. The triads (some of them ancient, some of them later literary extensions of the mode) list succinctly various heroes, beauties, wonders of Britain ("Three Red Ravagers of the Island of Britain," "Three Futile Battles of the Island of Britain," "Three Prominent Cows of the Island of Britain," "Three People who broke their hearts from Bewilderment").

29. Gwyn Jones and Thomas Jones, trans. *The Mabinogion,* Everyman's Library (97). New York: Dutton, 1949; 1970. In annotating Dafydd's many allusions to characters or incidents from *The Mabinogion,* I cite the page numbers of this translation.

Criticism

30. Theodor Max Chotzen. *Recherches sur la Poésie de Dafydd ab Gwilym, barde Gallois du XIVe siècle.* Amsterdam: H. J. Paris, 1927. A comprehensive study that stresses the international and contemporary character of Dafydd's work, showing him to be in touch not only with his Welsh world, but also with continental literary currents. Chotzen concludes (p. 334) that Dafydd "a entrepris de dépeindre la société contemporaine dans toutes ses couches et de mettre en scène dans ses *cywyddau* les dames nobles de Maesaleg commes les paroissiennes de Llanbadarn et les bourgeoises de Rhosyr. En cela il fait penser à Chaucer et semble déjà très moderne."

31. Thomas Parry. "Dafydd ap Gwilym," Yorkshire Celtic Studies, 5 (1949–52):19–31. This is the author's summary in English of the introduction to *GDG.*

32. D. J. Bowen. "Dafydd ap Gwilym a Datblygiad y Cywydd," *Llên Cymru,* 8, nos. 1–2 (1964): 1–32. An essay exploring Dafydd's contribution to the development of the *cywydd.* Professor Bowen draws attention to the variety of styles the poet employs, not only in

different poems, but also in the different parts of particular poems.

33. Eurys I. Rowlands. Review of the Second Edition of *GDG*, *Llên Cymru*, 8, nos. 1–2 (1964): 107–12. Among other matters, this review stresses the historical character of experiences embodied in Dafydd's poetry.

34. Rachel Bromwich. *Tradition and Innovation in the Poetry of Dafydd ap Gwilym*. Cardiff: University of Wales Press, 1967. A study of the poet's sources and what he did with them. For example, Celtic traditions such as the appeal to a dead man to speak; or the verse satire that is believed capable of killing the one satirized; or conventional metaphors for a woman's beauty — these elements of Dafydd's native heritage enrich his poems. Dr. Bromwich shows, with detailed instances, that Dafydd also makes masterly use of other European poetic traditions.

35. Gwyn Williams. "Dafydd ap Gwilym: Poet of Love," *Poetry Wales*, 8, no. 4:18–27. This and the following three articles (as well as no. 2 and no. 24 above) appeared in a special issue of *Poetry Wales* (Spring 1973) devoted to Dafydd ap Gwilym.

36. Gwyn Thomas. "Dafydd ap Gwilym the Nature-Poet," *Poetry Wales*, 8, no. 4:28–33.

37. Thomas Parry. "Dafydd ap Gwilym's Poetic Craft," *Poetry Wales*, 8, no. 4:34–43.

38. Rachel Bromwich. "Influences upon Dafydd ap Gwilym's Poetry," *Poetry Wales*, 8, no. 4:44–55. Dr. Bromwich explores, in particular, the similarity in achievement of Chaucer and Dafydd ap Gwilym.

39. Rachel Bromwich. *Dafydd ap Gwilym*. Writers of Wales Series. Cardiff: University of Wales Press, 1974.

40. John Rowlands. *Dafydd ap Gwilym a Chanu Serch yr Oesoedd Canol*. Cardiff: University of Wales Press, 1975. Papers from the 1972 Gregynog colloquium. See my comment at the beginning of this bibliographical note. Two papers are specifically concerned with the poetry of Dafydd ap Gwilym: Rachel Bromwich, "Dafydd ap Gwilym: Y Traddodiad Islenyddol," pp. 43–57; and Dafydd Elis Thomas, "Dafydd ap Gwilym y Bardd," pp. 76–94.

41. R. Geraint Gruffydd. "Sylwadau ar Gywydd 'Offeren y Llwyn' Dafydd ap Gwilym," in J. E. Caerwyn Williams, ed., *Ysgrifau Beirniadol*, 10, 181–89. See my note on this article following my translation of Poem 122.

42. *Y Traethodydd*, 133. The April 1978 issue of this journal is

devoted principally to Dafydd ap Gwilym. In addition to essays (all in Welsh) by Dr. Gruffydd, Dr. Parry, and Dr. Bromwich, there is a note by David Jenkins (then Librarian of the National Library of Wales) on Dafydd's native region, with a map (p. 83), and appreciations of three of Dafydd's poems, by John Gwilym Jones (on Poem 27), Eurys Rolant (on Poem 42), and Gwyn Thomas (on Poem 124).

43. Alan Llwyd, ed. *50 o Gywyddau Dafydd ap Gwilym.* Swansea: Christopher Davies, 1980. Fifty expositions in Welsh of poems of Dafydd ap Gwilym; a total of forty-eight poems are treated, two of the poems being discussed twice, by different scholars. In addition to the editor, Alan Llwyd, the contributing scholars are John Rowlands, R. Geraint Gruffydd, Gwyn Thomas, and Gwynn ap Gwilym. For each poem, there is a commentary, the text of the poem from *GDG*, and a line-by-line prose modernization.

44. A. O. H. Jarman and Gwilym Rees Hughes, eds. *A Guide to Welsh Literature*, 2 vols. Swansea: Christopher Davies, 1976 (Vol. I); 1979 (Vol. II). Essays by several scholars, on Welsh literature from the sixth century to the early sixteenth century. Chapter V of Volume II is "Dafydd ap Gwilym," by Rachel Bromwich; with bibliography. Chapter VI, also by Dr. Bromwich, is a critical discussion of contemporaries of Dafydd such as Gruffudd Gryg and Iolo Goch. These are the first volumes of a series projected to cover Welsh literature to the present day; all the essays are in English, with translation of cited passages of Welsh poetry and prose.

45. Saunders Lewis. "Dafydd ap Gwilym," *Blackfriars* 34, 131–5. An essay in English, reprinted in *Presenting Saunders Lewis,* ed. Alun R. Jones and Gwyn Thomas. Cardiff: University of Wales Press, 1973, pp. 159–63. In *GDG*, Dr. Parry often cites Saunders Lewis (see my notes to Poems 54 and 140); Saunders Lewis's Welsh review of *GDG*[1] appeared in *Llên Cymru 2, 199*–208, and is reprinted in a collection of his essays on Welsh literature, *Meistri'r Canrifoedd,* ed. R. Geraint Gruffydd (Cardiff: University of Wales Press, 1973), pp. 41–55. A distinguished poet and dramatist as well as critic and historian, Saunders Lewis has for more than half a century been a leading figure in the movement to advance the Welsh language as a medium of national self-expression and cosmopolitan culture.

Translations

Just as editors may include critical commentary in their introductions and notes, so do critics writing in English include passages of translation in their essays on Dafydd. Thus does Rachel Bromwich in her *Dafydd ap Gwilym* (no. 39); and of course, her new edition of 56 poems is to include translations with notes and introduction. Consequently, my list of translations below does not include all that are now in print, nor do I indicate every place where these translations have appeared in print. The *New Yorker,* for example, has published some of Rolfe Humphries' work based on translations from Welsh; D. W. Robertson, Jr., included seven of the Bells' translations of Dafydd ap Gwilym in his textbook, *The Literature of Medieval England* (New York: McGraw-Hill, 1970), pp. 187–93. A translation of Poem 129 ("Dawn") by Melville Richards is included in *Eos: An Inquiry into the Theme of Lovers' Meetings and Partings at Dawn in Poetry,* ed. A. T. Hatto (The Hague: Mouton, 1965), pp. 568–74. *The Oxford Book of Welsh Verse* (London, 1962; 1972), edited by Thomas Parry, gives the Welsh texts of Poems 137, 141, 23, 124, 63, 42, 117, 144 (in that order). *The Oxford Book of Welsh Verse in English,* chosen by Gwyn Jones (London, 1977), includes translations of two of these, namely, Poem 117 ("The Wind") in Joseph Clancy's translation; and Poem 144 ("The Ruin") in Rolfe Humphries' translation; together with these other four translations: Poem 118 ("The Seagull," Glyn Jones); Poem 53 ("In Morfudd's Arms," Rolfe Humphries); Poem 48 ("The Girls of Llanbadarn," Rolfe Humphries); Poem 122 ("The Woodland Mass," Gwyn Williams). Some translators include poems not accepted as canonical by Dr. Parry; since the appearance of *GDG,* it has been customary to print the aprocryphal poems as anonymous productions.

Here or elsewhere in this bibliographical note, I believe I have identified all the principal publications where a reader may find translations of Dafydd ap Gwilym. The following are seven collections of translations, in order of the date of their first publication as collections (some translations of individual poems appeared separately earlier) and with distinguishing symbols; most of these collections are accompanied by valuable introductions and notes; those by Kenneth Jackson, Gwyn Williams, Joseph Clancy, and Anthony Conran include translations of several other poets besides Dafydd ap Gwilym.

B H. Idris Bell and David Bell. *Dafydd ap Gwilym: Fifty Poems.* London: Honourable Society of Cymmrodorion, 1942. The translations are in rhymed couplets, tetrameter or longer, some lines being filled out with matter not in the original.

H Nigel Heseltine. *25 Poems: Dafydd ap Gwilym.* With a preface by Frank O'Connor. Banbury: The Piers Press, 1970. This was first published as *Selected Poems,* by the Cuala Press, Dublin, 1944. Heseltine's translations are in prose, enjoyably conveying sense and feeling, though a reader equipped with Dr. Parry's text and commentary will note inaccuracies.

J Kenneth Jackson. *A Celtic Miscellany.* Harmondsworth: Penguin Books, 1979. First published by Routledge and Kegan Paul, 1951. Kenneth Jackson is a leading Celtic scholar; his prose translations carry the authority of his erudition, yet are brisk and clear.

W Gwyn Williams. *Welsh Poems: Sixth Century to 1600.* London: Faber and Faber, 1973. These translations first appeared in a volume titled *The Burning Tree* (London, 1956). They are in a free verse line which Williams employs with sensitivity and grace.

C Joseph P. Clancy. *Medieval Welsh Lyrics.* London: St. Martin's Press, 1965. In this anthology, Joseph Clancy includes his translations of fifty-five of the *cywyddau* of Dafydd ap Gwilym, based on the text of *GDG.* His translations are in verse: in seven-syllable couplets ending alternately on accented and unaccented syllables. This is an imitation of Dafydd's *cywydd* meter, without rhyme or *cynghanedd* (though alliteration and internal rhyme occur occasionally). The seven-syllable limitation results in omission of some of the literal content of Dafydd's lines, but the translations are scholarly, colloquial, and vivid. Eight of them were reprinted in the *Poetry Wales* issue honoring Dafydd.

P Anthony Conran. *The Penguin Book of Welsh Verse.* Harmondsworth: Penguin Books, 1967. These translations carry the imitation of the *cywydd* a step further: Conran uses the seven-syllable couplet together with the *cywydd* rhyme. The demands of rhyming entail departures from the original, but the poems are neatly done and lively.

R Rolfe Humphries. *Nine Thorny Thickets.* With four translations by
Jon Roush. Kent State University Press, 1969. This volume was in
press when Humphries died. Rolfe Humphries' work, also imitative
of the Welsh verse forms, is free as to sense, but with vigorous and appropriate feeling. In an earlier work (inspired by his reading of Gwyn
Williams' *Introduction to Welsh Poetry*), Humphries comes close to suggesting the various patterns of Welsh verse in English: *Green Armor on
Green Ground: Poems in the Twenty-four Official Welsh Meters and Some, in
Free Meters, on Welsh Themes* (New York: Scribner's, 1956).

The following list indicates what poems are translated by these
authors (represented by symbols); the poems are numbered as in
GDG.

	B	H	J	W	C	P	R
17.	B				C		R
18.	B		J		C		R
24.					C		
26.					C		
27.	B				C		R
28.						P	R
29.					C		
32.	B				C		
34.	B						
39.	B				C		R
41.					C		
42.					C		
43.					C		
45.					C		R
48.	B	H	J	W	C	P	R
49.	B		J		C		
51.	B						
53.	B				C		R
54.					C		
56.	B						
57.	B				C		
58.	B				C		R
59.					C		
63.	B		J		C		

	B	*H*	*J*	*W*	*C*	*P*	*R*
64.		H					R
67.					C		
68.					C		
69.	B		J		C		
70.					C		
71.	B				C		
74.	B	H	J		C		
75.					C		R
76.					C		
79.					C		
80.	B				C		R
81.					C		
83.		H					R
85.	B				C		
89.		H			C		
90.	B				C		R
93.					C		
94.					C		
98.					C		
99.		H					R
102.	B				C	P	
105.		H			C		R
106.					C		
111.	B				C		R
112.	B						R
113.		H					
114.	B	H			C		
117.	B	H			C	P	R
118.	B	H	J		C	P	
119.	B	H			C		R
122.	B	H		W	C		Roush
124.	B		J		C	P	R
125.		H		W	C		Roush
126.							Roush
127.		H					
128.					C		
129.	B	H			C		R
137.	B	H	J		C	P	

	B	H	J	W	C	P	R
139.					C		
141.	B	H			C		R
143.					C		
144.					C	P	R
145.		H					

The 83 canonical poems not appearing in translation in the above seven collections are the following, as numbered in *GDG*: 1, 2, 3, 4, 5, 6, 8, 9, 10, 11, 12, 13, 14, 15, 16, 17, 19, 20, 21, 22, 23, 25, 30, 31, 33, 35, 36, 37, 38, 40, 44, 46, 47, 50, 52, 55, 60, 61, 62, 65, 66, 72, 73, 77, 78, 82, 84, 86, 87, 88, 91, 92, 95, 96, 97, 100, 101, 103, 104, 107, 108, 109, 110, 115, 116, 120, 121, 123, 130, 131 132, 133, 134, 135, 136, 138, 140, 142, 146, 148, 150, 152, 154.

It is clear that some of the poems have been particular favorites with the translators and their readers. Poem 48, "The Girls of Llanbadarn," appears in all seven collections. In five of the collections, there are translations of Poem 117, "The Wind"; Poem 118, "The Seagull"; Poem 122, "Mass of the Grove"; Poem 124, "Trouble in a Tavern"; and Poem 137, "The Poet and the Gray Friar." The reader who is unfamiliar with Dafydd ap Gwilym might well begin his reading of Dafydd with these popular poems. The next step could be to explore — following one's personal interest — a certain group of poems, such as I have pointed to in my introduction: the love-messenger poems, say, or the Morfudd poems, or the Dyddgu poems, or the friar poems. And then to read the rest. Each of the translators I have listed captures qualities of the original that help the English reader appreciate the art of Dafydd ap Gwilym. Like photographs of a fine building, the various translations provide different perspectives and textures from which we may derive a sense of the original structure. Of course, no translation equals the poem translated. Poetry baffles translation because poetry is the densest yet most delicate of linguistic structures: there is much matter there, and it is all light and breath. Verse translations alone impart something of the music that orders and sweetens a poem; on the other hand, drawing out the full substance of meaning, allusion, and imagery in a poem requires pages of annotation and commentary, not just a prose re-statement. Each translator must settle for a limited goal. Mine has been to express with reasonable clearness and force what Dafydd's

Welsh says, so far as I can understand that and put it into English. And I have translated all the poems in *GDG*. They have proved a pleasant and enriching discovery for me; and so I hope they will prove for other readers. The texts, the translations, the commentaries, the linguistic and historical studies now available should attract a wider audience to read Dafydd ap Gwilym in Welsh, in the masterful edition of Sir Thomas Parry. Dafydd is not a poet of a few memorable pieces. His achievement is more abundant and complex: he writes of many subjects, in many styles. His poems illuminate one another and, as an ensemble, provide us with profound poetic joy as we encounter his genius and the drama of his turbulent, radiant world.

The Welsh Arts Council has recently issued through Oriel Recordings a record of readings from Dafydd ap Gwilym, including poems read by John Gwilym Jones, Trefor Edwards, Catrin Lewis, and Sir Thomas Parry, with a linking narrative read by R. Alun Evans and three poems declaimed by Osian Ellis to his harp accompaniment; the presentation was arranged and produced by Professor Gwyn Thomas. It may be obtained from the Welsh Arts Council, 9 Museum Street, Cardiff; or Oriel, 53 Charles Street, Cardiff.

Glossary and Index of Names

See also the notes to individual poems. For place names, see the maps in the Introduction. This glossary is limited to the canonical poems in *GDG*. The names are listed as they appear in the translations (e.g., "England," not "Lloegr"). When the names in the original poems differ thus from those in my translation, I note the original Welsh forms in parentheses after the glossary entry. For fuller discussion of these names, readers are referred to *GDG* and other sources listed in my bibliographical note, especially no. 27, William Rees, *An Historical Atlas of Wales* (London, 1972), and no. 28, Rachel Bromwich, *Trioedd Ynys Prydein: The Welsh Triads* (Cardiff, 1978). In Welsh names, the patronymics are *mab* (son) and *merch* (daughter); these normally appear in mutated forms (*fab, ferch*) or abbreviated (*ab, ap*), the shorter forms being common in modern Welsh. The Welsh alphabet is followed in this glossary only for Welsh names beginning with *LL*, which appear after all names beginning with single *L*. The numbers following an entry give poem number and line number in which the name occurs in the translations.

Aberffraw, 153.34. The site of the ancient court of the princes of Gwynedd, in Anglesey; the birthplace of Gruffudd Gryg.

Abermaw, 99.25. Barmouth, coastal town in Merionethshire, at the estuary of the Mawddach.

Adail Heilin, 83.33. See note to Poem 83.

Adam (*Adda, Addaf*), 24.1, 31; 83.50; 92.30. Cf. **Eve; Paradise.**

Aeron, 99.35. River in mid-Cardiganshire.

Amlyn, 17.15. Amlyn and Amic are the heroes of a medieval Welsh version of a French *chanson de geste* recounting the friendship of Amis and Amiles.

Andrew (*Andras*), 4.26. The apostle, brother of Peter.

Angharad, 16, *passim;* 140.32. Daughter of a family from Buellt, east of Cardiganshire; wife of Ieuan Llwyd ab Ieuan ap Gruffudd Foel, who swore loyalty to the Black Prince in 1343; their home was in Pennardd, a district in mid-Cardiganshire.

Anglesey. See **Môn.**

Anna, 3.4, 5; 26.21; 52.42. St. Anne, mother of the Virgin Mary.

Annwn, 22.42; 68.44; (*Annwfn*) 27.40. The otherworld of Welsh myth; land of the *Tylwyth Teg,* the Welsh fairy troop.

April (*Ebrill*), 63.4; 69.18; 114.4.

Arabian Gold (*Aur Afia*), 13.122. A figure for Dafydd's bardic uncle, connoting excellence; Arabia (*Arafia, Afia*) is traditionally associated by Welsh poets with gold.

Ardudfyl, 149.48; 153.52. Mother of Dafydd ap Gwilym.

Arfon, 84.42; 89.27; 152.3. Region of North Wales opposite the island of Môn (Anglesey).

Arthur, 5.14; 147.35. The legendary hero and king of Britain.

Artro Fawr, 99.24. River in Merionethshire entering the sea about midway between Y Bychan Draeth and Barmouth.

August (*Awst*), 27.24.

Babylon, Tower of (*tŵr Babilon*), 140.26.

Bangor, 15.10; 111.6; 149.35. Coastal town in northwestern Wales; an episcopal see.

Bartholomew (*Martholamëus*), 4.33–34. The apostle.

Basaleg, 8.38; 9.54; 11.39. Location of the court of Dafydd's patron, Ifor Hael, near Cardiff.

Beli, 12.43. Legendary ancestor of Welsh royal dynasties.

Beuno, 78.47. Welsh saint of the seventh century, founder of churches, especially in North Wales.

Bleddyn, 15.39; 154.36. An unidentified inferior poet.

Brân, 15.9. A legendary king of Britain, son of Llŷr and kin to Beli; traditionally styled Brân Fendigaid (Brân the Blessed), he is credited with superhuman powers. In the *Mabinogi* of *Branwen ferch Lŷr,* he leads an army into Ireland, to avenge his sister's humiliation there.

Branwen Ferch Llŷr, 40.14. Heroine of the *Mabinogi* named for her (the name being usually spelled with a mutation: Branwen ferch Lŷr). Her brother, king of Britain, gave her in marriage to the king of Ireland; a tragic war ensued.

Britons (*Brytaniaid*), 140.1. Ancestors of the Welsh, colonized by Rome.

Bro Gadell, 150.33. Land of Cadell; that is, South Wales. See **Cadell.**

Bro Gynin, Dafydd's birthplace. See note to Poem 83.

Brychan Yrth, 94.54. Legendary founder of the Welsh kingdom of Brycheiniog (from which the name of Brecon is derived).

Buellt, 16.70. A region east of Cardiganshire; the town of Builth Wells is on its eastern border, *Builth* being the English rendering of *Buellt.*

Bwa Bach, Y, 117.44; 131.40. "The Little Bow"; a nickname for Morfudd's husband. Cf. **Cynfrig Cynin; The Dark Idler; Eiddig.**

Bwlch Meibion Dafydd, 83.19. See note to Poem 83.

Bwlch Y Gyfylfaen, 83.24. See note to Poem 83.

Bychan Draeth, Y, 99.21. Ocean spur extending into north Merionethshire, southeast of Y Traeth Mawr.

Bysaleg, 83.15. Stream flowing past Dafydd's birthplace at Bro Gynin; now known as Afon Stewy; see note to Poem 83.

Cadell (*Bro Gadell*), 150.33. Cadell was a son of Rhodri Mawr who ruled in South Wales; he died early in the tenth century; his son, Hywel Dda, is credited with codifying the Welsh laws.

Cadfan, 81.45; 86.23. A Welsh saint believed to have founded the church named for him at Tywyn in Merionethshire; if Morfudd's family lived in Merionethshire, these references to Cadfan could be marks of deference to a saint of their region.

Caer, County of (*swydd Gaer*), 122.9. Carmarthenshire? Earldom of Caerlleon Gawr (Chester)?

Caer in Arfon (*y Gaer yn Arfon*), 89.27. Caernarvon castle.

Caerfyrddin, 133.24. The town of Carmarthen. A "crown of Caerfyrddin" would probably be a coin, associated with Carmarthen because that town was an administrative center for South Wales.

Caerllion, 64.22. The town located on the site of the Roman legionary fortress of Isca, near Newport in South Wales; in English, Caerleon-on-Usk. Geoffrey of Monmouth represents it as a leading center for Arthur's court.

Caesar's Nation (*cenedl Sisar*), 140.2. Presumably the ancient Romans.

Cai, 114.13; **Cai Hir** ("Tall Cai"), 21.53. Arthur's companion (corresponding to the character known in English as "Kay the Seneschal"); the Welsh bards, unlike continental Arthurian narrators, consistently present Cai (or Cei) in a favorable light, as a brave warrior endowed with magical properties.

Calais (*Y Galais*), 140.22. The fortified port on the French coast.

Camber's Land (*Gwlad Gamber*), 84.70. Cambria, i.e., Wales. Geoffrey of Monmouth traces the name "Cymry" (the Welsh people) to a son of Brutus named Camber (as he traces the British to Brutus).

Caron (*Carawn*), 88.24. The land around Tregaron in mid-Cardiganshire.

Castell Gwgawn, 83.31. See note to Poem 83.

Celli Fleddyn, 83.12. Unidentified; see note to Poem 83.

Celliau'r Meirch, 83.7. See note to Poem 83.

Ceredigion (*Geredigiawn*), 16.68; 88.4. Ancient Welsh kingdom comprising the territory of the modern county of Cardiganshire; in both these references, the full phrase is *Gwawn Geredigiawn,* "Gossamer of Ceredigion," applied in Poem 16 to Angharad of Glyn Aeron, and in Poem 88 to an unnamed girl associated with the nearby region about Tregaron.

Ceri, 9.7; 85.23. Kerry, a border district in Powys.

Chester (*Caer*), 126.40; 127.38. The verses to the Cross of Chester ascribed to Dafydd Llwyd ap Gwilym Gam (*GDG* ³, p. 556) — now accepted by Dr. Parry as an ascription to Dafydd, though the work is not included in *GDG* — are another association of Dafydd ap Gwilym with the town of Chester. Chester might also be the scene of Poem 66 (cf. *GDG* ³, p. 558).

Christendom (*Cred*), 10.35; 13.36; 41.2; 94.32; 118.28; 123.19; 125.27.

Christmas (*Nadolig*), 145.6.

Clud, 13.29. A man's name; see **Gwawl Fab Clud.**

Coed Eutun, 25.52. "Eutun Wood"; Eutun was a medieval estate near the Dee, in Maelor.

Creator (*Creawdr*), 114.20; 139.28; **Lord Creator** (*Creawdrner*), 67.19. Cf. **Father; God; Jesus; Trinity.**

Creirwy, 123.19. A legendary beauty cited by the poets.

Cuhelyn, 25.41; 143.39. A twelfth-century ancestor of Dafydd's was named Cuhelyn Fardd, "Cuhelyn the Bard." His shield was cited by the poets. The name may correspond to the Irish name, Cuchulainn.

Cwm-Y-Gro, 94.32. Perhaps the modern Cwm-y-glo, near Bro Gynin; see note to Poem 83.

Cybi, 15.3; 52.27; 115.39. A sixth-century monk and founder of churches in Anglesey and Gwynedd.

Cynddelw, 15.40. Cynddelw Brydydd Mawr was a distinguished Welsh poet of the twelfth century.

Cyndeyrn, 21.72. St. Kentigern, patron saint of Glasgow; also known as St. Mungu or Mungo; he is associated with the Welsh heroes of Strathclyde, a tradition identifying him as the son of Owain ab Urien; he is also credited with founding St. Asaph's in North Wales.

Cynfelyn, 116.46. A saint associated with Cardiganshire.
Cynfrig, 16.50. Great-grandfather of Angharad, wife of Ieuan Llwyd of Glyn Aeron.
Cynfrig Cynin, 73.27. The name of Morfudd's husband. Cf. **Y Bwa Bach; The Dark Idler; Eiddig.**
Cyrseus, 143.24. The sword of Otfel (Otinel) in the Charlemagne cycle.

Dafydd, 9.59; 43.32; 44.1; 58.9; 77.14; 95.18; 128.43; 131.2, 13; 136.7; 137.87; 138.33; 144.42; 147–54 *passim;* **Dafydd Fab Gwilym,** 25.7–8.
Dark Idler, The (*y Du Segur*), 93.16. An epithet for Morfudd's husband. Cf. **Y Bwa Bach; Cynfrig Cynin; Eiddig.**
David, The Prophet (*Dafydd Broffwyd*), 137.60.
David, St. See **Dewi.**
Ddôl Goch, Y, 13.77. One of the courts of Dafydd's uncle, Llywelyn ap Gwilym; from the poem, Y Ddôl Goch appears to be the "fair court in Emlyn" where Llywelyn was murdered.
Deheubarth, 17.24. A kingdom of South Wales that comprised Pembrokeshire, Cardiganshire, and Ystrad Tywi (region along the river Towy).
Deidameia (*Diodemaf*), 51.9. The mother of Achilles' son Neoptolemus; the triad alluded to in this poem appears to have confused Deidameia with Dido.
Deifr, 58.48; 66.42. A woman's name, a variant of Dyfr; this is also the spelling of the Welsh word for Deira (see below), but Dr. Parry takes the reference in Poem 66 to be to a woman, not to "the English."
Deinioel, 50.34; 82.5; 111.6. Patron saint of Bangor in North Wales; the name is a Welsh form of the name Daniel.
Deira (*Deifr*), 5.42; 8.27; 11.10; 13.13; 14.36; 143.28. The ancient northern English kingdom against which the Welsh of North Britain fought; the persistence of the name is an archaic element in Dafydd's poetry and serves as a poetic equivalent to "the English." Cf. **England.**
Deirdre (*Derdri*), 139.21. The tragic heroine of Irish legend, married to Conchobar but in love with Naisi.
Dewi, 15.2; 99.4, 28; 121.23; 123.44; 149.11. St. David, patron saint of Wales, founder of the monastic church of Mynyw (Menevia) in Pembrokeshire.
Dinbyrn, 21.76. An obscure traditional hero.
Dwynwen, 94.1. A saint of North Wales, patroness of courting

lovers; though now a ruin, her picturesquely sited shrine on a headland near Newborough in Anglesey was still attracting pilgrims in the eighteenth century.

Dyddgu, 37.1; 45.54; 79.16, 54; 92.13, 39, 43; 95.1; 98.36; 116.30; 142.22; 151.50, 53. Daughter of a man praised by Dafydd named Ieuan ap Gruffudd ap Llywelyn, of a noble southern family; the names of daughter and father are too common to permit — as yet — a positive identification of the family. They may have lived at Tywyn in south Cardiganshire. Her name is pronounced with the accent on the first syllable, which rhymes with the first syllable of *southern;* the second syllable rhymes with *key.* A gracious but distant brunette, Dyddgu stirred love-longing in Dafydd that she seems neither to have encouraged nor appeased. He addressed poems of courtly tribute and solicitation to her, though she remained demurely aloof. He wept therefore, but he does not charge her with fickleness or trickery, as he does Morfudd; and he persisted in his courtship, though he never glories — as he does with Morfudd — in winning her love. Once thought only a literary exercise in troubadour homage to a lady, scholars now believe that Dafydd's love for Dyddgu was for a real woman.

Dyfed, 12.1, 38; 13.1, 140; 84.28; 95.17. Ancient kingdom of south-western Wales; known in Welsh tradition as *Gwlad yr Hud,* "the Land of Enchantment."

Dyfi, 10.7; 71.6; 99.29. River dividing South and North Wales (in English, the Dovey).

Dyfr, 52.13; 56.33; 93.32. A legendary beauty of Arthur's court, included in a late triad with Tegau and Enid, as a model of excellence. Cf. **Deifr.**

Dysynni, 99.27. A stream rising on Cader Idris that enters the sea north of Tywyn in Merionethshire.

Easter (Pasg), 132.11.

Edward, King (*Edwart Frenin*), 140.56. The allusion is probably to Edward III, who besieged the port of Calais in 1346-7.

Eidal, Land of (*Bro Eidal*), 44.11. Unidentified. *Yr Eidal* is the Welsh name for Italy, but Dr. Parry does not regard that as the intended reference here.

Eiddig, 40.5; 59.2; 61.42; 70.33; 72.4; 76.4; 77.25; 78.21; 80.2, 5, 14, 24, 58, 62; 81.17, 41; 94.27; 114.52, 56; 116.44; 143.22; 145.26. The word means "jealous" and is used as an epithet for the jealous husband. Poem 75 is a curse upon such a husband.

Poems 41 (line 33) and 82 (line 32) speak of *dyn eiddig,* "a jealous man," which I render as "Eiddig." Cf. the references to Morfudd's jealous husband: **Y Bwa Bach; Cynfrig Cynin; The Dark Idler.** But "Eiddig" may be any jealous husband.

Eiddilig Gor, 84.40. An Irish magician.

Eigr, 16.51, 54; 30.22; 50.16; 54.42; 56.30; 58.3, 21; 66.44; 77.6; 81.20; 87.61; 88.12; 99.4; 118.14. Igraine, mother of Arthur.

Einion Dot, 128.59. Character in some lost Welsh legend.

Eithinfynydd, 57.1. Perhaps a reference to a residence of that name in Merionethshire.

Eleirch, 83.8. The modern village of Elerch; see note to Poem 83.

Elen, 51.12; 141.2. Helen of Troy.

Elfed, 12.37. A district in Carmarthenshire bordered by the river Gwili.

Elien, 15.8. Eilian, a Welsh saint to whom a church and well are dedicated in Anglesey.

Emig, 17.16. Amic: Amic and Amlyn are the heroes of a medieval Welsh version of a French *chanson de geste* recounting the friendship of Amis and Amiles.

Emlyn, 12.4, 5; 13.66. Both the region of Emlyn and the town of Newcastle Emlyn on the Teifi, where Dafydd's uncle, Llywelyn ap Gwilym, was constable.

England (*Lloegr*), 12.10; 13.94; 95.34; **Englishmen** (*Eingl*), 5.23; 11.43; **Englishman, Englishmen** (*Sais*), 8.16; 9.56; 81.26; 116.42; 124.48; **English** (adjective: *Seisnig*), 9.56; 81.29; 125.31. Cf. **Deira.**

Enid, 52.50; 53.1; 55.7; 81.17; 105.7; 120.14; 128.6. A beautiful woman of Arthur's court; in Chrétien's romance, Enid is the wife of Erec; in the corresponding Welsh romance, she is the wife of Gereint fab Erbin; she is a model of patience.

Epiphany (*Ystwyll*), 97.3.

Esyllt, 16.14; 33.14; 45.41; 86.2; 111.29; 120.19. Isolt, wife of Mark and lover of Tristan.

Eve (*Efa*), 51.4; 97.1, 24, 26. The reference in Poem 51 is to the Eve of Genesis (cf. **Adam; Paradise**). The Eve in Poem 97 is a woman Dafydd has loved (perhaps one of his fictions).

Father, God the Father (*Tad*), 3.3; 114.39; (*Tad Duw*) 70.64; (*Duw Dad*) 68.7; 121.10; 133.9; 140.45; (*Dofydd Dad*), 16.48; 122.33; **True God My Father** (*Gwirdduw fy Nhad*), 140.36; **Father of Divinity** (*dwyfoliaeth dad*), 30.17. Cf. **Creator; God; Jesus; Trinity.**

Fflur, 44.17; 86.5; 111.8. Often cited as a standard of beauty, Fflur figures in an incompletely preserved legend relating to the Roman conquest of Britain.

France, Frenchmen (*Ffrainc*), 6.10; 12.29; 44.26; 58.30; 75.5, 40; 132.10; 142.29; **Frenchman, Norman** (*Ffranc*), 6.9; 58.34; **French** (adjective: *Ffrengig*), 10.32; 68.39; 133.5.

Fulke (*Ffwg*), 6.37. Perhaps the Marcher lord, Fulke Fitz Warine.

Gamallt, Y, 83.21. See note to Poem 83.

Garwy, 48.15. A lover traditionally cited by the poets for his manly passion.

Gascony (*Gasgwyn*), 132.11; **Gascony Mare** (*Gwasgwynes*), 75.28; **Gascony Stallion** (*gwasgwyn*), 150.51.

Giles, St. (*Silin*), 15.7. Athenian-born hermit who in the seventh century became abbot of a monastery near Arles.

Glyn, 17.19. Glyn Aeron, the upper valley of the river Aeron in Cardiganshire.

God (*Duw*), 1.34, 40; 3.8, 9; 4.15, 20, 22; 7.18; 8.8; 12.27, 52; 13.41, 96, 100, 124; 14.11; 16.41; 17.44; 19.48; 20.51; 23.1, 6, 51; 25.17; 29.20, 21; 30.18, 26; 31.5, 46; 32.38; 35.11, 72; 36.12, 18, 20; 39.42; 42.3, 40; 43.21, 36, 41; 45.17, 46; 46.36, 60; 48.22; 50.34; 51.4, 40; 53.14; 55.18; 56.6; 57.18; 67.2; 70.2, 46; 71.5; 76.6, 29; 77.27; 79.34; 80.63; 81.4; 83.11; 85.18, 47; 89.4; 91.12; 93.25; 94.20, 23, 33, 35, 37; 98.10, 37; 101.11, 36; 103.28; 108.34; 114.21, 42; 116.4, 45; 117.25; 120.2; 121.14; 123.43; 124.70; 126.14; 129.14, 21, 44, 46; 131.2, 9, 29; 133.52; 137.28, 37, 39, 44, 59, 62; 139.1, 10; 140.9, 19; 143.6; 150.9; 151.45; (*Deus*) 1.7; (*Dofydd*) 1.1; 4.8; 11.21; 16.41, 48; 23.23; 114.12; 122.33; 136.16; 140.42; (*Dwy*) 70.46; **God, Lord** (*Celi*), 2.11; 13.27, 33, 37; 36.27; 63.71; 113.3; 114.27; (*Iôn*) 4.15; (*Iôr*) 3.9; 43.33; (*Naf*) 5.18; 43.20; 58.13; 93.25; (*Nêr*) 4.20; 5.17; 16.11; 68.52; 140.9; **Lord** (*Dom'ne, Dom'nus*), 1.8; (*Gwawr*) 13.25, 124; (*Llywydd*) 76.29; 129.21; (*Rhi*) 13.41; 71.5; 120.2; **By God** (*rho Duw*), 24.3; 39.29; 70.66; 81.45; 98.30; 116.7; 143.2; 151.4; **By the Great God** (*myn Duw mawr*), 122.19; **By the God Who is Loved** (*myn Duw a gerir*), 27.11; **The Man Who Owns the World** (*'r Gwr biau'r byd*), 67.17; **By the Man Who Owns Today** (*myn y Gwr a fedd heddiw*), 106.3; 136.17; **By the Man Who Made Me** (*ym Gwr a'm gwnaeth*), 89.26. Cf. **Creator; Father; Jesus; Trinity.** The divine names appearing in the works of Dafydd ap Gwilym are so numerous, so varied in their distribution and connotation, and so potent in their signification that of themselves they provide the materials for a theology. He can be profane; but his poems proclaim belief in a universe sustained by generosity and mercy and ruled by truth. Dafydd need not turn a bird into a spirit in order to transcend the mundane; his skylark, in its gentle body, natural soaring, and instinctive song, manifests the Creator's love.

Gogfran Gawr, 64.26. In Welsh tradition, father of Gwenhwyfar (Guinevere).

Goleuddydd, 20.20. A woman to whom Gruffudd Gryg composed verses.

Greece (*Groeg*), 51.14.

Gruffudd ab Adda, 18. A *cywydd*-poet, contemporary with Dafydd, whose home was in Powys.

Gruffudd Gryg, 20; 47–54. The poet born in Aberffraw in Anglesey who contended with Dafydd on the subject of love poetry; though he adopts a conservative stance towards the emotional drama of Dafydd's *cywyddau,* he was younger than Dafydd and his extant poems are themselves *cywyddau* in Dafydd's mode.

Gwaeddan, 84.19. Character in a lost Welsh story.

Gwalchmai, 21.2. The Welsh Gawain.

Gwawl Fab Clud, 92.26. Gwawl son of Clud is a forthright suitor in "Pwyll Prince of Dyfed," the first of the *Mabinogion* tales.

Gweirful, 101.44; 151.52, 54; 153.1, 14. A woman's name. In Poems 151 and 153, the Gwynedd poet, Gruffudd Gryg, names Gweirful as a woman he loves; in Poem 101, the girl from the South who is the subject of that poem is contrasted with "an elegant Gweirful" from Gwynedd, perhaps Gruffudd's beloved.

Gwenhwyfar, 82.33. Guinevere.

Gwenwlydd, 149.4. Ganelon, the traitor at Roncesvalles, in the *Chanson de Roland.*

Gwenwynwyn-Land (*Gwenwynwyn dir*), 18.36. South Powys.

Gwern-y-Talwrn, 83.44. See note to Poem 83.

Gwgon, 34.30; **Gwgon Gleddyfrudd,** 46.67–8. Perhaps the last king of Ceredigion, Gwgon ap Meurig, who died about 871. *Gleddyfrudd* is a compound epithet (*cleddyf* + *rhudd*) meaning "red sword."

Gwili (*Wyli*), 12.39. A stream flowing into the Towy just above Carmarthen.

Gwinau Dau Freuddwyd, Y, 15.6. Great-grandfather of St. Llywelyn, the patron saint of Welshpool in Powys.

Gwri Golden Hair (*Gwri Wallt Euryn*), 12.35. Name given Pryderi in the *Mabinogi* of "Pwyll."

Gwyn ap Nudd (*Gwyn fab Nudd*), 26.40; 68.32, 40; 127.29; 150.52.

Leader of the *Tylwyth Teg* (literally, the "Fair Family"), the Welsh fairy troop.

Gwynedd, 8.4;10.4; 25.45; 34.14; 51.27; 86.15; 98.57; 101.44; 105.35; 111.22; 114.46; 128.5, 33, 45; 137.83; 148.36; 149.43; 152.24, 39; 154.35; **Man of Gwynedd** (*Gwyndyd*), 15.28,; 148.33; (adjective: *Gwyndodig*) 148.32. Gwynedd is the ancient kingdom of northwestern Wales.

Hawtyclŷr, 143.44. Hauteclaire, the sword of Oliver, Roland's companion.

Heaven (*nef*), 2.33; 3.12; 11.46; 20.66; 51.4; 63.27; 99.2; 134.10; 137.44, 49; (*nefau*) 10.26; (*nen*) 122.32; (*Geli*) 108.33.

Hector (*Ector; Echdor*), 5.14, 41. The Trojan warrior-prince.

Helen (*Elen*), 98.17. The wife of a rich merchant named Robin Nordd; his Anglo-Norman name suggests that her "stubborn accent" was English; she rewards Dafydd for his poetry with gifts of socks and motley-cloth, her husband's merchandise being wool.

Hercules (*Ercwlff*), 5.25; Ector and Ercwlff are named in a Welsh triad.

Hickin (*Hicin*), 124.50. Diminutive of the English name Richard; Dafydd refers to the three English hucksters by casual short names.

Hildr, 142.25. Evidently once a famous teacher of music.

Huail, 14.40. A legendary warrior, noted for high spirits; in Arthurian tradition, he challenged the authority of the king and was slain by Arthur.

Hywel, 15.15, 43. Probably the Hywel ap Goronwy of Anglesey who was Dean of Bangor Cathedral about 1350 and became Bishop in 1370.

Hywel Fychan, 29.23. Unidentified; apparently a love poet.

Ieuan ap Gruffudd ap Llywelyn, 45.1–3. Friend of Dafydd's and father of Dyddgu.

Ieuan Llwyd of Genau'r Glyn, 14, *passim.* Dafydd's patron living in Genau'r Glyn, a district (commote) north of Bro Gynin; he is named in state records as an official of Dafydd's native commote of Perfedd in 1351–52.

Ifor, 5–11; 83.35. Poems 5–11 deal with Dafydd's patron, Ifor Hael of Basaleg near Cardiff; the Ifor named in Poem 83 as having a court near Bro Gynin is unidentified.

Indeg, 16.9; 43.43; 54.24; 71.41; 79.11; 94.6; 96.1; 103.1. A woman whose beauty was cited by the poets as a standard of excellence.

A triad names her as daughter of Garwy Hir and mistress of Arthur, but her story has been lost.

Iolydd, 116.22. A dog's name; the word means "suppliant, worshipper."

Iorwerth ab y Cyriog (*Ierwerth; Mab y Cyriog*), 31.17, 31, 37, 58. A poet from Anglesey, contemporary with Dafydd.

Irishman (*Gwyddel*), 84.40; **Irish** (adjective: *Gwyddeleg*), 139.45.

Is-Aeron, 88.2. Region in Cardiganshire south of the river Aeron.

Jack (*Siac*), 124.50.

James (*Iago*), 4.27, 36. The two apostles named James: James son of Zebedee and James son of Alphaeus.

January (*marwfis*), 87.16. Also named (*Mis Ionawr*) in Dr. Parry's title to Poem 69.

Jenkin (Siencin), 124.50. Diminutive of Jan, an English name, like John, derived from Iohannes; one of the English hucksters who mistake Dafydd for a thief.

Jenkin the Goldsmith (*Siancyn Eurych*), 38.35–36. Presumably a thrifty goldsmith, whom Morfudd surpasses in her insistence on being paid; she expects a payment of love, since her gift of a birch-belt was in Welsh folklore a sign of love.

Jesus (*Siesus*), 1.1, 42; 52.43; (*Iesu*) 2.21; 4.10, 18; 124.66; **Jesus the Holy God** (*Iesu lwyd Iôn*), 4.11; **God Jesus** (*Duw Iesu*), 4.49; 78.13; **Christ** (*Christus*), 2.3; (*Crist*) 2.3, 5, 9, 13, 17; 4.46; 13.33, 37; 24.51; 36.22, 27; 67.41; 99.15; 125.27; 129.37; 132.4; 136.4; **Great Christ, God's Generous Treasure** (*haelgrair Duw Uchelgrist*), 20.51; **Mary's Son** (*Mab Mair*), 3.11; 30.24; 43.19; 44.29; 136.5; **Foster Son of Mary** (*Mab maeth Mair*), 52.34; **Son of Grace** (*Mab Rhad*), 50.56; **Only Son of the Lord God** (*Unmab Duw Naf*), 95.2; **God's Son Above Who Rules Us** (*Mab Duw fry a'n medd*), 4.2; **The Lord** (*'r Arglwydd*), 4.30; **By St. Anne's Grandson** (*myn ŵyr Anna*), 26.21; **By the Man of Sorrows . . . Who Suffered** (*Myn y Gŵr mewn cyflwr cawdd . . . a ddioddefawdd*), 77.13–14; **By the Five Wounds** (*er pum harcholl*), 128.47; **By the Cross** (*myn y grog*), 20.10; 86.24; 140.12. Cf. **Creator; Father; God; Trinity.**

Jew, Jews (*Iddew; Iddewon, Iddeon*), 1.24; 52.36; 76.4.

John (*Ieuan*), 4.24. The apostle and evangelist.

Joseph (*Sioseb*), 1.42; 52.44. Spouse of the Virgin Mary.

Judas Iscariot (*Suddas*), 1.17.

Jude (*Sud*), 4.37; 15.4, 5. The apostle Jude Thaddeus.

June (*Mehefin*), 27.46.

Land of Enchantment: See **Dyfed.**

Latin (*Lladin*), 35.48.

Lent (*Grawys*), 154.49; **Shrove Tuesday** (*ynyd*), 119.10.

Luned, 43.5; 86.9; 133.16, 44, 50. A woman's name, corresponding to the French Lunete.

Llanbadarn, 41.21; 48.19; 71.30. Dafydd's home parish in Cardiganshire; founded by the Welsh missionary monk, St. Padarn, in the sixth century, Llanbadarn was an important ecclesiastical center for mid-Wales.

Llanddwyn, 94.8, 31. A church dedicated to Dwynwen in Anglesey, near Newborough.

Llandudoch, 13.130. Village and parish (known in English as St. Dogmael's) near the town of Cardigan; the original home of Dafydd's family.

Llan-Faes, 20.38. Site of a friary near Beaumaris in Anglesey; the inhabitants of the town of Llanfaes were resettled by Edward I in Newborough; after the Dissolution, some of the treasure and furnishings of Llanfaes Friary were moved to the parish church in Beaumaris; these include the tomb of Joan, daughter of King John of England and wife of Llywelyn the Great.

Llanllugan, 113.10. Convent of Cistercian nuns in Powys.

Llawdden, 14.26. Great-grandfather of Ieuan Llwyd of Genau'r Glyn (a district in north Cardiganshire).

Llwyd, Dafydd, ap Gwilym Gam. See **Chester;** and note to Poem 43.

Llwyd, Morfudd. See **Morfudd;** and note to Poem 43.

Llwyd Fab Cel Coed, 84.46. An enchanter who figures in the *Mabinogion* tale of "Manawydan Son of Llŷr"; he casts a spell on Dyfed to avenge the beating of Gwawl son of Clud.

Llyfni, 99.18. A river in Caernarvonshire entering the sea to the south of the Menai Straits.

Llŷr, 11.43; 12.44; 14.45; 44.13. A legendary ancestor in Welsh royal genealogies; perhaps originally a Celtic sea-god.

Llystyn, Y, 13.56. One of the courts in Dyfed of Dafydd's uncle, Llywelyn ap Gwilym.

Llywelyn ap Gwilym, 12; 13. Dafydd's uncle and bardic master, constable of Newcastle Emlyn.

Llywelyn Fychan, 17.11–13. A soldier from the Aeron valley who served the English king; sworn friend to Rhydderch, the subject of this elegy.

Madawg Lawgam, 93.5. Name of Morfudd's father, with epithet ("Madog of the Crooked Hand").

Madog Benfras, 19. Poet and friend of Dafydd's whose home was in Maelor in northeastern Wales; the Madog of Poem 31 and the Madog fab Gruffudd of Poem 25 may be the same person.

Madog Hir, 128.58. Unidentified legendary character.

Mael, 95.3. Ancestral figure for whom the land of Maelienydd in mid-Wales is named.

Maelgwn, 135.44. King of Gwynedd in the early sixth century; he is mentioned by Gildas (the Latin form of his name being Maglocunus).

Maelor, 44.19. A district in northeastern Wales, on both sides of the River Dee, extending into England at the border of Cheshire and Shropshire.

Maestran, 25.43. A town in Merionethshire.

Mald y Cwd, 154.44. Perhaps a stock comic character.

Man, Isle of (*Manaw*), 6.10.

Manafan, 119.4. A meadow near Llanbadarn, on the bank of the Rheidol river.

March, The (*'r Mars*), 113.2. The Welsh border region.

Mary (*Mair*), 1.12, 28; 3.6, 7; 5.24; 23.52; 49.25; 51.34; 57.16; 60.34; 63.37; 67.34; 69.9; 72.31; 75.6; 76.35; 86.20; 89.6; 95.3; 99.45; 101.11, 46; 106.12; 110.16; 111.24; 113.8; 115.14; 128.10, 52; 131.7; 133.18; 135.34; 136.5, 14; 139.14; 141.15; 145.45; 149.28; 153.6; **The Precious Virgin** (*em Wyry*), 94.56; **Mother of God** (*Mam Dduw*), 147.8. Cf. **Jesus** (*Mab Mair*).

Math, 84.42. A legendary magician of North Wales.

Matthew (*Matheus*), 1.30; 4.35. The apostle and evangelist.

May (*Mai*), 14.1; 18.32; 19.38; 20.30; 23 *passim;* 28.22; 29.12, 16; 35.26, 44, 64; 59.8; 69.2, 10, 18; 87.31; 95.35; 102.2; 113.2; 120.23, 43; 121.4, 24; 122.14, 16; 123.1, 9; 135.33; 145.56, 63. Dafydd's (and Chaucer's) favorite month.

Melwas, 64.23, 29. The abductor of Gwenhwyfar (Guinevere), corresponding to Meleagant in the Lancelot romance of Chrétien de Troyes.

Menai, 21.10; 99.16. The straits lying between Anglesey and the mainland.

Menw, 84.31, 38; 152.53. Legendary Welsh magician.

Merddin: See **Myrddin.**

Merlin: See **Myrddin.**

Môn, 14.6; 15.23, 44; 20.12; 30.10; 31.37; 34.39; 82.2, 34; 84.41; 99.5, 14; 111.14; 128.4; 134.12; 147.43; 150.31; 152.4, 42; 153.32, 34, 54; 154.38, 40. Anglesey. Cf. these places in Môn also named by Dafydd: **Aberffraw, Llanddwyn, Llanfaes, Rhosyr/Newborough.**

Monday (*Dyw Llun*), 146.2.

Mordaf, 25.3. A northern British leader linked with Rhydderch and Nudd as a model of generosity.

Mordëyrn, 15.1; 101.11. An early Welsh monastic saint.

Morfudd, 34.51; 35.1, 21, 32, 40; 38.30; 42 *passim;* 43.3, 48; 50.26; 52.1; 53.18; 57.15, 26; 67.40; 69.29; 71.46; 72.23; 73.36; 76.44; 77.1, 20; 79.17; 83.38; 85.6, 7, 45; 87.16, 50; 89.11; 93.5; 94.16; 96.9, 34; 98.4; 102.2; 103.10, 26; 106.1; 108.40; 109.28; 113.22; 117.48; 122.13; 131.33; 139.26; 147.58. Pronouncing *Morfudd:* the *f* is pronounced like *v;* the last syllable rhymes with the first syllable of *hither;* the accent is on the first syllable: Moré vĭthe. Morfudd is named "Morfudd Llwyd" in Poems 43, 59, 73, 76, *Llwyd* being perhaps her family's name; the name *Llwyd* is also given to Dafydd ap Gwilym in one manuscript (Hendregadredd). In each of these four poems, the name "Morfudd Llwyd" appears in a position of emphasis in the last line; the poems focus on key stages of the relationship, from an exchange of vows to separation. The Morfudd poems, as much as the dialogues with birds, doubtless contain fictions, but recent scholarship has argued that the person and her relationship with Dafydd were real. She is Dafydd's beloved — beautiful, devout, loving, inconstant. The poems tell us that she had blonde hair and dark eyebrows, a light complexion, red cheeks, flashing eyes; that she was slender and vivacious, wore fine fur and jewelry, was proud, sensitive of her honor, easily angered, yet sophisticated and skilled in conversation, tender and generous in her embraces: a golden girl. They may have pledged love to one another in what Dafydd took to be a kind of marriage, but her family — perhaps the eminent Merionethshire family of Nannau — forced her to marry a certain Cynfrig Cynin, nicknamed Y Bwa Bach; she lived with Y Bwa Bach as wife and mother of his children in north Cardiganshire, near Dafydd's native Bro Gynin. Though Poem 98 tells us that he vowed not to, Dafydd continued to love her, and loved her still when age had diminished her beauty. She was evidently a woman of extraordinary spirit and charm; unlike Dyddgu, she returned Dafydd's love. There is a tradition that upon their non-canonical marriage, they fled to Glamorgan and were apprehended there, Morfudd being restored to her family and Y Bwa Bach, and a fine levied on Dafydd, which was paid by men of Glamorgan. Once dismissed as romantic fiction, this episode, too, is thought by some modern scholars to have historical foundation.

Morgannwg, 6.38; 8.3, 20. Glamorgan.

Mynyw, 82.33; 99.5, 42. St. David's; in Latin, Menevia; the church and monastery in Pembrokeshire founded by St. David in the sixth century; the principal shrine of Wales.

Myrddin, 118.23; **Merddin,** 19.27; **Myrddin Fab Saith Gudyn,** 130.7. Myrddin is alluded to by medieval Welsh writers as a warrior, a poet, a lover, a prophet; he has associations with both Dyfed and Cumberland, and his legend incorporates a tale of madness that parallels the frenzy of the Irish hero Suibhne. He is said to have fought in the sixth century. His name may derive by false etymology from Caerfyrddin ("Myrddin's Fort"); Geoffrey of Monmouth changed the name to Merlin, combining other legends to create a new character. Giraldus Cambrensis distinguishes two Merlins, one a counsellor, the other a wild man. Dafydd ap Gwilym cites this complex figure as a poet (Poem 19), a lover (118) and a madman (130).

Nannau. See **Ynyr.**

Nant-y-Glo, 83.40. See note to Poem 83.

Nant-y-Seri, 98.2. Perhaps the modern Cwmseiri, near Bro Gynin; see note to Poem 83.

Nentyrch, 122.12. An unidentified place name, according to Ifor Williams and Dr. Parry; see the note to Poem 122 for a variant reading proposed by R. Geraint Gruffydd.

Nest, 11, *passim.* Wife of Ifor Hael.

Newborough (*Niwbwrch*), 134.2. The name given by the English in 1305 to a borough on the site of the Welsh town of Rhosyr in Anglesey.

Noah (*Noe*), 5.47; **Noah's Ark** (*balchnoe*), 111.5.

Non, 99.3. Mother of St. David; a chapel dedicated to her stood near the sea about a mile from St. David's.

North Sea (*Môr Udd*), 60.34.

Nudd, 5.26; 6.1. Memorialized in a Welsh triad as notable for generosity, Nudd figures in tradition as a northern British leader of the late sixth century, kin to Rhydderch and Mordaf.

Nyf, 98.56; 129.8. A woman's name; corresponding to the Irish name Niamh.

Ovid (*Ofydd*), 6.16, 23; 22.3; 24.29; 28.21; 31.60; 35.43; 50.1; 58.20; 70.9; 83.42; 116.34; 143.51; 148.8. The noun *ofyddiaeth* appears in Dafydd's poems with the meanings of "love-craft" or poetic "art" like Ovid's (14.22; 20.60). Poem 71 (see my headnote) may be modelled on a poem of Ovid's.

Pali, 116.21. A dog's name; the word means "brocaded silk."

Pant Cwcwll, 83.30. Perhaps Talybont, a town lying between Aberystwyth and the River Dovey. See note to Poem 83.

Paradise (*Paradwys*), 24.15; 28.30; 29.29; 123.48; 137.70; 142.1. Cf. **Adam; Eve.**

Paris, 13.118; 44.24; 145.26. The city.

Paul (*Pawl*), 4.31. The apostle.

Pennardd, 16.13. A district in mid-Cardiganshire.

Penrhyn, Y, 42.52. Perhaps Penrhyncoch, near Bro Gynin.

Peredur Fab Efrog, 45.37–38. Hero of the Welsh romance named for him; he corresponds to Perceval in Chrétien's Grail romance.

Peter (*Pedr*), 4.23; 36.19; 128.1; 144.38. The apostle.

Philip (*Phylib*), 4.25. The apostle.

Pilate (*Pilatus*), 1.22.

Polixena (*Policsena*), 51.7. A daughter of Priam.

Pope, The (*y Pab*), 54.14; 82.19; 93.6; 104.31; 139.25; 146.27; 153.28; 154.4.

Powys, 18.17; 92.20. Kingdom of mid-Wales along the eastern border with England.

Priam (*Pria*), 51.7. King of Troy.

Pryderi, 12.40; 150.32. Hero of the Four Branches of the Mabinogi; son of Pwyll, Prince of Dyfed.

Pyll, 12.42. A son of Llywarch Hen, the legendary warrior of North Britain and Powys.

Rheged, 9.34. Ancient northern British kingdom in southwestern Scotland and northern Cumberland, centered about the Solway Firth; its sixth-century king was Urien, father of Owain (who appears in later French romance as Yvain).

Rheidol, 99.31. A river flowing from Pumlumon (Plynlimon), past Llanbadarn, to the sea at Aberystwyth.

Rhiw Rheon, 66.3. Perhaps a slope near Brecon (which may therefore be the "choice town" Dafydd speaks of in this poem). There is an old Roman fort nearby, once the capital of the Welsh kingdom of Brycheiniog; or the "round fort" mentioned in the poem could be the Norman castle of Bernard Newmarch in Brecon. A variant reading suggests Chester as the poem's location.

Rhodri, 12.42. Rhodri Mawr (Rhodri the Great) was a powerful ninth-century king of Gwynedd who defended the Welsh against Danish attacks.

Rhosyr, 128.2; 134.7. The name of the old Welsh town in Anglesey renamed Newborough in 1305; its parish church was dedicated to St. Peter, so that the occasion of Poem 128 was the feast of the patron saint.

Rhun, 51.11. A man's name; see note to the poem. Rhun ap Maelgwn was a ruler of Gwynedd, as was his father. Later poetry refers to leaders of North Wales as the descendants of Rhun. Could the beautiful woman from Gwynedd who is the subject of this poem be a "second Rhun" in the sense of being a noble descendant of Rhun (if she, not Elen, is referred to)?

Rhydderch, 17, *passim.* Probably the son of Angharad and Ieuan Llwyd of Glyn Aeron, a soldier and patron of poetry who outlived Dafydd (making this poem a feigned elegy).

Rhydderch, 7.10; 10.19; **Like Rhydderch** (*Rhydderchaidd*), 15.42. A ruler of the northern Britons in Strathclyde in the late sixth century, Rhydderch (with Nudd and Mordaf) is cited for his generosity in a triad; poetry and legend represent him as a foe to Myrddin and friend to St. Kentigern (Cyndeyrn).

Rhys, 75.2. Probably Rhys ap Gruffudd ap Hywel, Lord of Narberth and kinsman of Dafydd, who fought at Crecy in 1346.

Rhys Meigen, 21; 151.70; 152.55, 59. Dafydd's Shadwell: a lesser poet made famous by Dafydd's satirical attack on him (Poem 21).

Robert (*Rhobert*), 29.22. Unidentified; perhaps an artist or craftsman.

Robin Nordd, 98.16. Husband of the Helen who rewards Dafydd with socks and motley; he is probably the Aberystwyth burgess, Robert le Northern.

Roman Sages (*Doethion Rhufain*), 45.23. "The Seven Sages of Rome" is a collection of tales of oriental origin having the frame narrative of a Roman emperor's son educated by seven sages who tell stories of the craft of women, to help defend the emperor's son against his stepmother's accusations. See Johannes de Alta Silva, *Dolopathos: or The King and the Seven Wise Men,* transl. by Brady B. Gilleland, Medieval & Renaissance Texts & Studies 2 (Binghamton, N.Y., 1981).

Rome (*Rhufain*), 82.19; 139.5.

Scotland (*Prydyn*), 12.10; 58.30.

Seth, 92.30. Adam's son.

Severn (*Hafren*), 5.46; 29.35. River rising on Pumlumon and flowing east and south to the Bristol Channel.

Simon, 4.28; 15.4. The apostle, Simon the Zealot.

Solomon (*Selyf*), 8.9 (see the note to this line).
South, The (*y Deau*), 38.20; 75.6, 46; 79.39; 101.4; 149.7; 152.44; 153.43; South Wales (south of the River Dovey).
Sunday (*Sul; Dwysul*), 96.12, 35; 146.4.

Taliesin, 9.35; 10.34; 20.2; 118.24. Sixth-century bard, author of panegyrics to Urien, king of Rheged; he is the hero of a medieval Welsh tale of magic and poetic contention and, like Myrddin, acquired a reputation as a prophet.
Tegau, 52.1, 18; 53.36; 56.51; 65.1; 92.1; 110.36, 45. A woman cited as a standard of beauty who appears to have been remarkable also for chastity and fidelity.
Teifi, 12.5, 22; 21.10; 99.37; 104.35. River in Cardiganshire; its source is near Strata Florida, and its mouth, at Cardigan (Aberteifi).
Thomas, 4.32. The apostle.
Thursday (*Difiau*), 68.1, 9.
Traeth Mawr, Y, 99.19. A spur of ocean at the border of Caernarvonshire and Merionethshire, once extending far inland.
Trinity, The (*Y Drindod*), 3.1; 4.9; 12.51; 67.32; 106.11; **The True Father, The Son of Fair Grace, and the Spirit** (*Gwirdad a Mab rhad prydus ac Ysbryd*), 1.13; **God of Three** (*Duw Tri*), 1.15; **Heart of Three and One** (*annwyd Tri ac Un*), 2.1; **God One and Three** (*Duw Un a Thri*), 114.36. Cf. **Creator; Father; God; Jesus.**
Tristan (*Trystan*), 33.8. Tristan, nephew of King Mark of Cornwall and lover of Isolt.
Troy, Citadel of (*Caer Droea*), 140.24.
Tudor (*Tewdwr*), 95.40. The princely family of the kingdom of Deheubarth (from which Dyddgu was descended).
Tudur ap Cyfnerth, 150.16. A poet whose works are lost.
Tudur Goch, 153.17; 154.48. A now unknown inferior poet.
Tyrel (*Turel*), 133.40. Identified by D. J. Bowen as a French feudal lord who won a lawsuit against Edward III in 1359.
Tywyn, 116.24. Probably the medieval estate of Tywyn on the coast of south Cardiganshire (rather than the town in Merionethshire).

Uthr, 16.51. Uther Pendragon, father of Arthur.
Uwch-Aeron, 117.41. Region in Cardiganshire north of the River Aeron.
Uwch-Conwy, 154.45. Region in Gwynedd to the west of the river Conwy.

Virgil (*Fferyll*), 32.32; 84.58. Both these allusions are to Virgil as a magician.

Wales; Welshmen (*Cymry*), 11.4; 13.94, 120, 122; 78.41; 124.34; 137.15; **Welshman** (*Cymro*), 13.119; 15.41; 78.49; 124.53; 147.43; **Welsh** (adjective: *Cymroaidd*), 15.18; 76.38; **Welsh Language** (*Cymraeg*), 7.33; 76.38; 149.47. In medieval usage, the same word, *Cymry,* denoted both the land and the people. Cf. **Camber's Land.**

Wennallt, Y, 9.47. Wooded spot a few miles northwest of Gwerny-clepa, the home of Ifor Hael in Glamorgan.

Yale (*Iâl*), 60.17. A district of northeastern Wales, west of Wrexham, north of Llangollen.

Ynyr, 102.27. Perhaps Ynyr Nannau, ancestor of the Merionethshire family of Nannau, to which Morfudd may have belonged; the estate of Nannau was located near the River Mawddach, a few miles inland of the Mawddach estuary.

Ysgolan, 50.52. A legendary scholar.

Ystudfach, 137.71. A bard known only by his name.

Ystwyth, 99.33. River in Cardiganshire, entering the sea at Aberystwyth (*aber* being a topographical term for "mouth of river" or "confluence").

Index of Titles

Index of First Lines

References are to poem numbers

Dafydd ap Gwilym is the first English translation of the complete poems of the fourteenth-century Welsh poet now recognized as one of the great lyric poets of the Middle Ages. Dafydd ap Gwilym wrote of love, nature, nobility, anguish, and survival, in lyrics of vivid detail, passion, and wit. These lively prose translations, based on the magisterial critical edition by Sir Thomas Parry, follow closely the line divisions of the Welsh so that readers may perceive the strands of meaning, imagery, and dramatic utterance woven together in the original.

Professor Loomis's introduction discusses the poet and his world, language and versification, as well as the themes and artistry of his poems. Professor Loomis also analyzes some central problems in translating Dafydd ap Gwilym, and offers a description of previously published twentieth-century translations. The poems are annotated; the volume includes a glossary of names of places and persons. Three detailed maps, facsimiles of two manuscript pages attributed to the hand of Dafydd, and drawings of eight birds mentioned in the poems also grace this volume. The bibliographical note lists a selection of printed sources including bibliographies, editions, and historical, linguistic, and critical studies.

Richard Morgan Loomis is Professor of English at Nazareth College, Rochester. He has published a number of poems as well as translations of Welsh poetry (in *Poetry Wales*), articles on Robert Southwell (in *Recusant History*), and studies of Welsh language (in *Studies in the Humanities*).

m R t s

medieval & Renaissance texts & studies
is the publishing program of the
Center for Medieval and Early Renaissance Studies
at the State University of New York at Binghamton.

mRts aims to provide the highest quality scholarship
in attractive and durable format at modest cost.